D

GOD AND THE UNIVERSE OF FAITHS

GOD AND THE UNIVERSE OF FAITHS

OF FAITHS

Essays in the Philosophy of Religion

JOHN HICK

First edition 1973
Reprinted 1975

Published by
THE MACMILLAN PRESS LTD
London and Basingstoke
Associated companies in New York
Dublin Melbourne Johannesburg and Madras

SBN 333 15002 3

Printed in Great Britain by
REDWOOD BURN LIMITED
Trowbridge & Esher

Contents

Introduction

THIS BOOK reflects both the perennial and the changing character of the problems of religious thought. The starting point is religious language. Here the fundamental question is whether in speaking, for example, about God and eternal life the man of faith is making assertions about 'what there is' and 'how things are'. Is it a question of fact (though not of course physical fact) whether God is real? Or is God-talk a mythological expression of a state of the human mind involving no claims about that which is said to transcend both man and matter? Are the key religious statements true or false, in the sense of corresponding or failing to correspond with reality; or is it more appropriate to ask whether they satisfy or fail to satisfy us emotionally? I am sure that a great deal of the language of faith is variously emotive, poetic and mythic rather than fact-asserting, but I nevertheless want to insist that the core religious statements are true or false in a sense that is ultimately factual.[1] This leads in Chapter 2 to a criticism of non-cognitivist analyses of religious language, including the currently influential but in my view misleading Wittgensteinian language-game theory.

An insistence upon the basically cognitive character of religious discourse carries with it an obligation to face four major contemporary challenges to religious belief − first, the non-coerciveness of theism in view of the fact that every aspect of our experience, including the religious aspect, is capable of naturalistic explanation; second, the ancient and grisly problem of evil; third,

[1] Another paper closely relevant to this issue, which I considered including, is 'Theology and Verification' (*Theology Today*, April 1960). But this essay has been reprinted in a number of collections and is readily available − most accessibly, in paperback form, in *The Existence of God*, edited by John Hick (New York: The Macmillan Company, and London: Collier-Macmillan, 1964), and *The Philosophy of Religion*, edited by Basil Mitchell (London: Oxford University Press, 1971).

the question of the internal consistency of the concept of God; and fourth, the problem of the conflicting truth-claims of the different religions. The rest of the book deals, at varying lengths, with these four great issues.

In response to the first of them, the challenge of the non-coercive and apparently optional character of theistic belief, Chapter 3 presents a theory of faith as the interpretative element within religious experience, continuous in character with the element of interpretation in all our experience. The need for this voluntary act of interpretation preserves our status as free beings over against the infinite divine reality. The first half of Chapter 7, on the relation between the scientific and religious understandings of the world, is also concerned with this issue.

The next two chapters are a response to the theological problem of evil, and present a contemporary version of the Irenaean theodicy in relation both to human pain and suffering (Chapter 4) and human wickedness (Chapter 5). The last chapter of the book, on immortality, is also directly relevant to the mystery of evil, for I believe that any genuinely christian grappling with this problem has to take seriously the idea of a life to come.

Chapter 6, on the idea of necessary being, is a partial attempt to meet the third challenge, concerning the viability of the concept of God.

With the second half of Chapter 7 we approach the immense new problem that has been looming ever larger on the horizon of religious thought as the adherents of each of the world faiths have become more clearly aware of the spiritual reality of the other faiths. From my own point of view these chapters represent a fairly considerable process of rethinking in response to new experiences. The whole subject of the relation between Christianity and other religions is one which I had, in effect, largely ignored until coming to live in the multi-cultural, multi-coloured and multi-faith city of Birmingham, and being drawn into some of the practical problems of religious pluralism. I now no longer find it possible to proceed as a christian theologian as though Christianity were the only religion in the world. Surely our thinking must be undertaken, in the 'one world' of today and tomorrow, on a more open and global basis. Accordingly Chapters 8, 9 and 10 seek to develop a christian theology of religions which takes the decisive step from what I call a Ptolemaic (i.e.

one's-own-religion centred) to a Copernican (i.e. a God-centred) view of the religious life of mankind.

In this field the most difficult problem for the Christian is to reconcile his allegiance to the person of Christ, by whom he is irrevocably grasped, with his awareness of God's saving activity outside the borders of Christianity. Two main paths offer themselves at this point. A way that has often been taken is to give the idea of incarnation an adjectival instead of a substantival interpretation. One can then speak of divine incarnation in varying degrees in the great prophets, saints and seers of all ages. However I prefer, in Chapter 11, to reformulate the doctrine of the Incarnation in its full traditional meaning and then to ask, in Chapter 12, to what logical category the doctrine belongs. I suggest that it is a mythic expression of the experience of salvation through Christ; and as such it is not to be set in opposition to the myths of other faiths as if myths were literally true-or-false assertions.

The extent of the rethinking involved in coming to this conclusion is measured by the difference between Chapter 11 (published in 1966) and Chapter 12 (first published now). And yet it will I think be seen that this rethinking represents an expansion rather than a reversal of viewpoint. The earlier paper was an attempt to restate the content of the traditional christian teaching. The new paper raises the meta-question whether this teaching constitutes a theological theory or whether it represents, on the contrary, a mythological use of language.

To identify the language of incarnation as mythological in turn involves an expanded awareness of the varieties of religious language. Whilst insisting upon the cognitive, truth-claiming nature of the core of religious discourse it also seems to me important to recognise that much of the language that revolves around this core has mythological rather than literal meaning.

The last chapter, on death and immortality, returns to the insistence upon the factual core of religion and presents man's survival of bodily death as an actual future experience of which we should take account now, both for our living and for our thinking.

May 1973   JOHN HICK

Acknowledgements

A NUMBER of these chapters are either altered or unaltered versions of essays first published in various journals or books, and I am grateful to the editors and publishers concerned for permission to reproduce them here.

Chapter 1, 'Theology's Central Problem', was my inaugural lecture in the H. G. Wood chair of theology, delivered on 31 October 1967, and was first published by the University of Birmingham.

Much of the first half of Chapter 2, 'Religion as Fact-asserting', was a guest editorial in the Princeton journal *Theology Today*, April 1961, and is reprinted with the permission of that journal; and much of the second half of the same chapter first appeared as an article in *Theology*, March 1968.

Chapter 3, 'Religious Faith as Experiencing-as', was a lecture delivered under the auspices of the Royal Institute of Philosophy and first published in *Talk of God*, edited by G. N. A. Vesey (London: Macmillan and New York: St Martin's Press, 1969).

Chapter 4, 'God, Evil and Mystery', appeared in its original form in *Religious Studies*, April 1968, in reply to an article by Professor Roland Puccetti of the University of Singapore entitled 'The Loving God – Some Observations on John Hick's *Evil and the God of Love*' (*Religious Studies*, April 1967). Chapter 5, 'The Problem of Evil in the First and Last Things', was likewise originally a reply (*J.T.S.*, October 1968) to an article by Dom Illtyd Trethowan of Downside Abbey entitled 'Dr Hick and the Problem of Evil' (*J.T.S.*, October 1967), and is reprinted by permission of the editors of the *Journal of Theological Studies*.

Chapter 6, 'God as Necessary Being', was first published in *The Scottish Journal of Theology*, December 1961.

Chapter 7, 'The Reconstruction of Christian Belief', appeared as two articles in *Theology* in 1970.

The next three chapters, 8, 9, and 10, on 'The Essence of Christianity', 'The Copernican Revolution in Theology', and 'The New Map of the Universe of Faiths', were delivered as public lectures in Carrs Lane Church Centre, Birmingham, in February and March 1972. I remember with appreciation the high degree of theological interest shown by the Carrs Lane audiences. Part of Chapter 9 subsequently appeared in the *Expository Times*, November 1972, in a series on Learning from Other Faiths.

Chapter 11, 'Christ and Incarnation', was originally part of an article contributed to *Prospect for Theology: Essays in Honour of H. H. Farmer*, edited by F. G. Healey and published in 1966 by James Nisbet and Co. Ltd. It is now reprinted by permission of these publishers as copyright holders. The next chapter, on 'Incarnation and Mythology', has not appeared before, though part of it was delivered as a paper to the Society for the Study of Theology meeting at Lancaster in April 1973.

The last chapter, 'Towards a Theology of Death', first appeared in *Dying, Death and Disposal*, edited by Gilbert Cope (London: S.P.C.K., 1970), and foreshadows a full-scale work on the theology of death which is now two-thirds written.

1. Theology's Central Problem

BY THEOLOGY, in this chapter, I mean primarily the theology of the main religious option in our own culture, namely Christianity. Almost all that I say will also in fact apply to Judaism, for the problem I want to describe affects the judaic-christian tradition as a whole. It does not however affect the eastern religions in the same way, and I have neither the space nor the competence to discuss it in its eastern as well as in its western forms.

From time to time in the past, different topics have come to the fore as theology's central problem; but hitherto it has always been an internal or domestic issue. It was always a particular debate within theology, such as the struggle of monotheism versus polytheism fought by some of the great prophets of the Old Testament; or the question of the relation between God the Father and God the Son worked out in the fourth and fifth centuries A.D.; or in the sixteenth century the problem of the reformation of the church; or in the nineteenth century the task of digesting the implications of the discovery of the evolution of the forms of life. Today however – and this is a new situation – theology's central problem is not so much one within theology as around theology, enfolding it entirely and calling into question its nature and status as a whole.

This issue, at once central and all-embracing, presents itself to the philosopher as a problem concerning religious language. In a sentence the issue is whether distinctively religious utterances are instances of the cognitive or of the non-cognitive uses of language.

In its cognitive uses language is employed to state or assert or indicate facts or alleged facts. It conveys information (or mis-information) by making statements which are true or false. But it has always been clear that this is not the sole use that we have for language. Poetry, for example, does not typically operate in this way. Nor is it the function of such everyday locutions as 'Shut the door', or 'Damn', or 'How do you do' to state facts. Indeed commands, exclamations, greetings, congratulations and suggestions, and also performative utterances such as occur in the naming of a ship, the christening of a baby, the declaring of a verdict and the making of a promise, are all examples of familiar and established non-cognitive or non-indicative uses of language.

Of course the cognitive/non-cognitive distinction is not the only axis that can be driven through the realms of religious and theological language. Indeed for the detailed exploration of religious language it is too blunt an instrument, and one needs a network of distinctions such as was developed by the late J. L. Austin. In his later work he distinguished a variety of illocutionary forces – commissive, verdictive, behabitive, etc. – all of which can be detected within the range of religious utterances, and none of which is directly assessed in terms of truth value. But fully granting the rich and legitimate variety of the uses of human speech, still the cognitive/non-cognitive distinction gives rise to the first and most basic question that we have to ask concerning religious language. Although there are undoubtedly many aspects of religious meaning to which the true-false dichotomy does not apply, it nevertheless remains a question of prime importance whether such sentences as 'God loves mankind' belong to the class of sentences that are either-true-or-false.

We must see presently what kind of non-cognitive use or uses distinctively religious language might be supposed to have. But we can first narrow down a little the area of discussion. It is agreed by all that there are plenty of statements made in a context of discourse concerning religion that are straightforwardly indicative: for example all reports about what is believed or done within the different religions, such as 'Muslims believe that Mohammed was the prophet of Allah', 'Hindus accept the idea of reincarnation', or 'Christians claim that Christ was divine'. But although the sentences I have just quoted are about religion they are not themselves examples of the religious use of language; they are descriptive statements in anthropology or in the historical or comparative study of religion. Again, within the creeds and theological systems of a given religion there may be non-problematically declarative components: for example the historical affirmations that Jesus of Nazareth lived in the first century A.D.

in what is today Israel, and that he was crucified by order of the Roman Governor of Judea, Pontius Pilate. These are propositions that have been established by the ordinary methods of historical research and that might be found in a secular work of history dealing with that period. But however important these historical facts may be to Christianity, to state them is still not to be making distinctively religious statements. Religious doctrines are based upon these historical assertions, but go beyond them not only in what is claimed but also in the nature of the claim that is made. Thus 'God was at work in the life of Jesus of Nazareth' is related to 'Jesus of Nazareth lived in the first century A.D. in what is today Israel' in such wise that the religious statement cannot be true unless the historical statement is true, but that on the other hand the historical statement can be true without the religious statement being true. The cognitive/non-cognitive issue centres upon the metaphysical surplus, namely the reference to God, by which the religious statement exceeds the purely historical one. It is as an item of God-talk (which is the literal meaning of 'theology') that a religious utterance is problematic. It is God-talk, whether infiltrating historical discourse or not, that provokes our problem. For we are not troubled in the same way by grammatically similar sentences with no transcendent component. Compare, for example, 'The Prime Minister was acting through the Foreign Secretary' with 'God was acting through Jesus of Nazareth', and 'Tom loves Mary' with 'God loves mankind', and 'Human character is determined by genes' with 'The universe is divinely created'. The relevant difference between the first and second members of each of these pairs is that whereas there is general agreement about how to determine or at least try to determine the truth value of statements about the Prime Minister, Tom and genes, there is no such agreement about how to determine the truth value of statements about God. Hence the inevitable suspicion that they have no truth value, being neither true nor false, and that their proper function must be one quite other than that of making assertions.

This contention came to the fore in the 1920s and 1930s in the discussions initiated by the school of logical positivism. The focus of philosophical discussion has moved on a long way since then, but its progress has benefited from an increment of understanding gained in the course of the debates provoked by the positivists.

For it is thanks to them that we have come to see clearly that there can only be any point, and in that sense only any meaning, in the statement that *x* exists or is real – whether *x* be an electron, a human being, a quasar, God or anything else – if it makes an appropriate experienceable difference whether *x* exists. If *x* is so defined that it makes no difference within human experience, past, present or future, whether it be there or not, then the apparent assertion by one human being to another that it exists does not really assert anything. On the basis of this principle it has been claimed that God-talk is logically hollow in that it does not lay itself open to experiential confirmation or disconfirmation and is accordingly without indicative meaning. If it has any meaning at all – that is, any systematic use – this can only lie within the wide range of the non-cognitive functions of language.

Let me now mention some of the main non-cognitive uses which have been assigned by different philosophers to religious language. According to vintage logical positivism as it was proclaimed a generation ago in A. J. Ayer's *Language, Truth and Logic*, religious language, like the language of ethics and of aesthetics, is a form of emotive expression. Its function is to give vent to the speaker's emotional state, and perhaps also to try to induce a similar state in his hearers. So the language of religious thanksgiving expresses euphoria; the language of penitence and confession expresses a state of depression and self-criticism; and so on. But taken literally and at their face value the religious man's utterances, referring as they profess to do to a systematically unobservable entity called God, are meaningless.

A far more sophisticated and interesting non-cognitive theory of religious language is, to my mind, that of Professor J. H. Randall of Columbia University. Religious language, on his view, is the language of myth and symbol. 'What is important to recognize [he says] is that religious symbols belong with social and artistic symbols, in the group of symbols that are both non-representative and noncognitive. Such noncognitive symbols can be said to symbolize not some external thing that can be indicated apart from their operation, but rather what they themselves *do*, their peculiar functions'.[1] According to Randall the main (though not the only) function of religious symbols is to point to

[1] *The Role of Knowledge in Western Religion* (Boston: Starr King Press, 1958) p. 114.

aspects of the world which affect the human mind by evoking in it the feelings of numinous awe, cosmic dependence, and so on, which our religious vocabularies have been developed to express, just as other aspects of the natural world evoke in us the feelings which are expressed in aesthetic language. He says,

> The work of the painter, the musician, the poet, teaches us how to use our eyes, our ears, our minds, and our feelings with greater power and skill. . . . It shows us how to discern unsuspected qualities in the world encountered, latent powers and possibilities there resident. Still more, it makes us see the new qualities with which that world, in co-operation with the spirit of man, can clothe itself. . . . Is it otherwise with the prophet and the saint? . . . They make us receptive to qualities of the world encountered; and they open our hearts to the new qualities with which that world, in co-operation with the spirit of man, can clothe itself. They enable us to see and feel the religious dimension of our world better, the 'order of splendor', and of man's experience in and with it. They teach us how to see the Divine; they show us visions of God.[2]

This is in some ways an attractive form of religious naturalism. It is religious in that it expresses a positive appreciation of religion as a valuable aspect of human life; but it is naturalistic in that it recognises no element of transcendence. For it is to be clearly understood that when Randall speaks of the Divine and of God he is not referring to an alleged transcendent Mind. He is using traditional religious symbols to point to aspects of the world itself and of our human response to it.

But non-cognitive interpretations of religious language do not come only from outside the churches, and as we have already seen in the case of J. H. Randall they are by no means always motivated by the hostility to religion that was evident in logical positivism. Indeed it is precisely because non-cognitive religion (as I shall call it) has become a live option in the minds of many people within the churches that theology's central problem today is also a crisis in the self-understanding of Christianity. From within the churches we have, for example, the clearly defined theory of R. B. Braithwaite, of Cambridge, assimilating religious

[2] Op. cit., pp. 128–9.

language to the language of moral commitment.[3] According to Braithwaite a general ethical statement, such as 'Lying is wrong', is really a disguised expression of the speaker's intention – in this case his intention not to tell lies. And a religious statement, such as 'God loves mankind', is a disguised ethical statement, namely 'Love of mankind is supremely valuable', which in turn expresses the speaker's intention or policy of loving mankind. But taken literally and without this reinterpretation God-talk would be meaningless.

These philosophers (and many more whom I have not mentioned) are quite clear about the negative implications of their theories. On the basis of some form of verifiability or falsifiability criterion they have ruled out as meaningless belief in the reality of a transcendent personal God and have thereby ruled out also the traditional cognitive understanding of religious language. But there are a number of writers in the theological world who are attracted by the non-cognitive conception of Christianity without, as it seems to me, having counted and accepted the cost. I am thinking here of a number of recent writers of popular theology, such as Paul van Buren, Thomas Altizer, William Hamilton, Alistair Kee. These seem to me to be flirting with the idea of non-cognitive Christianity without having sufficiently considered what it would entail.

Yet another non-cognitivist response to the challenge to the meaningfulness of religious language has come about under the inspiration of the later thought of Ludwig Wittgenstein. The starting point for this development is the concept of a language game, or a relatively autonomous realm of speech activity with its own rules and criteria, occurring within some coherent pattern of human activity or, in Wittgenstein's phrase, form of life. There is, for example, the life and language of the law courts, or of biological research, or of the stock exchange, or of literary criticism, or of musical appreciation. Each of these has criteria for the appropriateness and reasonableness of what is said in its own sphere. We do not, for instance, rule out a pronouncement in the realm of musical criticism because it cannot be supported in the way in which a conclusion in low-temperature physics ought to be supported. Each language-game, it is said, has its own logic,

[3] *An Empiricist's View of the Nature of Religious Belief* (Cambridge University Press, 1955).

and one is not to be criticised from the standpoint of another – for the rules and criteria appropriate to the one will not be appropriate to the other.

Now as well as all these secular forms of life, each generating its own distinctive linguistic activity, there is religion as a mode of human existence, a form of life which includes the use of religious language. This latter employs special religious concepts such as God, the will of God, salvation, eternal life, and many more. The religious man talks to God and about God; he joins in the traditional liturgical speech of his church; he takes upon his lips its credal declarations. And to be religious, or to have faith, or to be a believer, is to have a use for this realm of language, to want to participate in it.

Thus far this sounds straightforward enough. Naturally the religious believer uses religious language; this is what we would expect. The paradox appears when the Wittgensteinian philosopher explains that these religious utterances constitute an autonomous language game. This means that the realm of religious discourse has its own internal criteria determining what is properly to be said, or in other words what is true. This in turn means that religious statements carry no implications outside the borders of their own realm, and therefore can be neither confirmed nor disconfirmed, supported nor challenged, by reference to what is known or believed in other spheres. For example, the statement that 'God loves mankind' does not entail that God exists in any sense that would permit there to be evidence for or against divine existence either in the facts of the world or in the results of philosophical reflection. This comes out clearly in a work from a Wittgensteinian point of view by D. Z. Phillips. Discussing atheism he says that the only sort of atheism that is philosophically in order is 'the recognition that religion means nothing to one; one is at a loss to know what to make of prayer, worship, creeds and so on. It is the form of atheism summed up in the phrases, 'I shouldn't call myself religious', 'Religion has no meaning for me'.[4] Phillips is here ruling out equally the negative claims that there are no adequate grounds for believing in the reality of God, or that it is extremely improbable or even logically impossible that there is a God; and the corresponding positive claims that

[4] *The Concept of Prayer* (London: Routledge and Kegan Paul, 1965) p. 19.

there are good grounds for believing in a divine reality, or that there is a high probability that God exists, or that given certain religious experiences it is rational to believe this.

In considering this Wittgensteinian suggestion we must be clear about the implications of what is proposed. For when we attend to the language of judaic-christian faith in its natural sense, as we find it in the scriptures, in liturgies, in creeds and confessions, in sermons and in works of theology, we cannot doubt that the God-talk within it has always been meant by its users to operate as cognitive discourse. We cannot doubt that the great prophets of the Old Testament, or Jesus of Nazareth himself, or St Paul, or Augustine, Aquinas or Luther, when they spoke about God believed that they were referring to a real being who exists independently of ourselves and with whom in the activities of worship we may enter into personal relationship. Not only do their words express such a conviction but their lives bear witness to their sincerity in it. They believed in the reality of God as strongly as they believed in the reality of the material world and of other human beings; and their belief in God affected their lives as profoundly as did these other more universally held convictions. And what the great primary religious figures have believed with an intensity that determined the shape of their lives, ordinary believers down to and including ourselves today have also believed in our own varyingly weak and wavering fashions.

Thus from the point of view of one whose faith forms part of a history going back through the generations of the church's life to the faith of the New Testament, and behind that to the insights of the great hebrew prophets, the non-cognitivist is not offering an objective analysis of the language of faith as living speech but is instead recommending a quite new use for it. For the non-cognitivist theories are not descriptive but radically revisionary. They are not accounts of the meaning of religious language as the speech of actual religious communities, but proposals about the meaning that it ought to be given in the future. And their negative premiss is that religious language cannot mean what its users have in fact always meant by it. When, for example, they speak of God, intending thereby to refer to an infinite creative Mind which is ultimately responsible for the existence of the physical universe and of ourselves as part of it, this intention of theirs is, according to the various non-cognitivist theories, to be rejected. It is to be rejected broadly on the positivist ground that the proposition intended would be meaningless because not open to empirical verification or falsification. Thus the non-cognitivist philosopher, who was called in as a consultant to analyse the operation of the old-established firm of God-Talk, Ltd., having examined the books has decided to make his own take-over bid, proposing under the old name to carry on a different trade altogather. He is of course perfectly entitled to seek to take the business over as a going concern. But equally the old firm is entitled to calculate the gains and losses in prospect and to come to its own conclusion. And my advice is not to accept the bid; for I believe that the loss would considerably outweigh the gain.

The principal loss would be the irreversible retreat of religious discourse within the borders of its own autonomous language-game, where it must renounce all claim to bear witness to the nature of the universe, and must cease to interact with other departments of human knowledge. Religious language would become a protected discourse, no longer under obligation to show its compatibility with established conclusions in other spheres, because it makes no claims which could either agree or conflict with scientific knowledge or philosophical reflection.

It would follow that the customary moves in the debate between Christians and Humanists are pointless. The christian apologist has been accustomed to draw attention to such considerations as the existence of the universe as an ordered but non-self-explanatory fact; to man's moral and religious experience; and sometimes to the alleged occurrence of contra-natural events through divine agency; and so on. But if the autonomist view of religious language is correct, the testimony of the great religious figures, reports of miracles, and philosophical arguments for the existence of God are all equally irrelevant to the validation of religious beliefs. For having a religious belief simply consists in the fact of using (as distinguished from mentioning, quoting or referring to) the appropriate range of religious language. One uses it because one finds it meaningful. It is not of course to be excluded that this state of mind may be brought about by reflection upon the kind of considerations I have just mentioned; but if so these considerations will be connected to it only as psychological causes, and not as validating reasons. And likewise the kind of counter-arguments which have customarily been levelled against the rationality of religious belief would become equally pointless – such considerations as the fact of human and animal suffering, which seems incompatible with the existence of a loving creator; the minute proportion of the space-time continuum occupied by our precarious human life, suggesting as this does man's utter insignificance and the unlikelihood that his beliefs about the universe as a whole should be true; the fact that everything, including moral and religious experience, can be explained naturalistically, without reference to a deity. According to the autonomist, whilst these considerations might have the psychological effect of bringing someone to abandon religious belief they have no bearing upon its logical propriety. For religion is simply an established form of human life and language. Like eating and drinking, it cannot properly be characterised as either true or false. It is just a fact that, in the words of Wittgenstein, this language game is played. Religion stands on its own feet as a form of human life, and anyone is free to participate in it or not.

Now of course in a way it would be a great relief to the religious apologist not to be expected to defend his faith against attack. If the problem of evil, and the verification challenge, and the comprehensibility of the universe without reference to the supernatural are all irrelevant to the validity of religious faith, then one is licensed to pursue one's religious predilection without let or hindrance from either science or philosophy. But on the other hand we do well to remember that there is literally all the difference in the world between fact and fiction, and also, though a different difference, between fact and poetry. If the christian message presents itself as poetry, or as something analogous to poetry, it can only hope to be relevant to those who appreciate poetry. Its status will be that of a special interest for those who are so minded. It will no longer speak to human beings as such, in all their human variety, or be entitled to be listened to as alleged news about a transcendent order of fact which is immensely significant for human life. The traditional word 'gospel' translates the Greek *euangelion*, meaning good or favourable news. In the New Testament, and within the church ever since, the christian message has been presented as the news that the whole physical universe, including the human life which has emerged on this earth (as well as any other intelligent life that there may be elsewhere), exists by the will and for the purpose of an infinite creative Mind. Further, the christian message claims that this Mind has made itself known to man's religious insight and conscience as a personal reality. If this alleged news is true it is obviously enormously important, profoundly affecting both the way in which we think about our human situation and the way in which we live our human life. For the distinctively christian way of participating in human existence only exhibits the rational character of living in terms of reality if the christian gospel is true. This particular form of life, to use Wittgenstein's phrase again, consists in living in the world as God's world and in relation to other people as God's children. It has political, economic and moral consequences which constitute the christian ethic. It also involves activities of worship and dispositions of mind, both intellectual and emotional, which directly refer to the supreme Being about whom the christian message speaks. If there is no such Being these activities are misdirected and non-functional. Transposing the matter into the terms of rational or warranted belief: if one who participates in the theistic form of life is not convinced of the reality of a supreme Being, he is behaving irrationally. He is irrational in the sort of way in which someone who talked and tried to behave as though he had inherited a million pounds, when he knows that in fact he has not, would be irrational. For to be rational is to live in terms of reality as one responsibly believes it to be. And the religious form of life can only count as reasonable if it is based upon a sincere conviction, or at least an effective working presupposition, that the God whom we worship and seek to serve does indeed exist. There is therefore something deeply irrational about the non-cognitivist proposals to use the traditional language of religion, and to participate in the form of life of which it is the linguistic expression, after consciously rejecting the premiss upon which these depend for their appropriateness.

It therefore seems to me that, whatever the risk may be from the religious point of view (and I shall point out the risk in a moment), clarity demands that we keep before our minds as distinct alternatives the two different conceptions of the universe and of man's place in it which can be called humanism and transcendent theism. According to humanism man is just what he seems to be, or rather just what he seems to be to ourselves as inhabitants of our twentieth-century science-oriented western culture. And what he seems to be is a complex and highly developed form of animal life which enjoys self-consciousness and intelligence in a universe by which he has been produced non-purposefully. The thread of consciousness runs, normally, for some thirty to ninety years and is then permanently broken by death. The quality of the life lived during that span is good (i.e. welcome) for some but bad (i.e. unwelcome) for many more. It is predominantly good for most of those who live in a relatively affluent country and in a period when wealth, education and cultural opportunities are widely distributed. But those who live or have in the past lived in such privileged circumstances amount only to a small minority of the total number of human beings who are now living and an infinitesimal proportion of all those who have lived since human life began. For the majority, indeed the very great majority, existing in direst poverty and under-nourishment, ill-health and insecurity, life has been a burden of toil, pain and anxiety relieved by occasional pleasures. Nor, so far as all the millions of millions who have lived until now are concerned, is there any possibility of salvation in the sense of their coming to enjoy a better life which justifies their existence to them. For they are dead, and death (in the humanist vision) is extinction. Nor again, so far as a purely rational judgement can guide us, is there any assurance that the general condition of human life is about to improve; for we face the three enormous perils of an accelerating population explosion by which the human race is gradually strangling itself, the fatal pollution of the human environment by a self-destructive industrial civilisation, and the ever-present peril of massive self-inflicted thermo-nuclear destruction. Thus, when one thinks not of oneself as an individual but of mankind as a whole, the humanist vision is seen to be a profoundly tragic one. To say this is not to criticise it. A vision of the world could be both tragic and true. Indeed its tragic character has always been emphasised by the more clear-minded and realistic humanist thinkers. Bertrand Russell, for instance, presented it with great eloquence in a famous early essay:

> That Man is the product of causes which had no prevision of the end they were achieving; that his origin, his growth, his hopes and fears, his loves and his beliefs, are but the outcome

of accidental collocations of atoms; that no fire, no heroism, no intensity of thought and feeling, can preserve an individual life beyond the grave; that all the labours of the ages, all the devotion, all the inspiration, all the noonday brightness of human genius, are destined to extinction in the vast death of the solar system, and that the whole temple of Man's achievement must inevitably be buried beneath the debris of a universe in ruins – all these things, if not quite beyond dispute, are yet so nearly certain, that no philosophy which rejects them can hope to stand. Only within the scaffolding of these truths, only on the firm foundation of unyielding despair, can the soul's habitation henceforth be safely built.[5]

This is a noble utterance, by one of the intellectual giants of our century, and it perfectly expresses the tragic vision which forms the background of so much contemporary art, particularly novels and drama.

It seems to me preferable not to call that which stands over against humanism, as its radical alternative, religion or religious-ness in general, but (even though the phrase is an awkward one) transcendent theism. By this I mean belief in a transcendent personal God, together with the major corollaries of this belief. These corollaries include a view of man's place in the universe which can be compared point by point with that of humanism.

In contrast to the unpurposed character of human existence, as seen by humanism, transcendent theism affirms a divine pur-pose behind the entire natural process within which, as a detail, our solar system has come into being and life has developed on this planet and has produced man. Human existence is intended, though within a cosmic intention which may well be of such vast scope and multi-dimensional complexity as to be in its totality beyond our mental grasp. The aspect of it that religious thought has discerned is a process of the gradual creating of perfected finite personal life through free responses to the challenges and opportunities of this world as also of other environments after bodily death.

[5] *Mysticism and Logic* (London: Longmans, Green & Co., 1918) pp. 47–8. In a 1962 letter Russell commented on this early essay that whilst he regarded its style as 'florid and rhetorical', nevertheless 'my outlook on the cosmos and on human life is substantially unchanged': *Autobiography*, III (London: Allen & Unwin, 1969) pp. 172–3.

Again, in contrast to the tragic character of life as seen by humanism, transcendent theism, in its jewish and christian forms, affirms that the divine Mind which religious faith has seen at work in various revelatory situations is wholly good. It follows from this that the hard travail of human life, as it has been for so many people, is neither pointless nor wasted. For it falls within a purpose which, being divine, is assured of ultimate fulfilment, and being good cherishes the welfare of each individual human being. This present life thus constitutes a chapter in a story which is going eventually to have a happy ending.

Of course in formulating in this way the implications of transcendent theism I am following that strand of christian tradition which stems from the New Testament proclamation of good news – the good news of the reality and love of God – rather than that other strand, classically formulated by St Augustine, which offers the bad news of a divine wrath which can only be satisfied by the eternal torment of most of the human race.

I mentioned a little while ago the risk that might be involved from the religious point of view in stressing the contrast between these two alternative visions; and I must now end by stressing this risk. Transcendent theism makes assertions which are logically capable of being either true or false. Thus in claiming to be true it inevitably runs the risk of being false. All the doubts about its truth that have been developed in both ancient and modern times are inescapably relevant, and demand to be met. They constitute in the end four great matters of debate. Two of these issues were clearly formulated by Thomas Aquinas in the thirteenth century. The first consists in the non-coerciveness of theistic belief in view of the fact that one need not refer to God in order to explain the workings of nature. As Aquinas said, presenting an objection to belief in the existence of God, 'It is superfluous to suppose that what can be accounted for by a few principles has been produced by many. But it seems that everything we see in the world can be accounted for by other principles, supposing God did not exist. For all natural things can be reduced to one principle, which is nature; and all voluntary things can be reduced to one principle, which is human reason, or will. Therefore there is no need to suppose God's existence'.[6] Or as Laplace said, '*Je n'avais pas besoin de cette hypothèse*'. And today it is not only the astronomer

[6] *Summa Theologica*, 1, q. 3, art. 2.

and the physicist, the chemist and the biologist who find no need for the God-hypothesis, but equally the cosmologist – for neither the steady state nor the big bang theory of the age and structure of the universe requires there to be a creator; and again the psychologist, who can study religious experience and religious belief without having to take account of God as a reality external to the human mind; and yet again, the sociologist, who can examine the roles of religion within human society without reference to any transcendent divine Being. Not only the starry heavens above, but also the moral law and man's religious experience within, can now be brought within the scope of the ever expanding discourse of either the natural or the human sciences. It follows that if theism be treated, as it so often has been in the past, as an explanatory hypothesis of cosmic dimensions, it has become entirely gratuitous. This in turn requires the abandonment of the traditional natural theology and the development of a quite new approach to the question of the grounds of rational theistic conviction.

The second great challenge comes from the ancient and grisly problem of evil, and is in a way an even more severe challenge than that of the explanatory superfluousness of the theistic hypothesis, in that the problem of evil constitutes not merely an absence of reason for believing in the reality of God but a positive reason for not so believing. There is no need to labour here the problem itself. It too was well known to Aquinas, who formulated it as follows: 'It seems that God does not exist; because if one of two contraries be infinite, the other would be altogether destroyed. But the name *God* means that He is infinite goodness. If, therefore, God existed, there would be no evil discoverable; but there is evil in the world. Therefore God does not exist'.[7] Or as Stendhal more succinctly put it, 'God's only excuse is that he does not exist'! And behind these thoughts there lies the great ocean of human and animal suffering, and the terrifying power of demonic evil as we saw it at work, for example, in the Nazi programme for the extermination of the European Jews, as well as in all too many more recent events. Many people who positively reject the christian belief in an omnipotent God of love would point to this as their over-riding reason.

The third great challenge is one which has come to the fore

[7] Ibid.

through the contemporary philosophical method of the analysis of concepts. Is the judaic-christian concept of God coherent? Or is it an assemblage of incompatible elements, analogous to those impossible figures which we meet in some recent works on the psychology of perception – figures which can be drawn on paper but which are incapable of being constructed as three-dimensional objects. We say, for example, that God is perfect and self-sufficient, needing nothing, and yet that he has willed to create a universe over against himself and that he desires the worship of his creatures; that he is infinite, and yet with the limitedness of personal characteristics; that he is eternal and immutable, and yet that he acts within human history; that he is impassible, and yet that he loves his creatures and sympathises with them in their sorrows. These paradoxes have led some thinkers to conclude that the idea of God is so full of contradictions that there cannot possibly be any such Being. And there is the closely related problem of the verifiability or testability of theological statements. What observable or experienceable difference does it make whether propositions about an unobservable deity are true?

The fourth great challenge arises from the conflicting truth-claims of the different world religions. The problem can be presented very simply. If I had been born in India I would probably be a Hindu; if in Egypt, probably a Muslim; if in Ceylon, probably a Buddhist; but I was born in England and am, predictably, a Christian. However, these different religions each profess to be true. The profession is made with varying degrees of exclusiveness, Hinduism for instance being much more tolerant of the claims of other religions than are Judaism or Christianity. But in the end it is far from evident that they can all be true. Are we then to say that one is true and all the others false – whether equally false or false in varying degrees? Or are we to say that each is true subjectively, for its own adherents – with the implication that probably none is objectively true? There is here an agonising dilemma for anyone committed to a particular faith. It seems that he must either abandon the truth-claims of his own religion, on which (I have been arguing) its whole point and value depends; or else he must allow only a conditional and secondary value to other religions. But to adopt the first option, abandoning the claim of his own faith to declare the nature of reality and the way of salvation, would be to commit religious suicide; whilst to take the alternative option, and relegate all the other religions of the world to an outer darkness of illusion and idolatry, would be to imply that God has revealed himself to mankind in a remarkably limited and ineffective way. Neither of these choices, then, can be a happy one.

What I am urging here is simply that these great issues must be squarely faced, and that a religious faith that is to be rationally credible must reveal within itself resources for meeting them. These immense problems must be soluble, if not fully and definitively then at least to the extent that faith remains an open possibility. I believe that this is in fact how the matter stands. These challenges to faith cannot be fully dissolved away, but it can be shown that they are nevertheless not fatal to a rational religious commitment. But needless to say I am not proposing to try to demonstrate this in the present chapter. I have been concerned here only to urge that these profoundly difficult, complex and challenging problems should not be evaded in the way offered by the various non-cognitive theories of religious language. Theology's central problem today is whether to take the easy road to extinction offered by the contemporary non-cognitivist theories of the function of religious language, or to face this formidable phalanx of challenges – the non-coerciveness of religious belief, the problem of evil, the question of meaning and verifiability, and that of the conflicting truth-claims of the different religions. My vote – recorded soberly and not in any spirit of bravado – is to take the risk of facing them.

2. Religion as Fact-asserting

IN THE LAST CHAPTER I claimed that religion is concerned with reality and that its central affirmations are, ultimately, true or false factual assertions. In this chapter I want to criticise the opposite view, both in the crude assumption that the important question is not whether religious affirmations are true but whether they are useful; and in the highly sophisticated form of the current neo-Wittgensteinian treatment of religious discourse as an autonomous language-game.

I

As regards the crude pragmatic approach to religion, I can indicate the tendency which I have in mind by recalling an impression received on going to teach in the United States in the midst of the religious boom of the 1950s. Observing America through the ears of a philosopher interested in the problems of language, I was struck by the frequent use of the word 'religion'·(or 'faith', used virtually as a synonym) and, within the same realm of discourse, the relatively infrequent occurrence of the word 'God'. In contexts in which a generation or so ago questions used to be raised and debated concerning God, his existence, attributes, purpose and deeds, the corresponding questions from at least the 1950s onwards have focused upon religion, its nature, function, forms and pragmatic value. A shift has apparently taken place from the term 'God' as the head of a certain family of words and locutions, to the term 'religion' as the new head of the same linguistic family.

One accordingly hears much talk of religion considered as an aspect of human culture. In many American universities and colleges there are departments devoted to studying the history and varieties of this phenomenon, and the contribution which it has brought to man's culture in general. And among the ideas treated in this connection, along with cult, priesthood, taboo, and many others, is the concept of God. For academic study God is thus a sub-topic within the larger subject of religion.

At a more popular level religion is widely conceived – sometimes articulately, often inarticulately – as a human activity whose general function is to enable the individual to achieve harmony within himself and with his environment. One of the distinctive ways in which religion fulfils this function is by preserving and promoting certain great ideas or symbols which have a power to invigorate men's finer aspirations; and the most important and enduring of these symbols is God. Both at the academic and at the popular levels, then, God is in effect defined in terms of religion, as one of the concepts with which religion works; rather than religion being defined in terms of God, as the realm of men's varying responses to a real supernatural Being.

This displacement of 'God' by 'religion' as the focus of a wide realm of discourse has brought with it a change in the character of the questions that are most persistently asked in this area. Concerning God the traditional question has naturally been whether he exists or is real. But this is not a question that arises with regard to religion. It is obvious that religion exists; the important queries concern the purposes which it serves in human life, whether it ought to be cultivated and, if so, in what directions it may most profitably be developed. Under the pressure of these concerns the question of the truth of religious beliefs has fallen into the background and the issue of their practical usefulness has come forward to occupy the centre of attention.

This situation was first impressed upon my own mind by reading hundreds of students' essays in a Philosophy of Religion course in a secular American university. It was evident from this sample that large numbers – indeed the majority – of the writers had only a very dim conception of religious beliefs as being true or false, but a much keener sense of their being (or failing to be) psychologically and socially valuable. The question of truth had not been explicitly repudiated; but the alternative question of practical usefulness was far more effectively to the fore.

The same basic standpoint lies behind sermons heard from many pulpits, in which the true relevance of the biblical teachings and narratives is seen to lie in their illustration of current principles of psychotherapy and mental hygiene. This tendency reaches its well-known peak in the virtual equation of the christian gospel with the proclamation of the power of positive thinking; but to this extreme there are many approximations. The resulting favourable public image of the Protestant minister – conformity to which earns community approval – is that of a man who performs services of social welfare (validated by statistically certifiable results), primarily in such areas as moral education, mental health, national morale and family life.

I am very far from wishing to question the real importance of such services, or their character as authentic expressions of christian love. I am rather seeking to focus attention upon the way in which arguments centering upon pragmatic value have replaced the traditional conception that there are great and saving truths to be proclaimed and all-important transcendent realities to be witnessed to.

Is the new pragmatic emphasis a surrogate for the older religious conviction, a substitute natural to an age of waning faith? Such a diagnosis is suggested by the observations of the agnostic John Stuart Mill at the opening of his famous essay on *The Utility of Religion*:

If religion, or any particular form of it, is true, its usefulness follows without other proof. If to know authentically in what order of things, under what government of the universe it is our destiny to live, were not useful, it is difficult to imagine what could be considered so. Whether a person is in a pleasant or in an unpleasant place, a palace or a prison, it cannot be otherwise than useful to him to know where he is. So long, therefore, as men accepted the teachings of their religion as positive facts, no more a matter of doubt than their own existence or the existence of the objects around them, to ask the use of believing it could not possibly occur to them. The utility of religion did not need to be asserted until the arguments for its truth had in a great measure ceased to convince. People must either have ceased to believe, or have ceased to rely on the belief of others, before they could take that inferior ground of defence without a consciousness of lowering what they were endeavouring to raise. An argument for the utility of religion is an appeal to unbelievers, to induce them to practice a well meant hypocrisy, or to semi-believers to make them avert their eyes from what might possibly shake their unstable belief, or finally to persons in general to abstain from expressing any doubts they may feel, since a fabric of immense importance to mankind is so insecure at its foundations, that men must hold their breath in its neighbourhood for fear of blowing it down.

Mill's words refer to mid-nineteenth-century England, which had much in common religiously with recent American society. One also recalls the caustic remark of Bertrand Russell (likewise a nineteenth-century rationalist, although happily he lived on into the second half of the twentieth century): 'I can respect the men who argue that religion is true and therefore ought to be believed, but I can feel only profound moral reprobation for those who say that religion ought to be believed because it is useful, and that to ask whether it is true is a waste of time'.[1]

Comparing our current emphasis upon utility rather than truth with the thought of the great biblical exemplars of faith, we are at once struck by a startling reversal. There is a profound and momentous difference between serving and worshipping God, and being 'interested in religion'. God, if he is real, is our Creator. We stand before him as One who is infinitely superior to ourselves, in worth as well as in power, and 'in whose eyes all hearts are open, all desires known, and from whom no secrets are hid'. But on the other hand religion stands before us as one of the various concerns which we may, at our own option, choose to cultivate. In dealing with religion and the religions we occupy the appraiser's role. And God is subsumed within that which we appraise. There need be no bareing of our lives and souls before the divine judgement and mercy. We can deal instead with religion, within which God is only an idea, a concept whose history we can trace, and which we can analyse, define, and even revise – instead of the living Lord of heaven and earth before whom we bow down in awe to worship and rise up with joy to serve.

There is, I think, no great mystery as to the historical sources of this prevalent view of religion as essentially an aspect of human

[1] *Why I am Not a Christian* (London: Allen & Unwin, 1957) p. 172; (New York: Simon & Schuster, 1957) p. 197.

culture, and of the consequent transformation of God into one of the terms of religious thought. It represents a logical development within an increasingly technological society of what has been variously called scientism, positivism and naturalism – the assumption engendered by the tremendous, dramatic and still accelerating growth of scientific knowledge and achievement, that the truth concerning any aspect or alleged aspect of reality consists in the results of the application to the relevant phenomena of the methods of scientific investigation. God is not a phenomenon available for scientific study; but religion is. There can be a history, a psychology, a sociology, and a comparative study of religion. Hence religion has become an object of intensive investigation, and God has perforce become identified as an idea which occurs within this complex phenomenon of religion.

Stated explicitly, the philosophical presupposition of the current mood is that the categories of truth and falsity do not apply to religious beliefs. Hence as a problem in contemporary theology and philosophy the issue centres upon the debate between the cognitive and non-cognitive, or the factual and mythological, understandings of religious language. Do such sentences as 'God loves mankind' or 'Men live after death', profess to describe objective realities; or do they perform a different function altogether? For language in its rich versatility can accomplish many other tasks than simply the making of assertions about what is alleged to be the case. We do not ask of a sonnet, for instance, whether it is literally true; poetry serves a quite different purpose from that of formulating factual assertions. And so the question naturally arises, Is the veracity properly claimed for religious statements more akin to 'poetic truth' than to ordinary factual truth? Are religious statements perhaps to be regarded as mythological and as having their own special kind of quasi-poetic truthfulness?

The problem is many-sided, and different aspects of it are at present engaging the attention of biblical scholars, theologians and philosophers of religion. A convenient way to raise some of the issues in short compass is by presenting a specific thesis. I shall therefore argue that: (*a*) it is vitally important to maintain the genuinely factual character of the central affirmations of the christian faith; and (*b*) given a basic structure of factual belief, there is ample scope for the non-factual language of myth, symbol and poetry to express the believer's awareness of the illimitable mysteries which surround that core of religious fact. We may begin with this latter contention. That there is a large admixture of mythological material (in the sense of statements which are non-factual but nevertheless religiously significant) in our scriptures, creeds, and other religious writings has long been recognised. It was as evident to Origen in the third century as it is to Bultmann in the twentieth. There will doubtless always be keen and even heated discussions about whether this or that specific item is to be regarded as factual or as mythological; but few thoughtful Christians today are disposed to deny that their religious discourse does include considerable mythological elements. Bishop James A. Pike, for instance, wrote:

> There are several phrases in the creed that I cannot affirm as literal prose sentences, but I can certainly sing them – as a kind of war song picturing major convictions in poetic terms. ... Stated in plain prose, I certainly do not believe that Christ 'sitteth on the right hand of the Father'. ... But I can sing this phrase with a real affirmation as to the place of Christ in the whole situation. I feel the same about 'ascended into Heaven'. And the same about 'conceived by the Holy Ghost, and born of the Virgin Mary'.[2]

Some would no doubt categorise differently one or other of the credal phrases cited. But it is impossible to repudiate the category itself which Bishop Pike used, or to deny that at least some religious utterances properly belong in it. Nor is there anything revolutionary in holding that the structure of fact-type christian beliefs contains gaps which have to be filled, if at all, by myth. Such myths are distinguished from whimsical or arbitrary exercises of the poetic imagination by their relation to a framework of factual belief which they supplement and adorn. For myths of this kind are always products of a serious theological intention. For example, the myth of the ascended Christ's session at the right hand of the Father expresses the conviction that in some way which cannot be literally visualised our Lord is enthroned over the world. The myth derives its appropriateness and its

2 *The Christian Century*, 21 Dec. 1960, p. 1497.

point from the environment of non-mythological beliefs within
which it lives – beliefs in the literal reality of God and of his
action in Christ. It is thus possible to see large tracts of christian
discourse as significant although non-factual if one holds them
within a context of genuinely factual beliefs.

If, however, the entire range of religious beliefs were regarded
as non-factual, none of them could possess the kind of significance which depends upon a connection with objective reality.
Myths that are embedded within a body of facts bear this kind
of significance secondarily and derivatively, but myths which live
in a system which is mythological throughout merely define an
imagined realm of their own. I suggest, then, that what might be
called valuable or significant myth is necessarily parasitic upon
non-mythological beliefs, and that if a set of myths becomes
complete and autonomous it thereby forfeits its cognitive value.

This conclusion points to my other thesis, namely that
Christianity, if it is not to deny itself, must insist upon the
properly factual character of its basic affirmations. The reason
for reaffirming this position, which has always been taken for
granted by the religious mind, is brought out by considering the
alternatives now being proposed. A growing number of contemporary philosophers have concluded that religious language is
(apart from its empirical-historical elements) non-cognitive. It
seems clear to them that whatever may be the legitimate point of,
for example, 'God loves mankind', that point cannot be to assert
a fact, since there are and can be no facts of this kind to be
asserted. They have accordingly considered what function such
a sentence may perform. Perhaps, for example, it expresses a way
of looking at the natural world (John Wisdom, J. H. Randall,
Peter Munz); or perhaps it declares an intention to live in a
certain way (R. B. Braithwaite, T. R. Miles); or perhaps it is a
'convictional' statement, this being an utterance of a type which
is to be classified as non-indicative (W. Zuurdeeg).

Possibly the clearest recent expression of the conception of
religion as exclusively a phase of human culture is that of
J. H. Randall. He argues, with impressive force and clarity, that
religion is to be identified as 'a distinctive human enterprise with
a socially indispensable function'.[3] Enlightened religion should
have nothing to do with the superstitious belief in a really existing

[3] *The Role of Knowledge in Western Religion*, op. cit., p. 6.

divine Being. Rather theology is 'an imaginative and symbolic rendering of men's moral experience and ideals: all religious beliefs are symbolic'.[4] The function of religious symbols (in conjunction with their associated rituals and ceremonies) is fourfold: to stimulate the will to moral activity; to bind a community together through its common symbols; to communicate a quality of experience which can only be expressed by poetry and symbol; and to open our eyes to the 'order of splendour' in the world, comprising nature's more elusive depths and mysteries. On the one hand, then, Randall sees religion as an important and valuable enrichment of human life, and on the other hand as a purely intra-mundane concern in which the idea of a transcendent God has no proper place.

On the assumption – for which, in his book, Randall offers no reasons – that belief in the reality of God is absurd, and out of the question for twentieth-century man, there is much to be said for a religious naturalism of this kind. But it is important to see that this initial assumption does not constitute merely an enlightened *revision* of christian tradition but spells the *obituary* of historic Christianity. The faith embodied in the biblical writings, and the faith of the church as an extension of this, depend upon the conviction that God exists, not merely as an idea in some men's minds, but as the creator and sustainer of the universe, the ultimate reality with whom we have inescapably to do and whose self-disclosed purpose towards us is supremely good and loving.

II

Here I enter into dialogue with the contemporary neo-Wittgensteinian approach to the philosophy of religion as represented by Professor Dewi Z. Phillips in *The Concept of Prayer* and *Faith and Philosophical Enquiry*.[5] And against that approach I wish to propound three theses:

My first thesis is that it is presupposed in the christian scriptures, creeds, confessions, prayers, sermons and theologies that it is a factual truth that God exists.

Phillips does not agree with this. For example, he says that 'To have the idea of God is to know God'.[6] This seems to entail

---

[4] Ibid., p. 9. [5] London: Routledge and Kegan Paul, 1970.
[6] *The Concept of Prayer*, op. cit., p. 18.

that for someone to have the idea of God is for God to exist – or perhaps to exist 'for' the one who has the concept. This in turn suggests that there is no proper question whether God exists, in distinction from the question whether people have the concept of God. Again, he says, 'What [the believer] learns is religious language; a language which he participates in along with other believers. What I am suggesting is that to know how to use this language is to know God' (p. 50). Or yet again, consider Phillips's discussion of the possibility of atheism. He says that the only sort of atheism that is philosophically in order is 'the recognition that religion means nothing to one; one is at a loss to know what to make of prayer, worship, creeds and so on. It is the form of atheism summed up in the phrases, "I shouldn't call myself religious", "Religion has no meaning for me"' (p. 19).

If this is the only philosophically proper form of atheism then one form that must be philosophically improper is that expressed by: 'It is irrational to believe that there is a God', 'There are no adequate grounds for believing in the reality of God', 'It is logically impossible that God, as defined in Christianity, should exist, since this particular concept of deity is radically incoherent', 'In view of considerations x, y, and z, it is more probable that there is not a God than that there is'. Presumably Phillips believes that the issue which such atheism professes to settle is not a genuine issue. And if this is a non-issue then the corresponding contrary conclusion that God does exist, or that it is rational to believe that God exists, or that there are adequate grounds for believing in the reality of God, etc., must also be philosophically out of order.

To rule out the question whether God exists as logically improper is by implication to deny that the core religious statements, such as 'God loves mankind' or 'God is guiding the universe to his own end for it', are factually true-or-false. The debate which Phillips here enters between cognitive and non-cognitive analyses of religious language constitutes, I believe, the central issue in the philosophy of religion today. It connects on the one hand with the notion (representing the valid deposit of logical positivism) that 'existence' is to be defined in the operational terms of making an experienceable difference; and on the other hand with the discovery of the immense variety of the uses of language and in particular of its manifold non-cognitive functions. The notions of the existence of God and of the factual truth of statements about him are bound up with the principle that any possible history of the universe which satisfies, for example, 'God loves mankind', must differ experientially from any possible history of the universe which does not satisfy it. On the one side of the debate are those who hold that the existence of God is ultimately a factual issue. And on the other side are those who hold that the function of, for example, 'God loves mankind', is not to assert an alleged matter of fact but to do something quite different, such as to express an emotion, attitude or intention. (The mutual tolerance between the two positions is asymmetrical. The 'cognitivist' can hold that in asserting a matter of fact one is also expressing emotion, etc., but the 'non-cognitivist' cannot hold that in expressing emotion, etc., one is also asserting a matter of fact – beyond, of course, the fact that one has that emotion or intention.)

In denying, in his treatment of atheism, that there is a proper question as to whether God exists, and declaring instead that the proper question is whether one wants to use religious language, Phillips assumes that the use of religious language does not itself involve belief in the existence of God. But it seems clear to me that such utterances as 'God is a very present help in time of trouble', 'The Lord God omnipotent reigneth', 'In the beginning was the Word, and the Word was with God . . .', 'O God, from whom all holy desires, all good counsels, and all just works do proceed . . .' entail (in the case of the statements) or presuppose (in the case of the prayer) that God exists; and it also seems clear to me that normal or typical users of such language have intended this entailment or presupposition. That is to say, if asked 'Are you assuming that there actually is a Being whom you are addressing (or referring to) and who is eternal, omnipotent, etc.?' the typical religious man would unhesitatingly reply, 'Yes, of course I am.' And if we pressed him further, in the light of modern discussions about the distinction between factual and non-factual statements, and asked 'Do you regard it as an objective fact that God exists – a fact which obtains whether or not any particular person knows it or believes it' he would still unhesitatingly say 'Yes'. In other words, christian language, as the actual speech of a living community, presupposes the extra-linguistic reality of God.

My second thesis follows from the first: Since christian discourse affirms the factual reality of God, it gives rise to an entirely proper question concerning the truth or otherwise of this affirmation. For it is always logically in order, in face of a factual claim, to ask whether that claim is justified. There is always a proper question whether an indicative statement is true. It would be illogical to say that the central religious assertions are factually true or false, but that there is nevertheless no proper question *whether* they are true.

However, Phillips apparently admits no such question. In an important passage on pp. 22–3 of *The Concept of Prayer* he says:

> To ask a question, then, about the reality of the physical world, is not to ask whether the physical world exists (what would that mean?) but to ask for an elucidation of the concept of reality in question. Similarly, the question of the reality of God which is of interest to the philosopher is a question about a *kind of reality*; a question about the possibility of giving an account of the distinction between truth and falsity, sense and nonsense, in religion. This is not a question of experimentation any more than the question of the reality of the physical world, but a question of conceptual elucidation; that is, the philosophers want to know what is meant by 'real' ('exists') in the statement 'God is real (exists)'.

The argument here seems to be: the user of physical-object language cannot meaningfully ask whether the physical world exists, though he can seek as a philosopher to elucidate the *kind* of reality it has. Similarly the user of theistic language cannot meaningfully ask whether God exists; though he can as a philosopher seek to elucidate the kind of reality God has. But this is a question-begging parallel. Whereas everyone is a user of physical-object language, so that there is no one in a position to ask seriously whether the physical world exists, by no means everyone is a user of theistic language, and there are many who ask seriously whether God exists. In the context of universal agreement that there is a material world, the question about its existence or reality is (as Phillips rightly says) a conceptual question asking for an elucidation of the notion of a material object. But in the quite different context of dispute as to whether God exists the question about the reality of God is not only a conceptual question but also a question of fact and existence. To ask 'What kind of reality has that which is spoken about in material-object language?' and

'What kind of reality has that which is spoken about in theistic language?' is to embark upon two very diverse kinds of inquiry. At this point, however, Phillips would perhaps want to refer to Malcolm's discussion of the second form of the ontological argument, presented in Anselm's *Proslogion* 3 and in his *Reply* to Gaunilon. In his much disscused article, 'Anselm's Ontological Arguments' (*Philosophical Review*, January 1960), of which Phillips makes frequent use, Malcolm shows that the concept of God is such that it is not a contingent question whether God exists. God can neither contingently exist nor contingently fail to exist; divine existence must be either necessary or impossible. He further believes that the second case, equivalent to the necessary non-existence of God, can be excluded, thereby proving that God necessarily exists. I have criticised this argument in detail elsewhere.[7] But the point at the moment is that the concept of God is such that God's existing or not existing is not a contingent existing or not existing. That is to say, God is conceived as being without beginning or end and as without dependence for his existence upon anything other than himself. But it does not follow from this, as Phillips seems to suppose, that there is no question *whether* there is such an eternal independent Being. There is, to be sure, no question whether God contingently exists. But there is a question whether he eternally and independently (i.e. necessarily) exists, in distinction from eternally not existing. Even if Phillips were to claim that this question can be definitively settled by philosophical reasoning (as Malcolm perhaps and Hartshorne certainly claim), the question thus settled would still be a perfectly good question.

This leads me to my third thesis: Philosophical considerations are relevant to a decision as to whether or not it is reasonable to believe that God exists.

Here it seems that Phillips would accept the negative contention that philosophical criticism may render an existing belief untenable,[8] but would deny to philosophy any converse positive office. He says:

The whole conception, then, of religion standing in need of

---

[7] In *The Many-Faced Argument*, edited by Hick and McGill (New York: The Macmillan Company, 1967, and London: Macmillan, 1968) ch. 19.   [8] *Faith and Philosophical Enquiry*, ch. 13.

justification is confused. Of course, epistemologists will seek to clarify the meaning of religious statements, but, as I have said, this means clarifying what is already there awaiting such clarification. Philosophy is neither for nor against religion: 'it leaves everything as it is'. This fact distinguishes philosophy from apologetics. It is not the task of the philosopher to decide whether there is a God or not, but to ask what it means to affirm or deny the existence of God.[9]

I should like to raise some questions about this passage. Certainly, philosophy in general is neither for nor against religion; but does it follow that there cannot be philosophical arguments for and against the belief-worthiness of religious claims, such as the claim that there is an infinite personal being who has created everything that exists other than himself? Again, certainly philosophy leaves everything as it is; but does it follow that it may not help us to discern how things are? Certainly, again, philosophy cannot decide whether God exists in the sense of determining whether he shall exist or not; but may philosophy not nevertheless help us to decide whether it is reasonable to believe that God exists; and may it not do this along precisely the path that Phillips indicates, namely by clarifying what it means to affirm or deny the existence of God? For example, given Yuri Gagarin's concept of God as an object that he would have observed, had it existed, during his first space flight, may one not put two and two together and conclude that it is unreasonable to believe that God, so conceived, exists? Of course, this latter operation of drawing conclusions concerning the truth or falsity of a belief is very much harder in the case of more sophisticated concepts of God; and if Phillips is saying just this, well and good. But that philosophy clarifies concepts, such as the concept of deity, does not entail that it can have nothing to say about whether there (logically) *can* be and, if so, whether it is reasonable to believe that there actually *is*, a reality answering to the concept. Nevertheless Phillips evidently holds, as a matter of definition, that it is properly philosophical to note what people say and to extract therefrom the concepts they are using, but not to consider reasons for and against believing what they say. The philosopher of religion is thus given the role of an observer who

[9] *The Concept of Prayer*, p. 10.

seeks to understand how religious persons talk and to discern the 'logic' of their language. He is committed as a spectator (or auditor) to noting, though not to accepting or rejecting, their religious beliefs and presuppositions. It is thus not open to him to conclude, either rightly or wrongly, that there cannot be a divine being such as religious people suppose there to be, and that they are therefore fundamentally mistaken. The philosopher, it would seem, is in this respect like an anthropologist or a sociologist who studies a living society, describing its structure and dynamics, but who does not in his capacity as anthropologist or sociologist form moral judgements about its life or truth-valuations about its beliefs. He accepts the society he is studying as a going concern, a part of the total phenomenon of human life, and he is not concerned to promote or oppose, praise or condemn, but simply to describe and understand it.

This conception of the philosophy of religion would cut out many of the topics that are normally discussed under that name. In excluding the critical consideration of possible grounds for believing or disbelieving in the reality of God it excludes study of the traditional theistic arguments; of the question of the cognitive value of religious experience and mysticism; of the relation between religious and scientific beliefs; of the apparently competing truth-claims of different religions; of naturalistic theories of the nature of religion; of the problem of evil considered as a challenge to theistic faith; of the alleged incoherences in the concept of God. Alas, some of us are not only profoundly interested in these questions but also earn our living by discussing them!

However, if some of us have a vested interest in traditional philosophy of religion and others haven't, this in itself hardly constitutes a philosophical issue. If a thinker prefers to omit certain topics from his range of interest, or even to adopt a definition of 'philosophy' which excludes them, this is his own business. It may appear to some of us as a needlessly quixotic act of self-denial, and we may be inclined to congratulate Phillips when in practice he infringes it by the interest that he shows in the ontological argument. But if there is nothing more to it than an individual preference there seems little more to be said.

There still remains, however, what *may* be a genuine difference of religious attitude and understanding. Phillips seems to think that there is such a difference, and he expresses it as follows:

There are some people the truth of whose religion depends on the way things go in their lives. Things may not go well here and now, but unless the ultimate facts, the eschatological situation, are favourable in some sense or other, faith has been a hoax and a failure. For Hick, the kind of difference religion makes to life is the difference between a set of empirical facts being or not being the case. This belief is illustrated by a comment I heard a mother make about her mentally handicapped child: 'Only my religious faith keeps me going. Of one thing I am sure: my child's place in heaven is secure.' On Hick's account, the mother would be saying, 'It is terrible for my child at the moment, but he is to be compensated later on'. Her hope is in certain facts being realized.

Although I sympathize with the mother's hope, I do not find it impressive religiously. Indeed, I should want to go further and say that it has little to do with religion, being much closer to superstition. Two other mothers of mentally handicapped children expressed what their religious faith meant to them in very different terms. One of them discussed the view that there is a *prima facie* incompatibility between belief in God and the terribleness of having a mentally handicapped child. People kept asking her why such a thing should have happened to her, to which she replied, 'Why shouldn't it have happened to me?' I found this answer extremely impressive, although I suspect that it needs a certain kind of religious belief to find it so . . .[10]

I am not sure whether this points to a real religious difference or not. I, for one, have no inclination whatever to regard religion as an explanatory hypothesis. I regard it rather as consciousness of God and as living on the basis of that consciousness. Contained within it – though varying in degree of explication in different minds – are a number of beliefs, including the belief that God is real and that the whole universe is ultimately under the sovereignty and within the providence of divine love. This means, in the case of the two mothers of mentally handicapped children, that those children, whom they love and whose development as persons is stunted by a defective brain or mind, are objects of God's care and will in the end participate in the 'good *eschaton*' of his creation. It is this that we call symbolically the Kingdom of

[10] *Faith and Philosophical Enquiry*, pp. 127–8.

Heaven, in which 'all shall be well, and all shall be well, and all manner of thing shall be well'. One of the two mothers may not spell out at all in her own mind the implications of this christian hope; she may simply be conscious of the reality and presence of God in her situation. And those who are least inclined to try to spell out the implications of their faith may be the ones who are living most firmly on the basis of it. (Perhaps this is what Phillips is concerned to emphasise.) But any faith that is recognisably continuous with that of the New Testament has an eschatological aspect of it. This is not a matter of 'pie in the sky' – any more than was Jesus' own awareness of God's sovereignty as ensuring the eventual triumph of the divine purpose for the whole creation. It was rather a sense of the *reality* of God and of the ultimate sovereignty of the divine love in relation to the temporal process.

III

In his paper on 'Religious Beliefs and Language Games'[11] Phillips faces the charge made by a number of writers (he cites Ronald Hepburn, Kai Nielsen and myself) that to regard religious language as a language-game with its own internal criteria of meaning and validity is to treat it as a form of protected discourse. As such it would be invulnerable to external criticism but, as the price of such invulnerability, of significance only to those who chose to play this 'game'. The teaching of Jesus, for example, could then no longer be seen as declaring in common human language truths which are of infinite importance to mankind but which are also capable of being questioned from an agnostic or atheist standpoint.

In facing this criticism (made, for example, in the previous section of this chapter) Phillips writes, he says, 'as one who has talked of religious beliefs as language-games, but also as one who has come to feel misgivings in some respects about doing so'.[12] And in the course of the paper he goes quite a long way in acknowledging that religious language cannot be an autonomous language-game, discontinuous with the rest of our speech and immune from the possibility of conflict with our other beliefs. 'So far', he says, 'from it being true that religion can be thought of as an isolated language-game, cut off from all other forms of

[11] *Faith and Philosophical Enquiry*, ch. 5.   [12] Op. cit., p. 78.

life, the fact is that religious beliefs cannot be understood at all
unless their relation to other modes of life is taken into account.'[13]
Again, 'one must stress the connection between religious beliefs
and the world, not only in bringing out the force which these
beliefs have, but also in bringing out the nature of the difficulties
which the belief may occasion. If religion were an isolated
language-game, cut off from everything which is not formally
religious, how could there be any of the characteristic difficulties
connected with religious belief?'[14]

This is a welcome clarification of Phillips's position, developing
it in what is, I believe, the right direction. But I want to suggest
that having set out on this path it is necessary to go a great deal
further. For religious beliefs not only have connections with this
familiar world, and with all our life within it, but also with
aspects of reality transcending this world and our present earthly
life. An obvious example is the religious faith in God's purpose to
raise us to life again after death. So far as christian language is
concerned it would be utterly arbitrary and dogmatic to cut out
all references to resurrection, the life to come, heaven and hell,
immortality, the fulfilment of God's purpose for men and women
beyond as well as within this world. Further, there is a manifest
connection between this area of religious belief and expectations
concerning the future course of human experience after death.
But faced with this particular connection between language and
fact, Phillips reverts to the autonomy-of-religious-language thesis
and refuses to admit the connections which the language itself
claims. Thus in *Death and Immortality*, after expounding the
standard philosophical arguments against the intelligibility of the
idea of personal survival after death, he offers his own this-
worldly reinterpretation of the language of immortality. 'Eternity', he says, 'is not *more* life, but this life seen under certain
moral and religious modes of thought.'[15]

The religious truth which lies in the offing is that eternal life, in
its fullness, is a quality of life, a life that is not only lived for ever
but is above all *worth* living for ever, and that this quality of life
may be entered upon now in the midst of this earthly existence.
But the untruth of Phillips's position lies in its unfaithfulness to

[13] Ibid., p. 97.   [14] Ibid., p. 99.
[15] *Death and Immortality* (London: Macmillan, and New York: St
Martin's Press, 1970) p. 49.

actual religious language, by cutting off its implications concerning 'what there is' and 'how things are'. Consider the connection between belief in the love of God for all his human creatures and belief in the final perfecting of human life after bodily death. In the context of christian faith, God's love for mankind is not an isolated unit of language, devoid of concrete implications, but refers to the creative divine purpose of bringing men and women to enjoy the supreme quality of life, in community with one another and in conscious dependence upon God, that is symbolised as the Kingdom of Heaven. In so far as human beings live in the misery of fear, hatred, jealousy, suspicion, anxiety, ignorance, oppression and frustrated potentiality, God's love for them is defeated and his loving purpose unfulfilled. Phillips ignores the thousands of millions of people down the ages for whom God's good purpose has not in fact been fulfilled in this earthly life, and develops his theories in terms of the more fortunate minority who have been able to find God in the midst of oppression or calamity, pain or failure. It is happily true that suffering does sometimes ennoble and deepen the human personality and bring one nearer to God. But it would be unrealistic to think that this is always or even usually the case. Phillips looks at the problem of evil through the eyes of such writers as Simone Weil, Kierkegaard, some of Dostoievsky's heroes, and saintly individuals who have found God in the midst of suffering. But the result is a spiritually élitist view which disregards the large and very imperfect mass of humanity. God's love enfolds sinners as well as saints, ordinary struggling and failing mortals as well as spiritual giants. For very many ordinary people God's loving purpose is manifestly not brought to completion in a world in which the majority of the human beings who have ever been born have died in infancy; and in which the majority of those who have survived to adulthood have lived in poverty, undernourishment and ill-health, in slavery or oppression and lack of freedom, and without any possibility of being enlarged by the emotional and intellectual riches opened up by literature and the arts, science and philosophy. Thus if we think of God's love in concrete terms, as a creative purpose seeking an authentically human existence for every individual, we are led to see life in a much larger context than this earth. For on this earth God's loving purpose succeeds only very partially. If babies who die in infancy, and the multitude of the oppressed in all ages, and the many who are defeated rather than elevated by suffering and injustice are ever to participate in the fulfilment of the divine intention there must be a further life to come; and accordingly talk of the love of God must have implications for the future course of human experience beyond bodily death.

I therefore suggest that having recognised in principle that religious beliefs do not constitute an autonomous language-game, but ramify out to connect with the whole of reality, one must accept the implications of belief in a loving God. If the word 'loving' has any meaning when applied to God it must bear the kind of positive analogy to human love that is indicated in so many of Jesus' sayings and parables. For *God*, the Creator and Lord of the universe, to be loving entails that evil is not ultimate and that infinite good will, however slowly and painfully, be brought out of it. And this in turn entails the completion of God's good purpose for human beings beyond this earthly life.

What is at issue here is not compensation in another life for men's sufferings in this, but the fulfilment of God's purpose for his creation. If that purpose involves that all his human children shall eventually be drawn into the divine life, this purpose has unavoidable implications concerning the structure and process of the universe. Expressions of christian faith are thus also, by implication, expressions of belief about the character of our total environment. This is, as I have been suggesting, brought home to us when we confront the theological problem of evil; and accordingly in two later chapters we shall be looking more closely at this problem.

3. Religious Faith as Experiencing-as

THE PARTICULAR sense or use of the word 'faith' that I am seeking to understand is that which occurs when the religious man, and more specifically the christian believer, speaks of 'knowing God' and goes on to explain that this is a knowing of God by faith. Or again, when asked how he professes to know that God, as spoken about in Christianity, is real, his answer is 'by faith'. Our question is: what does 'faith' mean in these contexts? And what I should like to be able to do is to make a descriptive (or if you like phenomenological) analysis that could be acceptable to both believers and non-believers. A Christian and an atheist or agnostic should equally be able to say, Yes, that is what, phenomenologically, faith is – though they would of course then go on to say radically different things about its value.

The modes of cognition have been classified in various ways. But the distinction that is most relevant to our present purpose is that between what I shall call cognition in presence and cognition in absence; or acquaintance (using this term less restrictedly than it was used by Russell) and holding beliefs-about. We cognise things that are present before us, this being called perception; and we also cognise things in their absence, this being a matter of holding beliefs about them. And the astonishing fact is that while our religious literature – the Bible, and prayers, hymns, sermons, devotional meditations, and so on – confidently presuppose a cognition of God by acquaintance, our theological literature in contrast recognises for the most part only cognition in absence. That is to say, whereas the Bible itself, and other writings directly expressing the life of faith, are full of men's encounters with God and men's personal dealings with the divine

Thou, the dominant systems of christian theology nevertheless treat faith as belief, as a propositional attitude. In the Catholic tradition deriving from St Thomas, and no less in the Protestant orthodoxy that supervened upon the Reformation movement, faith has been quite explicitly defined as believing on God's authority certain truths, i.e. propositional truths, that he has revealed. Thus faith, instead of being seen as a religious response to God's redemptive action in the life of Jesus of Nazareth, has been seen instead as primarily an assent to theological truths. For good or ill this was a very major and radical step, taken early on in the church's history and displaying its implications over the centuries in many different aspects of the life of Christendom. I believe that it was a wrong step, which the Reformers of the sixteenth century sought to correct. If this is so, we want to find a viable way, or perhaps even ways (in the plural), of thinking of faith as a form of cognition by acquaintance or cognition in presence. Instead of assimilating faith to propositional belief – whether such belief be produced by reasoning or act of will or both – we must assimilate it to perception. I therefore want to explore the possibility that the cognition of God by faith is more like perceiving something, even perceiving a physical object, that is present before us than it is like believing a statement about some absent object, whether because the statement has been proved to us or because we want to believe it.

But surely – if I may myself at once voice an inevitable protest – the cognition of God can no more be like sense perception than God is like a physical object. It is true that christian tradition tells of an ultimate beatific vision of God, but we are not now speaking of this but of the ordinary believer's awareness of God in our present earthly life. And this is not a matter of perceiving him, but of believing, without being able to perceive him, that he nevertheless exists. It is in fact, as it has traditionally been held to be, a case of cognition in absence, or of holding beliefs-about.

However the hypothesis that we want to consider is not that religious faith *is* sense perception, but that as a form of cognition by acquaintance it is *more like* sense perception than like propositional belief. That propositions may be validly founded upon the awareness of God, and that they then play an indispensable and immensely valuable part in the religious life, is not in question. But what we are interested in now is the awareness of

God itself; for this is faith – that is to say, distinctively religious cognition – in its primary sense.

It is today hardly a contentious doctrine requiring elaborate argumentation that seeing – to confine ourselves for the moment to this one mode of perceiving – is not a simple straightforward matter of physical objects registering themselves on our retinas and thence in our conscious visual fields. There are complexities, and indeed a complex variety of complexities. The particular complexity that concerns us now was brought to the attention of philosophers by Wittgenstein's discussion of seeing-as in the *Philosophical Investigations.*[1] Wittgenstein pointed to puzzle pictures and ambiguous diagrams of the kind that are found in abundance in some of the psychological texts – for instance the Necker cube, Jastrow's duck-rabbit, and Köhler's goblet-faces. The cube diagram, for instance, can be seen as a cube viewed either from below or from above, and the perceiving mind tends to alternate between these two perspectives. The goblet-faces diagram can be seen as the outline of a goblet or vase or as the outlines of two faces looking straight into each other's eyes. The duck-rabbit can be seen as the representation of a rabbit's head facing to the left or of a duck's head facing to the right. In these cases every line of the diagram plays its part in both aspects (as Wittgenstein called them) and has equal weight in each: these may accordingly be called cases of total ambiguity. Another sort, artistically more complex, might be called cases of emergent pattern; for example, those puzzle pictures in which you are presented with what at first seems to be a random and meaningless scattering of lines and dots, but in which as you look at it you come to see, say, a face; or again, as another example, the well-known 'Christ in the snow' picture. And in between there are various other sorts of intermediate cases which we need not however take account of here. We speak of seeing-as when that which is objectively there, in the sense of that which affects the retina, can be consciously perceived in two different ways as having two different characters or natures or meanings or significances; and very often, in these two-dimensional instances, we find that the mind switches back and forth between the alternative ways of seeing-as.

Let us at this point expand the notion of seeing-as into that of

[1] Pt. II, sec. xi.

experiencing-as. The elements of experiencing-as are the purely visual seeing-as which we have thus far been discussing, plus its equivalents for the other senses. For as well as seeing a bird as a bird, we may hear it as a bird – hear the bird's song as a bird's song, hear the rustle of its wings as a bird in flight, hear the rapping of the woodpecker as just that; and so on. Again, a carpenter may not only see the wood as mahogany but also feel it as mahogany; he may recognise it tactually as well as visually. Or again, we may taste the wine as Burgundy and smell the cheese as Gorgonzola. Not of course that the different senses normally function in isolation. We perceive and recognise by means of all the relevant senses co-operating as a single complex means of perception; and I suggest that we use the term 'experiencing-as' to refer to the end-product of this in consciousness.

The next step is from these two-dimensional pictures and diagrams to experiencing-as in real life – for example, seeing the tuft of grass over there in the field as a rabbit, or the shadows in the corner of the room as someone standing there. And the analogy to be explored is with two contrasting ways of experiencing the events of our lives and of human history, on the one hand as purely natural events and on the other hand as mediating the presence and activity of God. For there is a sense in which the religious man and the atheist both live in the same world and another sense in which they live consciously in different worlds. They inhabit the same physical environment and are confronted by the same changes occurring within it. But in its actual concrete character in their respective 'streams of consciousness' it has for each a different nature and quality, a different meaning and significance; for one does and the other does not experience life as a continual interaction with the transcendent God. Is there then any true analogy or parallel between, on the one hand, these two ways of experiencing human life, *as* an encounter with God or *as* an encounter only with a natural order, and on the other hand the two ways of seeing the distant shape, *as* a rabbit or *as* a tuft of grass?

An immediate comment might be: if there is any such analogy, so much the worse for religious cognition! For does not the analogy between seeing a puzzle picture in a certain way and experiencing human life in a certain way underline once again the purely subjective and gratuitous character of religious knowledge-claims in contrast with the compelling objectivity of ordinary sense perception?

So far as the argument has thus far gone, perhaps it does. But the next point to be introduced must considerably affect the upshot of what has gone before. This is the thesis that *all* experiencing is experiencing-as – not only, for example, seeing the tuft of grass, erroneously, as a rabbit, but also seeing it correctly as a tuft of grass. On the face of it this sounds paradoxical. One might put the difficulty in this way: we may if we like speak of seeing the tuft of grass *as* a tuft of grass because it is evidently possible to misperceive it as a sitting rabbit. But what about something utterly familiar and unmistakable? What about the fork on the table? Would it not be absurd to say that you are seeing it *as* a fork? It must be granted that this particular locution would be distinctly odd in most circumstances. However we have more acceptable names for ordinary seeing-as in real life; we call it 'recognising' or 'identifying'. Of course we are so familiar with forks that normally we recognise one without encountering even enough difficulty to make us notice that we are in fact performing an act of recognition. But if the fork were sufficiently exotic in design I might have occasion to say that I can recognise the thing before me on the table as a fork – that is, as a man-made instrument for conveying food into the mouth. And, going further afield, a Stone-Age savage would not be able to recognise it at all. He might identify it instead as a marvellously shining object which must be full of *mana* and must not be touched; or as a small but deadly weapon; or as a tool for digging; or just as something utterly baffling and unidentifiable. But he would not have the concept of a fork with which to identify it as a fork. Indeed to say that he does not have this concept and that he cannot perform this act of recognition are two ways of saying the same thing. That there is no ambiguity or mystery about forks for you or me is simply due to the contingent circumstance that forks are familiar parts of the apparatus of our culture. For the original nature or meaning of an artefact is determined by the purpose for which it has been made, and this purpose necessarily operates within a particular cultural context. But simply as a physical object of a certain size and shape an artefact does not bear its meaning stamped upon it. To recognise or identify is to be experiencing-as in terms of a concept; and our concepts are social products having their life within a particular linguistic environment.

Further, this is as true of natural objects as it is of artefacts. Here, too, to recognise is to apply a concept; and this is always to cognise the thing as being much more than is currently perceptible. For example, to identify a moving object in the sky as a bird is not only to make implicit claims about its present shape, size and structure beyond what we immediately observe but also about its past (for instance, that it came out of an egg, not a factory), about its future (for instance, that it will one day die), and about its behaviour in various hypothetical circumstances (for instance, that it will tend to be frightened by loud noises). When we thus equate experiencing-as with recognising it is I think no longer a paradoxical doctrine that all conscious experiencing is experiencing-as.

But – if I may raise a possible objection – is it not the case that 'He recognises *x*' entails that the thing recognised is indeed *x*, while 'He is experiencing *a* as *x*' does not entail that *a* is indeed *x*: and must we not therefore acknowledge a distinction between recognising and experiencing-as? As a matter of the ordinary use of these words the objection is, I think, in order. But what it indicates is that we lack a term to cover both recognition and misrecognition. We are accordingly driven to use 'recognition' generically, as 'knowledge' in 'theory of knowledge' is used to cover error as well as knowledge, or as 'morality' in 'theory of morality' is used to cover immorality also. I have been using 'recognition' here in an analogous way to include unjustified as well as justified identification assertions.

I proceed, then, from the proposition that all conscious experiencing involves recognitions which go beyond what is given to the senses and is thus a matter of experiencing-as. This means that ordinary secular perceiving shares a common epistemological character with religious experiencing. We must accordingly abandon the view – if we ever held it – that sense perception at the highly sophisticated human level is a mere automatic registering by the mind of what is on the retina, while religious perception is, in contrast, a subjective response which gratuitously projects meanings into the world. We find instead that all conscious perceiving goes beyond what the senses report to a significance which has not as such been given to the senses. And the religious experience of life as a sphere in which we have continually to do with God and he with us is likewise an awareness in our experience as a whole of a significance which transcends the scope of the senses. In both cases, in a classic statement of John Oman's, 'knowing is not knowledge as an effect of an unknown external cause, but is knowledge as we so interpret that our meaning is the actual meaning of our environment'.[2] And, as Oman also taught, the claim of the religious believer is that in his religious commitment he is relating himself to his total environment in its most ultimate meaning.

The conclusion that *all* experiencing is experiencing-as enables us to meet a fundamental objection that might be made against the analogy between experiencing-as in ordinary life and in religious awareness. It might be pointed out that it is only possible to see, let us say, a tuft of grass as a rabbit if one has previously seen real rabbits; and that in general to see *A* as a *B* presupposes acquaintance with *B*s. Analogously, in order to experience some event, say a striking escape from danger or a healing, as an act of God it would seem that we must first know by direct acquaintance what an act of God is like. However all that has ever been witnessed in the way of divine actions are earthly events which the religious mind has seen as acts of God but which a sceptical observer could see as having a purely natural explanation. In other words, we never have before us unambiguously divine acts, but only ambiguous events which are capable of taking on religious significance to the eyes of faith. But in that case, it will be said, we have no unproblematic cases of divine actions available to us, as we have in abundance unproblematic instances of rabbits and forks; and consequently we can never be in a position to recognise any of these ambiguous events *as* acts of God. Just as it would be impossible for one who had never seen rabbits to see anything *as* a rabbit, so it must be impossible for us who have never seen an undeniable act of God, to see an event *as* an act of God. This seems on the face of it to be a conclusive objection.

However the objection collapses if, as I have been arguing, *all* experiencing, involving as it does the activity of recognising, is to be construed as experiencing-as. For although the process of

[2] *The Natural and the Supernatural* (Cambridge University Press, 1931) p. 175.

recognising is mysterious, there is no doubt that we do continually recognise things, and further that we can learn to recognise. We have learned, starting from scratch, to identify rabbits and forks and innumerable other kinds of thing. And so there is thus far in principle no difficulty about the claim that we may learn to use the concept 'act of God', as we have learned to use other concepts, and acquire the capacity to recognise exemplifying instances.

But of course – let it at once be granted – there are obvious and indeed immense differences between the concept of a divine act and such concepts as rabbit and fork. For one thing, rabbits and forks are objects – substances, if you like – whereas a divine act is an event. This is already a considerable conceptual contrast. And we must proceed to enlarge it still further. For the cognition of God recorded in the Bible is much wider in scope than an awareness of particular isolated events as being acts of God. Such divine acts are but points of peculiarly intense focus within a much wider awareness of existing in the presence of God. Indeed the biblical cognition of God is typically mediated through the whole experience of the prophet or apostle after his call or conversion, even though within this totality there are specially vivid moments of awareness of God, some of which are evoked by striking or numinous events which thereby becomes miracles or theophanies. However, we are primarily concerned here with the wider and more continuous awareness of living within the ambience of the unseen God – with the sense of the presence of God – and this is surely something very unlike the awareness of forks and rabbits.

But although the sense of the presence of God is indeed very far removed from the recognition of forks and rabbits, it is already, I think, clear that there are connecting links in virtue of which the religious awareness need not be completely unintelligible to us. In its epistemological structure it exhibits a continuity with our awareness in other fields.

In seeking further to uncover and investigate this continuity we must now take note of another feature of experiencing-as, namely the fact that it occurs at various levels of awareness. By this I mean that as well as there being values of x and y such that to experience A as x is incompatible with experiencing it as y, because x and y are mutually exclusive alternatives, there are also values of x and y such that it is possible to experience A as simultaneously *x* and *y*. Here *y* is supplementary to *x*, but on a different level. What is meant by 'levels' in this context? That *y* is on a higher level than *x* means that the experiencing of *A* as *y* presupposes but goes beyond the experiencing of it as *x*. One or two examples may be useful at this point. As an example, first, of mutually exclusive experiencings-as, one cannot see the tuft of grass simultaneously as a tuft of grass and as a rabbit; or the person whose face we are watching as both furiously angry and profoundly delighted. On the other hand, as an example of supplementary experiencings-as, we may see what is moving above us in the sky as a bird; we may further see it as a hawk; and we may further see it as a hawk engaged in searching for prey; and if we are extremely expert bird watchers we may even see it as a hawk about to swoop down on something on the far side of that low hump of ground. These are successively higher-level recognitions in the sense that each later member of the list presupposes and goes beyond the previous one.

Now let us call the correlate of experiencing-as 'significance', defining this by means of the notion of appropriate response. That is to say, to recognise what is before us as an *x* involves being in a dispositional state to act in relation to it in a certain distinctive way or range of ways. For example, to recognise the object on the table as a fork is to be in a different dispositional state from that in which one is if one recognises it as a fountain pen. One is prepared in the two cases for the object to display different characteristics, and to be surprised if it doesn't; and one is prepared to use it in different ways and on different occasions, and so on; and in general to recognise something *as* a this or a that (i.e. as significant in this way or in that way) involves being in a certain dispositional state in relation to it.

Our next step must be to shift attention from isolated objects as units of significance to larger and more complex units, namely situations.

A situation is composed of objects; but it is not simply any random collocation of objects. It is a group of objects which, when attended to as a group, has its own distinctive significance over and above the individual significances of its constituent members. That is to say, the situation evokes its own appropriate dispositional response.

As in the case of object-significance there can be different levels of situational significance, with higher levels presupposing lower. An example that is directly relevant is the relation between the ethical significance of a human situation and its purely natural or physical significance. Think of any situation involving an element of moral obligation. Suppose, for example, that someone is caught at the foot of a steep cliff by an incoming tide and I at the top hear his cries for help. He asks me to run to the nearest telephone, ring the police and ask them to call out the lifeboat to rescue him. Consider this first at the purely natural or physical level. There are the cliff and the sea, a human creature liable in due course to be submerged by the rising tide, and his shouted appeals for help. And, morality apart, that is all that there is – just this particular pattern of physical events. However as moral beings we are aware of more than that. As well as experiencing the physical events as physical events we also experience them as constituting a situation of moral claim upon ourselves. We experience the physical pattern as having ethical significance; and the dispositional response that it renders appropriate is to seek to help the trapped person in whatever way seems most practicable. We can, however, conceive of someone with no moral sense at all, who simply fails to be aware of the ethical significance of this situation. He would be interpreting or recognising or experiencing-as only at the physical level of significance. And there would be no way of proving to someone who was thus morally defective that there is any such thing as moral obligation. No doubt an amoral creature could be induced by threats and promises to conform to a socially desirable pattern of behaviour, but he could never be turned by these means into a moral being. In the end we can only say, tautologously, that a person is aware of the ethical significance of situations because he is a moral being; he experiences in moral terms because he is built that way.

The ethical is experienced as an order of significance which supervenes upon, interpenetrates and is mediated through the physical significance which it presupposes. And if on some occasion the moral character of a situation is not at first apparent to us, but dawns upon as we contemplate it, something happens that is comparable to the discovery of an emergent pattern in a puzzle picture. As the same lines and marks are there, but we have now come to see them as constituting an importantly new pattern, so the social situation is there with the same describable features, but we have now come to be aware of it as laying upon us an inescapable moral claim.

Now consider religious significance as a yet higher level of significance. It is a higher level of significance, adding a new dimension which both includes and transcends that of moral judgement, and yet on the other hand it does not form a simple continuation of the pattern we have already noted. As between natural and ethical significance it is safe to say that every instance of the latter presupposes some instance of the former; for there could be no moral situations if there were no physical situations to have moral significance. But as between ethical and religious significance the relationship is more complex. Not every moment of religious awareness is superimposed upon some occasion of moral obligation. Very often – and especially in the prophetic type of religion that we know in Judaism and Christianity – the sense of the presence of God does carry with it some specific or general moral demand. But we may also be conscious of God in solitude, surrounded only by the natural world, when the divine presence is borne in upon us by the vastness of the starry heavens above or the majestic beauty of a sunrise or a mountain range or some lake or forest scene, or other aspect of earth's marvellously varied face. Again, the sense of the presence of God may occur without any specific environmental context, when the mind is wrapt in prayer or meditation; for there is a contemplative and mystical awareness of God which is relatively independent of external circumstances. And indeed even within the prophetic type of religious experience there are also moments of encounter with God in nature and through solitary prayer as well as in the claims of the personal world. But on the other hand even when the sense of the presence of God has dawned upon us in solitude it is still normally true that it leads us back to our neighbours and often deepens the ethical significance of our relations with them. Thus the dispositional response which is part of the awareness of God is a response in terms of our involvement with our neighbours within our common environment. Even the awareness of God through nature and mystical contemplation leads eventually back to the service of God in the world.

Let us then continue to think here primarily of the prophetic awareness of God, since although this is not the only form of religious cognition it is the typically judaic-christian form. And let us test the notion of faith as religious experiencing-as by applying it to the particular history of faith which is reflected in the biblical records.

The Old Testament prophets were vividly conscious of Jahweh as acting in relation to the people of Israel in certain of the events of their time. Through the writings which recall their words and deeds we feel their overwhelmingly vivid consciousness of God as actively present in their contemporary history. It was God who, in the experience of Amos, was threatening selfish and complacent Israel with Assyrian conquest, while also offering mercy to such as should repent. It was God in his holy anger who, in the experience of Jeremiah, was bringing up the Babylonian army against Jerusalem and summoning his people to turn from their greed and wickedness. It is equally true of the other great prophets of the Old Testament that they were experiencing history, as it was taking place around them, as having a distinctively religious significance. Humanly explicable events were experienced as also acts of God, embodying his wrath or his mercy or his calling of the Jewish nation into covenant with him. The prophets experienced the religious significance of these events and declared it to the people; and this religious significance was always such that to see it meant being conscious of a sacred demand to behave in a new way towards one's neighbours.

It is, I think, important to realise that this prophetic interpretation of hebrew history was not in the first place a philosophy of history, a theoretical pattern imposed retrospectively upon remembered or recorded events. It was in the first place the way in which the great prophets actually experienced and participated in these events at the time. Hosea did not *infer* Jahweh's mercy; second Isaiah did not *infer* his universal sovereignty; Jeremiah did not *infer* his holy righteousness – rather they were conscious of the Eternal as acting towards them, and towards their nation, in his mercy, in his holy righteousness, in his absolute sovereignty. They were, in other words, experiencing-as.

Again, in the New Testament, the primary instance of faith, the rock on which Christianity is based, consisted in seeing Jesus as the Christ. This was the faith of the disciples, epitomised in Peter's confession at Caesarea Philippi, whereby their experience of following Jesus was also an experience of being in the presence of God's personal purpose and claim and love. They may or may not at the time have used any of the terms that were later used in the New Testament writings to express this awareness – Messiah, Son of God, divine Logos. However, these terms point back to that original response, and the faith which they came to express must have been implicit within it. And once again this primary response of the first disciples to Jesus as Lord and Christ was not a theory about him which they adopted, but an experience out of which christian language and theory later grew. That he was their Lord was a fact of experience given in their personal dealings with him. And the special character of their way of seeing and responding to him, in contrast to that of others who never found him to be their Lord, is precisely the distinctive essence of christian faith.

The experiencing of Jesus of Nazareth as Lord – Jesus of Nazareth, that is to say, not as a theological symbol but in his historical concreteness, including his teaching concerning God and man – meant coming to share in some degree both his experiencing of life as the sphere of God's redemptive activity and his practical response to God's purposes in the world. What that involved for Jesus himself is spelled out in his life, and especially in the drama of his death. What it involves for Christians – for those who have begun to share Jesus' vision of the world in its relation to God – is indicated in his moral teaching. For this is simply a general description, with concrete examples drawn from the life of first-century Palestine, of the way in which someone tends spontaneously to behave who is consciously living in the presence of God as Jesus has revealed him.

I have now, I hope, offered at least a very rough outline of a conception of faith as the interpretative element within our cognitive religious experience. How is one to test such a theory, and how decide whether to accept or reject it? All that can be done is to spell out its consequences as fully as possible in the hope that the theory will then either founder under a weight of implausible corollaries, or else show its viability as it proceeds and float triumphantly on to acceptance. I have already tried to indicate its epistemological basis in the thesis that all experiencing is experiencing-as, and the way in which this thesis is relevant to the stream of distinctively religious experience recorded in the Bible. Let me now sketch some of its lines of implication in other directions.

It suggests, as I have already mentioned, a view of the christian ethic as the practical corollary of the distinctively christian vision of the world. Taking a hint from the modern dispositional analysis of belief we may say that to experience the world as having a certain character is, among other things, to be in a dispositional state to live in it in the manner which such a character in our environment renders appropriate. And to experience it in a way derived from Christ's own experience is accordingly to tend to live in the kind of way that he both taught and showed forth in his own life.

Another implication of this theory of faith concerns the nature of revelation. For in christian theology revelation and faith are correlative concepts, faith being a human response to the divine activity of self-revelation. If faith is construed as a distinctively religious experiencing of life as mediating God's presence and activity, this clearly fits and even demands a *heilsgeschichtliche* conception of revelation as consisting in divine actions in human history. God is self-revealingly active within the world that he has made. But his actions are not overwhelmingly manifest and unmistakable; for then men would have no cognitive freedom in relation to their maker. Instead God always acts in such a way that man is free to see or fail to see the events in question as divine acts. The prophets were conscious of God at work in the happenings of their time; but many of their contemporaries were not. Again, the disciples were conscious of Jesus as the Christ; but the scribes and pharisees and the Romans were not. Thus revelation, as communication between God and man, only becomes actual when it meets an answering human response of faith; and the necessity for this response, making possible an uncompelled cognition of God's presence and activity, preserves the freedom and responsibility of the finite creature in relation to the infinite creator.

This in turn suggests an understanding of the special character of the Bible and of its inspiration. The Bible is a record of the stream of revelatory events that culminated in the coming of the Christ. But it differs from a secular account of the same strand of history in that the Bible is written throughout from the standpoint of faith. It describes this history as it was experienced from within by the prophets and then by the apostles. And the faith of the writers, whereby they saw the revelatory events *as* revelatory, is their inspiration. The uniqueness of the Bible is not due to any unique mode or quality of its writing but to the unique significance of the events of which it is the original documentary expression, which became revelatory through the faith of the biblical writers. As such the Bible mediates the same revelation to subsequent generations and is thus itself revelatory in a secondary sense, calling in its own turn for a response of faith.

This theory of faith can also be used to throw light on the nature of the miraculous. For a miracle, whatever else it may be, is an event through which we become vividly and immediately conscious of God as acting towards us. A startling happening, even if it should involve a suspension of natural law, does not constitute for us a miracle in the religious sense of the word if it fails to make us intensely aware of being in God's presence. In order to be miraculous, an event must be experienced as religiously significant. Indeed we may say that a miracle is any event that is experienced as a miracle; and this particular mode of experiencingas is accordingly an essential element in the miraculous.

Finally, yet another application of this theory of faith is to the sacraments. In the sacraments some ordinary material object, bread or wine or water, is experienced as a vehicle of God's grace and becomes a focus of specially intense consciousness of God's overshadowing presence and purpose. A sacrament has in fact the same religious quality as a miracle but differs from other miracles in that it occurs within a liturgical context and is a product of ritual. In themselves, apart from the sacramental context of worshipping faith, the bread and wine or the water are ordinary material things; they have no magical properties. What happens in the sacramental event is that they are experienced as channels of divine grace. They thus invite a peculiarly direct moment of religious experiencing-as, fulfilling for subsequent believers the faith-eliciting and faith-nourishing function of the person of Christ in the experience of the first disciples.

Now I must repeat something that I said near the beginning of this chapter. What I have been attempting to formulate is an epistemological analysis of religious faith, not an argument for the validity of that faith. Faith, I have been suggesting, is the interpretative element within what the religious man reports as his experience of living in the presence of God. But whether that experience is veridical or illusory is another question. My own view is that it is as rational for the religious man to treat his experience of God as veridical as it is for him and others to treat their experience of the physical world as veridical. But that requires another argument, which I have not attempted to supply here.[3]

[3] I have, however, attempted to supply it in the last chapter of *Arguments for the Existence of God* (London: Macmillan, 1970, and New York: Herder and Herder, 1971).

4. God, Evil and Mystery

CAN A LOVING God exist, in view of the reality of sin and suffering? In response to this challenge the Irenaean theodicy offers the limited and negative conclusion that the world's evil does not rationally require one to renounce belief in God. Nor on the other hand, needless to say, does the fact of evil lead one towards belief in God. The positive grounds of belief are not an inference from the world to God. We cannot argue from 'the appearances of nature' – which include all sorts of cases of unmerited suffering – to the existence of a good and loving creator. The positive grounds of theistic belief are, I believe, experiential rather than inferential. But our question now is whether the reality of evil, particularly in the forms of wickedness and suffering, renders it unreasonable to retain a belief in God which has arisen from other grounds. And I want to suggest, in the light of the considerations which constitute the Irenaean theodicy, that whilst the reality of evil undoubtedly challenges christian faith and sets it under a severe strain, it does not finally render that faith untenable by a rational person.

The Irenaean starting point is a conception of the divine purpose for man, from which follows an understanding of both moral and natural evil. The basic postulate is that of a divine purpose to make finite persons who have a genuine autonomy and freedom in relation to their creator and who are therefore capable of entering into personal relationship with him. To this end man has not been brought into existence as a perfect being, but as an imperfect and immature creature who is only at the beginning of a long process of development. This conception was expressed by Irenaeus in his distinction between the image (*imago*) and the likeness (*similitudo*) of God in man. The former is, roughly, man's nature as a rational animal capable of moral judgement and choice. But the creature who has thus been made in the image of God is only the raw material for a further stage of God's creative work, consisting in the unfolding of the fuller potentialities of humanity in the perfecting of our nature through our own free responses to the challenges and opportunities of life – this perfecting eventually constituting man's finite 'likeness' to God in conscious relation with him. And therefore, according to the Irenaean view of the matter, our present world is not intended to be a paradise, in the sense of a proper habitation for perfect beings, but rather a place of soul-making, an environment in which creatures made as rational and personal in the image of God can grow towards the finite likeness of their maker.

The value of this process lies in the creatures' uncoerced recognition of and response to the good – for which they have been made and which they need for their full self-realisation – in right relationship to their fellow creatures and in worship of the supreme Good. It follows that in order freely to *come* to God man must not be created in the immediate presence of his maker but at a distance from him – not a spatial but an epistemic distance, constituted by the circumstance that man has been brought into being in a world and as part of a world in which God is not compulsorily evident, and in which awareness of the divine Thou includes a free interpretative act, traditionally called faith.

Thus man has evolved out of the lower forms of life in a world in which his attention is monopolised by the problems of physical survival. This initial situation produces the self-centred point of view and self-regarding outlook from which human sinfulness in its many forms has arisen. It is this original moral immaturity that is symbolised in the Genesis creation myth by the fall of man. Thus we have to say, in the language of the myth, that man was created as a fallen being! But the traditional language is more misleading than illuminating, for man never in fact fell from a prior state of perfection; he started in primitive animality, and his perfecting lies before him in the future. Here we meet one of the main differences between the Augustinian and Irenaean types of theodicy; the former looks to the past, and to a good which has been lost, for its clue to the meaning and justification of human evil, whilst the latter looks to the future and to a good that has yet to be realised.

The implications of this Irenaean conception for the character of our present world are that it should be religiously ambiguous, making possible a faith-response to God, and that it should constitute an environment in which moral judgements and decisions are called for. It is the latter point that provides a clue to the problem of pain and suffering. For the moral life presupposes a world inhabited in common by the community of those who have rights and obligations in relation to one another – namely, the human race. As a common environment it cannot be a dream-like world, plastic to each individual's wishes, but must have its own objective structure which its inhabitants must learn and in terms of which they have to live. And given the existence of bodily persons (whose existence is therefore continuous with that of their physical environment) in a causally law-abiding world, a pain mechanism seems necessary such as has in fact developed in sentient life. Otherwise, vulnerable fleshy organisms moving about and seeking sustenance in a hard material environment would be unable to survive and propagate their species.

This general character of the world as an objective, causally law-governed environment of psycho-physical life sets the stage for the emergence of moral life. For only a world that is imperfect, in the sense that it is no stress-free and pain-free paradise, can be an environment in which moral choices are called for and in which the development of moral personality can take place. In a paradise no one would be able to help or to harm another, since there could be no forms of want or need, danger or injury.

The development of moral concepts presupposes a situation like that provided by our actual life in this world. Among the features relevant to its character as a moral sphere are our mortality and the precarious existence of the human race within an indifferent environment; our human passions and temptations; and the limited size and resources of the earth. As Ninian Smart has said, 'Moral utterance is embedded in the cosmic status quo'.[1]

According to the Irenaean theodicy, then, this world is not intended to be a paradisal habitation for perfect beings, but an environment in which imperfect creatures can live as moral agents and begin to realise the highest potentialities of their nature. (These two developments are closely intertwined, for such valuable qualities as love, integrity, respect for truth, all have ethical aspects.) And I think we can see, at least in broad and

[1] 'Omnipotence, Evil and Supermen', *Philosophy*, vol. xxvi, no. 137, p. 191.

general terms, that our world is compatible with such an intention. One can see that a creation produced by an omnipotent and
loving maker might, for a good reason, be very imperfect from
the point of view of its inhabitants, containing many rough edges
and constituting a challenging setting for human life.

It is of course an essential part of this theological picture that
our present earthly life is not the totality of human existence.
Moral growth and development are conceived of as continuing
in a post-mortem life, leading eventually to the eternal fulfilment
of the potentialities of humanity in what is depicted symbolically
as the Kingdom of God. This is relevant, not in rendering human
tragedies any less tragic as aspects of present human experience,
but by setting them in a larger and therefore different context in
which there is hope of good beyond the tragedy. If the infant
toddler who is accidentally drowned really does live on in another
world, her little unformed personality not after all extinguished
but continuing to develop, and ultimately attaining to her perfection and fulfilment, does not this make a very considerable
difference? And if the lingering terminal pains of the cancer
sufferer do not end in her extinction but in her release into
another life, freed from the pain-racked diseased body, does not
this again make a very considerable difference? And if the
brilliant young pianist, afflicted with Huntington's Chorea, is not
to be annihilated by his untimely death, after his distressing
physical disintegration, but will continue to explore, enjoy and
create beauty in a renewed existence, does not this too make a
considerable difference? It does not – I repeat – mean that the
tragedy, in each case, is not after all a tragedy. It hardly makes
them, as present experiences, less devastating and hard to bear.
But it does nevertheless make a very large and indeed transforming difference to the total situation, both for calm reflection outside immediate involvement in the tragedy, and also for the
actual future experience of those who are directly involved. For it
means that endless and therefore infinite good lies beyond the
sufferings which so many undergo in this present life.

If, then, the general point is granted that a soul-making world
cannot be a paradise but must on the contrary be like our own
very un-paradisal world in being a stable law-governed environment to which we must adapt our behaviour, and which presents
to us problems to be solved, challenges to be met, and difficulties

to be overcome, the central issue now becomes the *amount* of the suffering caused by the structure of the world. As I have stated the problem elsewhere:

> Let the hypothesis of a divine purpose of soul-making be adopted, and let it be further granted that an environment which is to serve this purpose cannot be a permanent hedonistic paradise but must offer to man real tasks, challenges, and problems. Still the question must be asked: Need the world contain the more extreme and crushing evils which it in fact contains? Are not life's challenges often so severe as to be self-defeating when considered as soul-making influences? Man must (let us suppose) cultivate the soil so as to win his bread by the sweat of his brow; but need there be the gigantic famines from which millions have so miserably perished? Man must (let us suppose) labour on the earth's surface to make roads, and dig beneath it to extract its coals and minerals; but need there be volcanic eruptions burying whole cities, and earth-quakes killing thousands of terrified people in a single night? Man must (let us suppose) face harsh bodily consequences of over-indulgence; but need there also be such fearful diseases as typhoid, polio, cancer, angina? These reach far beyond any constructive function of character training. Their effect seems to be sheerly dysteleological and destructive. They can break their victim's spirit and cause him to curse whatever gods there are. When a child dies of cerebral meningitis, his little personality undeveloped and his life unfulfilled, leaving only an unquenchable aching void in his parents' lives; or when a charming, lively and intelligent woman suffers from a shrinking of the brain which destroys her personality and leaves her in an asylum, barely able to recognise her nearest relatives, until death comes in middle life as a baneful blessing; or when a child is born so deformed and defective that he can never live a properly human life, but must always be an object of pity to some and revulsion to others . . . when such things happen we can see no gain to the soul, whether of the victim or of others, but on the contrary only a ruthlessly destructive process which is utterly inimical to human values.[2]

[2] *Evil and the God of Love* (London: Macmillan, 1966 and New York: Harper & Row, 1967; Fontana ed. 1968) pp. 365–6.

We are here, I believe, at the 'crunch' of the theological problem of evil. What response can there be to this fact of apparently needless, excessive, purposeless, dysteleological suffering?

The starting point must be the acknowledgement that although Christianity (in its Irenaean version) claims that good is ultimately to be brought out of evil, so that all suffering is finally to become a stage in the sufferer's journey to the Kingdom of God, yet we cannot in this present life foresee in each particular case along what specific routes of future experience good is to be brought out of evil. Sometimes we find that there have been sown or there come to flower in calamity graces of character that make even that calamity itself worth while. A selfish spirit may be moved to compassion, a thoughtless person discover life's depths and be deepened thereby, a proud spirit learn humility, a soft self-indulgent person be made strong in the fires of adversity. But sometimes the contrary happens and, instead of ennobling, affliction crushes the soul and wrests from it whatever virtues it possessed. The overall situation is thus that, so far as we can tell, suffering occurs haphazardly, uselessly, and therefore unjustly. It appears to be only randomly related either to past desert or to future soul-making. Instead of serving a constructive purpose, pain and misery seem to fall upon men patternlessly and meaninglessly, with the result that suffering is often undeserved and often occurs in amounts exceeding anything that could have been morally planned.

In response to this problem let us adopt the method of counterfactual hypothesis. At this stage of the discussion it is assumed that a soul-making world cannot be a pain-free paradise but must contain real challenges, with the virtual inevitability of real setbacks, failures and defeats – in short, of real suffering. Let us then conduct the experiment of considering what would be involved in a world order in which suffering did *not* take place apparently randomly and without any constructive purpose. Let us suppose that it occurred, not haphazardly and therefore unjustly, but on the contrary justly and therefore non-haphazardly. In such a world whenever anyone met with any disaster or disease, any accident or calamity, it would be obvious either that he deserved this as a punishment for some specific wrong-doing, or else that the evil was manifestly in process of redounding to his good within a constructive programme of soul-making.

As regards the first case: if we knew that tangible reward or punishment was going to be the immediate consequence of our good or evil deeds we should no longer be free to make genuinely moral choices. As Kant pointed out,

most actions conforming to the [moral] law would be done from fear, few would be done from hope, none from duty. The moral worth of actions, on which alone the worth of the person and even of the world depends in the eyes of supreme wisdom, would not exist at all. The conduct of man, so long as his nature remained as it now is, would be changed into mere mechanism, where, as in a puppet show, everything would gesticulate well but no life would be found in the figures.[3]

The same point is made graphically in the science fiction novel *Eye in the Sky* by Philip Dark, in which some people find themselves in a world ruled by a jealous God whose vengeance upon wrong-doing always strikes promptly. For example, Hamilton frightens the unpleasant Miss Reiss with tales about the vicious nature of his cat.

A terrified squeak escaped from Miss Reiss' lips. In panic, she scrambled back, pathetic and defenceless. Instantly, Hamilton was sorry. Ashamed of himself, he opened his mouth to apologise, to retract his misplaced humor. From the air above his ·head a shower of locusts descended. Buried in a squirming mass of vermin, Hamilton struggled frantically to escape. The two women and the tomcat stood paralysed with disbelief. For a time he rolled and fought with the horde of crawling, biting, stinging pests. Then, dragging himself away, he managed to bat them off and retreat, panting and gasping, to a corner.[4]

One can see that in such a world morality would inevitably be replaced by prudential self-interest.

As regards the second case, a divine arrangement by which suffering could always be seen to work for the good of the sufferer would likewise be self-defeating.

[3] *Critique of Practical Reason*, trans. L. W. Beck (New York: Liberal Arts Press, 1956), pt I, bk II, sec. ix.
[4] *Eye in the Sky* (London: Arrow Books, 1971) p. 39.

In such a world [to repeat what I have written elsewhere] human misery would not evoke deep personal sympathy or call forth organised relief and sacrificial help and service. For it is presupposed in these compassionate reactions both that the suffering is not deserved and that it is *bad* for the sufferer. We do not acknowledge a moral call to sacrificial measures to save a criminal from receiving his just punishment or a patient from receiving the painful treatment that is to cure him. But men and women often act in true compassion and massive generosity and self-giving in the face of unmerited suffering, especially when it comes in such dramatic forms as an earthquake, a famine, or a mining disaster. It seems, then, that in a world that is to be the scene of compassionate love and self-giving for others, suffering must fall upon mankind with something of the haphazardness and inequity that we now experience. It must be apparently unmerited, pointless, and incapable of being morally rationalised. For it is precisely this feature of our common human lot that creates sympathy between man and man and evokes the unselfishness, kindness and goodwill which are among the highest values of personal life.[5]

This does not imply that God *sends* disease, accident, famine, earthquakes, etc., to provide opportunities for sympathy and mutual help. The context of the present phase of the argument is the view that God has set us in an objective world order, with its own inherent structure and laws, within which there are real contingencies and accidents, both good and bad. For only in such a world can the creation of moral character take place in the meeting of real challenges to attain real ends. Further, it is clear that the character of the world as a sphere of 'real life' decisions, involving real risks and opportunities, and with real possibilities of both achievement and failure, would be vitiated if God were continually intervening to alter the course of nature by preventing suffering that would otherwise have occurred. Thus it is not (so far as the Irenaean tradition is concerned) the theological view of the contingent events of the world that they are not contingent but instead divinely caused. The contingencies of the world process are genuine; though the existence of the whole process, with its contingencies, represents a divine creative act, the purpose

[5] *Evil and the God of Love*, pp. 370-1.

of which is to make it possible for finite persons to inhabit an autonomous world in which their creator is not involuntarily evident and in which, accordingly, their moral and spiritual nature may freely develop. In and through and out of this religiously and morally ambiguous situation – which is human existence as we now experience it – and out of its continuation, variation and transformation beyond this present life, the infinite good symbolised by the Kingdom of God is finally to come. Within the context of this theory the positive contribution of mystery to the soul-making process consists in the fact that in a world in which rewards and punishments were justly apportioned to our deeds, our moral nature would never have occasion to develop; and that a world in which the ultimately constructive use of adversity was an established scientific fact would not function as a soul-making sphere. Our world would no longer be a moral order in which moral choices are to be made and which elicits self-giving for others amidst common needs and fears and joys and problems and achievements. Thus, paradoxically, if this life is to be an ethical and spiritual preparation for participation in an infinite good, it must remain a matter of faith and not of sight that this is indeed the purpose that it serves.

5. The Problem of Evil in the First and Last Things

THE NOTIONS of the fall and of eternal damnation should, I believe, be regarded as mythological expressions of aspects of our own self-awareness. The myth of the fall expresses our sense of distance from the proper fulfilment of the God-given possibilities of our nature; and the myth of the double destiny, made vividly concrete in the polarity of heaven and hell, expresses our sense of the unqualified seriousness of the free choices and responses which are all the time inexorably forming our characters for good or ill. As ancient and long-lived poetry expressing important facets of our human self-consciousness these myths may properly be said to be true. That is to say, they are true as myths: they are products of the imagination which stir the will in a right direction. If, however, the mistake is made of taking them non-mythologically, and the question of their value is accordingly posed in terms of literal truth or falsity, then we are likely to dismiss them as false and yet at the same time to miss their significance as myths.

We are concerned with the ideas of the fall and damnation here only in their bearing upon the theodicy problem. I shall seek to show how these two myths, when understood (or rather misunderstood) as pointing to actual past and future events, have distorted the Christian response to the mystery of evil; and then to show how their demythologisation may unblock the path to a more credible christian theodicy.

To understand the idea of the fall of angels and men as referring to actual past events does not, of course, involve accepting literally the story of Adam and Eve. No educated person today, I suppose, does that. To go to the heart of the idea of the fall we must follow the whole medieval tradition of discussion of evil in taking seriously the notion of the fall of the angels. For if we discuss the fall of man, and consider the inevitable criticism that finitely perfect beings would never have fallen, the argument then regresses to the prior fall of the angels in virtue of which evil was already present in the human environment so as to be able to infect man's will. It is only when we turn to the fall of the angels that we are looking (according to the Augustinian theodicy tradition) at the true origin of evil. Before this angelic fall no evil of any kind existed. The created realm was pure and flawless. The finite intelligences whom God had created were marred by no taint or trace of evil in their nature; and their environment likewise was totally free from evil, both in itself and as it impinged upon the life within it. It contained nothing that was not good in God's sight, and nothing that could set up the moral stress of temptation in the angels. There was no tempter; no disorderly desire, or wanton impulse or instinct; no pain or unhappiness; no anxiety or fear. The angelic beings lived in an unclouded awareness of God and of his love. And yet it was in this flawless realm that evil first occurred, appearing as an absolute novelty, completely discontinuous with the previous state of affairs. It came into existence when an angel first rejected God and decided, in effect, to worship and serve himself instead of his maker. This wrong choice, this deliberate and perverse turning from the supreme Good to a lesser good, and consequent self-disorientation in relation to the divine Reality, was the origin of evil; and from it all other evils have subsequently flowed.

In its relation to the theodicy problem (which is not, however, the myth's only or perhaps its original context) the function of the fall story is to shift responsibility for the existence of evil from the omnipotent creator – to whom, *prima facie*, it belongs – to the creature. God created a universe that was totally free from any taint of evil; but the free beings who were part of it wilfully and wickedly misused their freedom, bringing 'death into the world, and all our woe'. The traditional critique of this foundation stone of the Augustinian theodicy is that the doctrine of the spontaneous going wrong of finitely perfect beings involves an impossible self-creation of evil *ex nihilo*. It is sheerly self-contradictory to hold that a perfect creation went wrong all by itself. Flawless creatures would not sin even though they were formally free to do so. If they did sin, this showed that they were not initially flawless after all. It will not do simply to say that the angels were free beings, and that free beings must be free to go wrong as well as to go right. For we can conceive of free beings with a nature such that although free to go wrong they are nevertheless under no temptation to do so; or, again, we can conceive of beings who are tempted to go wrong but whose moral nature is such that they always resist that temptation. Therefore if the angels fell from grace, either they had been endowed by their creator with a sin-prone nature, or else this was a case of evil creating itself *ex nihilo*. The first of these alternatives fails to fulfil the function of the fall doctrine in the Augustinian theodicy, namely to clear God of any responsibility for the existence of evil by laying that responsibility without remainder upon the creature; while the second alternative is self-contradictory and therefore not a genuine option.

St Augustine himself saw this problem and wrestled with it in Books xi and xii of the *City of God*. Here the cat is let out of the bag, and has never since been successfully put back. Augustine is to be honoured for having seen so clearly the final logic of his own position and for adhering to it without evasive ambiguities. He asks himself how it was that some of the angels fell whilst others remained steadfast. And his answer in the end is that the latter 'attached themselves to Him who created them, with the love He created in them', but that the former 'either received less of the grace of the divine love than those who persevered in the same; or if both were created equally good, then, while the one fell by their evil will, the others were more abundantly assisted, and attained to that pitch of blessedness at which they became certain that they should never fall from it'.[1] Thus Augustine saw that the notion of finitely perfect beings, endowed with all the goodness that God's love prompts him to bestow upon its objects, deliberately and sinfully turning away from their maker, is an impossible idea, to which some alternative has to be found. I do not wish to invoke Augustine's own alternative of an iron doctrine of double predestination. But I do wish to invoke the support of Augustine's perception at this crucial point that a theory which postulates the self-creation of evil *ex nihilo* is not a viable option.

[1] *City of God*, xii 9. See also xi 13. Calvin's parallel treatment of the fall of man occurs in the *Institutes*, iii 21–3.

A contemporary Catholic philosopher, Dom Illtyd Trethowan, seeks to meet this problem as follows:

> The fact of sin – the refusal to accept God's offer in favour of 'digging oneself in' – is certainly an obstacle to thought. But do we not mean by 'sin' an *unreasonable* refusal? We are responsible for it precisely to the extent to which we turn deliberately away from what we know to be good. It seems to be the fact, however baffling, that this does happen – and it is the first duty of a philosopher to accept the facts and then, if he can, to fit them together.[2]

Now certainly it is a fact that we 'fallen' humans often act unreasonably and against our own true interests. But this is not what was in question. The question was whether the holy angels, as they came forth in pristine perfection from God's hand, can be conceived to have perversely and irrationally rejected the infinite Love which had made them. The question is whether we can affirm both their original flawlessness and, in this flawless state, their wicked and wanton misuse of their freedom. And it is not to the point here to observe that earthly men and women sin; for they are not flawless beings in a flawless universe. It does not seem to me, then, that any alleviation has been offered of the Augustinian self-contradiction. We are left with the impossible doctrine of the self-creation of evil *ex nihilo*.

Another way of formulating this criticism of the Augustinian theodicy, in respect of its central fall-damnation axis, is this: it offers the morally unacceptable picture of God as creating beings whom, in his divine omniscience, he knows will freely and culpably fall and so deserve eternal punishment. This would be analogous to the deliberate production of 'test-tube babies' with a DNA structure of tendencies which are almost sure sooner or later to be expressed in criminal actions, for which these unfortunate individuals will then be justly punished. Although it might be claimed that they freely act out their nature, and are then justly dealt with, yet we should never regard their initial production as an expression of love or of moral goodness. We should feel towards the scientists who undertook such an experiment as many have felt towards the strict predestinarian image of

[2] 'Dr Hick and the Problem of Evil', *Journal of Theological Studies*, Oct. 1967, p. 407.

God projected by Augustine and Calvin and their respective followers. Trethowan is as anxious as anyone else could be to dissociate himself from this apparent corollary of the Augustinian theodicy. And it is avoided, on his view, by the notion of the logical priority of God's creative act to the possibility of his knowing his creature's future free choices. 'God cannot decide to call off a man's creation because he knows that the man will sin, because the decision to create (logically) precedes the "fore-knowledge" (from God's point of view, simply the "knowledge") that sin will occur. And God does not change his mind'.[3]

The argument here is that God decides to create a particular human being, and can then (but only then) know that individual's future free actions, including his fall; and that it is a logical truth that the decision to create has already occurred if there is a determinate being with a future to be (fore)seen. So far this seems to be a valid discrimination. But it does not affect the original point that for God to create a human being (or an angel) is for him to create a being with a determinate structure or nature, involving determinate potentialities and, in the case of man, with related instincts, tendencies, drives and needs. Accordingly we must still ask what characteristics God has chosen to bestow upon his creature; for that creature's history must depend, at least in its basic character, upon the nature that God has given him. Is it a finitely perfect nature such that, in a perfect world, the creature will never fall; or is it an imperfect nature, or a nature interacting with an imperfect environment, such that he is virtually certain sooner or later to fall? The difficulty is a glaring one, which even thinkers with little interest in theology have observed. For example, Jean-Paul Sartre notes that in the Augustinian tradition on this matter as relayed by Leibnitz, 'we are free since our acts derive from our essence. Yet the single fact that our essence has not been chosen by us shows that all this freedom in particulars covers over a total slavery. God chose Adam's essence.'[4]

It is I think clear that for Trethowan the central issue is that of God's ultimate responsibility or non-responsibility for the actuality of our creaturely world, including the origin and eventual resolution of evil within it. To Trethowan it is an abhorrent thought

[3] Ibid., pp. 408–9.
[4] *Being and Nothingness*, trans. by Hazel Barnes (New York: Philosophical Library, 1956) p. 538.

that God should not only have the attributes of omnipotence and omniscience but also of ultimate omniresponsibility. The nearest he will approach to this is to say that God's creation of free beings involved the risk that they might go wrong: 'God takes a risk in creating us, for our acceptance or rejection of him is logically posterior to our creation.[5] I have already indicated why, as it seems to me, this is no solution: it does not escape the dilemma that either God created the angels, or men, as finitely perfect creatures, with a nature such that although free to fall they never would in fact fall; or else with an imperfect nature, such that he must reasonably expect that sooner or later they would fall. The only option that avoids both horns of this dilemma is the self-contradictory doctrine of the self-creation of evil *ex nihilo* through finitely perfect creatures spontaneously going wrong.

In view of this radical incoherence at the heart of the Augustinian theodicy it seems advisable to explore the alternative strand of christian thought which may be named after St Irenaeus as the first great post-biblical christian thinker to have expressed some of its basic themes. So far as the origin of sin is concerned, one development from the Irenaean starting point is as follows: In creating finite persons for fellowship with himself God has given to them the only kind of freedom that can endow them with a genuine (though relative) autonomy in relation to himself, namely cognitive freedom, the freedom to be aware or unaware of their creator. He has created them at an 'epistemic distance' from himself through their emergence in a world which God has set apart from himself as a separate creaturely sphere. This world has an ambiguous character in that it is capable of being responded to either religiously ·or non-religiously. An innate tendency to experience it religiously – in terms of sacred realities transcending the visible world – has always belonged to our human nature. But the full monotheistic conception of God, with its profound and far-reaching ethical implications, as it has gradually formed in men's minds has come to require for the religious experiencing of life a willingness to live consciously in an infinitely holy presence which confronts us with judgement and demand as well as grace and new life. Such a relationship with God must be entered into freely if the personal autonomy of the creature is to be preserved within it. Accordingly we only become aware of God

[5] Op. cit., p. 415.

by an uncoerced response, the interpretative element within which we call faith.

Man's creation at an epistemic distance from God corresponds to what the Hebrew myth of the beginning calls his fallenness. That is to say, man was not brought into existence in the direct presence of God and with an unclouded awareness of his maker, but in a natural environment of which he is himself a part and with which his will is directly engaged as he strives to maintain himself within it. This initial situation of man as an animal in a natural environment within which he can live only by continual struggle, and in virtue of a self-regarding survival instinct with its attendant competitiveness and aggressiveness, constitutes what the Genesis myth recognises as our actual (i.e. 'fallen') situation. But man has not lapsed into this state from a prior condition of primitive righteousness. The idea of a period of human existence, before the dawn of recorded history, when human nature was radically different, and in which man stood in a paradisal relationship to his environment and his fellows, must be dismissed as a fantasy. All the evidence that we have suggests man's continuity with lower forms of life and indeed with nature as a whole, and his complete involvement from the beginning in the harsh necessities of the struggle for survival. The ideal perfection of our human existence does not lie behind us in a long-lost past, but before us in the future completion of the divine creative purpose. We are indeed at the great distance from the fulfilment of God's intention for us which the myth of the fall recognises; and to this extent the myth truly depicts our situation. But even though the myth thus has a poetic appropriateness and truth, it is questionable whether this particular universe of poetic discourse is any longer serviceable. Prior to the development of the science of anthropology the picture of the fall of man communicated freely, without interference from knowledge already present in people's minds. The fall was projected on to the blank of an unknown human prehistory. But today that blank has been partially filled in, and the new picture that has emerged has a shape of its own which clashes with the story of the fall. Thus the language of the fall has become a victim of anthropology, as the language of the heavenly spheres was ousted by astronomy, and that of alchemy by chemistry. Once we are clear that the 'fall of man' does not refer to an actual earthly event which occurred some definite (even if not ascertainable) number of years ago it becomes misleading to use language which assumes a pre-fallen state from which man has fallen. I for one am therefore content to categorise the fall, together with the making of the world in seven days, the special creation of man in discontinuity with the other animals, and the reinauguration of human history by Noah after the world-wide flood, as religious poetry.

But if man was brought into existence by the slow process of evolution out of lower forms of life, it follows that our initial distancing from God through our immersion in the natural order, and our morally imperfect nature, have their place within the divine creative purpose. Our actual human situation, with all its ambiguities, is not the work of the Evil One seeking to thwart God's will, but represents a phase in the outworking of God's intention. In order to see that purpose expressed in the Bible we have to take the biblical writings as a whole, noting both the existential attitude to evil of the prophets and Jesus himself, immersed as they were within the struggle against sin and pain and seeing these as deadly enemies to be overcome; and also the attitude of theological reflection, as from a cosmic vantage point, in which the good and evil of the world are both seen as God's instruments and the divine purpose is recognised to have a universal scope, embracing all time and all space.

Should we then dare to speak of a divine responsibility for the existence of evil as well as of good? Clearly God is not answerable *to* anyone. But he is responsible for his creation, including the evil within it, in the sense that his will is the primary necessary condition of its existence, and in the sense also that its character can be justified only by the successful fulfilment of the divine purpose for which it exists. It is said that President Truman had a notice on his desk reminding him that 'This is where the buck stops'. In the universe as well as in a state there has to be a point beyond which responsibility can no longer be passed on. And it is part of the meaning of christian monotheism that there is an ultimately responsible moral being, who is absolute goodness and love, whom we may trust amid the uncertainties and anxieties of the gradual unfolding of reality to us in time. We are led to this trust by seeing the divine responsibility at work on earth in the life of Christ. For there we see the Love which has ordained the long, costly soul-making process entering into it and sharing with us in its inevitable pains and suffering. The cross of Christ reconciles us to the God who is ultimately responsible both for that cross and for the whole vast complex of human existence as it has been, as it is, and as it will be.

This ultimate divine responsibility for human existence does not remove our own personal responsibility for our deeds. That we are responsible means that our actions are *our* actions, flowing from our own individual nature; and the fact that both the initial structure of our being and the sphere within which we exercise it express the creative action of God does not render our actions any less our own or any less subject to moral assessment. The ultimate divine responsibility for the existence of the world and of ourselves as part of it, on the one hand, and our human responsibility for our own choices on the other, do not clash, for they do not obtain within the same frame of reference. This is not a case of shared responsibility, but of the dependence of our actions upon our own wills itself depending upon the divine will, which is thus a higher, and indeed highest, necessary condition of all that occurs.

I turn now, more briefly, from the idea of the fall to that of the double destiny of mankind in an everlasting heaven and hell. The Irenaean response to the mystery of evil, at any rate since it reached a full development in the nineteenth century in the thought of Schleiermacher, has always tended to reject the doctrine of eternal damnation. For this type of theodicy is eschatologically oriented, finding its clue to the meaning of ·evil in the hoped-for fulfilment of God's purpose for his creation in an infinite, because eternal, good which is such as to justify all that has occurred on the way to it. All experience of evil, in the forms both of wickedness and of suffering, will have been turned by its end into a history that has led to the Kingdom of God. But if that eschaton is to be unqualifiedly good, no preceding sin or pain must be left outside the scope of its retrospective justification. God's purpose of good must be universally fulfilled; or else, to the extent to which it has been thwarted, the divine sovereignty is shown to be limited. An eternally persisting evil would represent a definitive failure on the creator's part. And the doctrine of hell therefore rules itself out; for it postulates the eternally evil existence of the wicked and the eternal evil of their torment – or, if not positive torment, their infinite loss. If the universe contains these permanently unredeemed evils, it follows that God is limited either in goodness or in power. This is the logic leading to the rejection of the doctrine of hell in the Irenaean type of theodicy.

In the Augustinian theodicy these two evils – sin and the suffering involved in its just punishment – were seen as cancelling one another out so as to leave the universe unblemished. As Augustine said, 'But since there is happiness for those who do not sin, the universe is perfect; and it is no less perfect because there is misery for sinners. . . . The voluntary state of being sinful is dishonourable. Hence the penal state is imposed to bring it into order . . . so that the penalty of sin corrects the dishonour of sin.'[6] But this principle of moral balance is surely as sub-moral as it is sub-personal in its concern for the balancing of the accounts rather than for human beings and their salvation.

If one is impressed by the Irenaean argument, but impressed also by the weight of tradition in favour of a double destiny, one might incline towards a compromise doctrine of the gradual fading out of existence of the finally lost. They are not endlessly punished; they are not even destroyed; they simply come by the disintegrating effect of their own evil to embody less and less being until they cease to exist. This is a tempting compromise between heaven (for all) and hell (for some). I do not think, however, that it succeeds in avoiding the difficulty noted above. It does indeed eliminate one aspect of it, namely the eternal evil of the suffering (whether it be positive torment or consciousness of infinite loss) of the damned; but it does not eliminate another aspect, namely the eternal evil of God's failure to bring to a good end the finite personal life he has created. It means that in the case of those whose fate is extinction the evil that has brought them to this end remains eternally unredeemed, not made to serve any eventual good, and thus constitutes a perpetual marring of the universe. There remains an eternal (or more strictly a sempiternal) dualism of God and the evil that he is powerless to undo.

The only real alternative, then, to a doctrine of lost souls, whether living in misery or having totally perished, is the contrary doctrine of universal salvation. This does not entail that human choices are unreal and not of eternal significance, or that hell does not stand before all men as a terrible possibility. It means

[6] *On Free Will*, iii ix 26.

that this terrible possibility will not in fact be realised. In mythological language, hell exists, but is empty. It is 'there' awaiting
any who may be finally lost to God; but in the end none are to be
finally lost. Thus the language of the double destiny is existen-
tially valid, truly expressing the momentous character of our
moral choices as we face them in the concrete moments of life;
and yet it is also subject to qualification in the light of the final
sovereignty of God. That is to say, it is morally appropriate for us
to be challenged by the thought of the harm, in principle unlimited, which an evil-doer inflicts upon himself. But it may both
be a true perception from within the temporal process that unless
a man opens himself to God he will eventually perish, and also a
true deduction from God's power and goodness that in the end
that man *will* somehow be drawn freely to open himself to his
maker. Thus the doctrine of ultimate universal salvation does not
deny that men can damn themselves; but it affirms that although
they can, yet in the end none will. For human volition is not
exercised in a void. It always occurs in interaction with circumstances and forces beyond itself. The ultimate context of all our
volitions, according to christian faith, is the active love of God
seeking to save his human creatures. We can never escape from
this divine reality, for it has determined the nature of the environments in which we exercise our freedom, both in this world and
in other worlds to come. We must therefore assume that God's
love continues to be active towards us in and through a series of
aeons until at last we see the divine goodness and respond in glad
adoration. This process, in which the infinite resourcefulness of
infinite love will sooner or later find a way to us, depends upon
the fact that it is God who has created us and that he has created
us for himself. The God-given bias of our nature will not for ever
be frustrated. It is because 'our hearts are restless until they find
their rest in thee' that in the end, however far off that end may
be, human nature will arrive at its own self-fulfilment in a right
relation to God. It remains logically possible that any (or all) will
eternally persist in rejecting God; but it is also morally and
practically certain that in unlimited time, in a universe ruled by
a love that is actively seeking their deepest good, each will come
into harmony with the divine ground of his own being.

Logically, the affirmation that all will be saved without their
freedom being at any point overridden has the status, not of a

scientific prediction, but of a hope. It is not, however, an ungrounded hope. For it is part of the total christian hope, which is simply christian faith turned towards the future and seeing there the divine love finally and fully triumphant. From a secular standpoint this hope is, of course, merely a piece of wishful thinking; but from the christian point of view it is an aspect of our faith, with the same purchase within the christian mind as the assurance of the present reality and love of God.

Such a doctrine is, I suggest, compatible with the New Testament teaching about the sufferings of the wicked after death. For the context of this teaching is ethical rather than theological 'hell' is a result of lovelessness towards the neighbour in this life.[7] Even if the divinely ordained suffering which we call hell were purely retributive it could not in equity be an eternal and therefore infinite penalty. But surely we may infer from God's love that it is remedial and is part of the long, complex, soul-making process by which God is fashioning children who shall freely love him and one another. It is therefore not an unending punishment, but something more like the purgatory of traditional Roman Catholic doctrine, which is at this point wiser than the Protestant tradition – although the latter has the excuse that historically it began in a protest against the shocking abuse of the idea of purgatory in the sale of indulgences. Purgatory signifies real suffering occurring as a consequence of moral evil and rightly to be set before our minds as a real aspect of the moral order under which we live; but it is not an everlasting penalty. In the nature of the case, everlasting suffering would be an evil out of which no good could ever be brought. Such eternally unresolved evil would constitute the most intractable aspect of the theodicy problem! But although there is no divine sentence of eternal misery, yet there is a sharp reaction of the nature of things against moral evil, a reaction which has to be borne and worked through, if not in this life then in the life to come. It is this, I suggest, that appears in the Augustinian picture under the exaggerated form of eternal damnation.

This reinterpretation of hell is profoundly unacceptable to Trethowan; and he shows how powerful is the theological commitment which makes him reject such reinterpretations when he grants that 'The doctrine of hell is undoubtedly the most difficult

[7] Matt. 25: 31–46.

of all Christian doctrines' and that 'when we are asked how heaven could really be heaven if in fact there is a hell, we have to say that we do not know'.[8] But many of us do not share that initial commitment to the Augustinian tradition. This is not a matter of Protestant versus Roman Catholic views, for the Augustinian vision is as evident in the theology of Calvin as in that of Aquinas. Today, however, when the spell of the medieval outlook has been broken by the rise of modern science, many Christians wish to try to build again from the New Testament starting point with the aid of reason and conscience; and in this new light the doctrine of eternal damnation appears more credible as a revelation of men's attitudes to one another than of God's attitude to mankind. Indeed it has been suggested that the theme of sinners in the hands of an angry God reflects God in the hands of angry sinners!

I find, then, that at the end of these renewed reflections on the fall and hell I do not find myself any nearer to the Augustinian tradition than I was at the beginning. I can however readily acknowledge the points of difficulty in a theodicy of the Irenaean type. It grants God's ultimate responsibility for all existence, including the evil within it; and this is hard to reconcile with a full recognition of the demonic character of much evil, both moral and natural. And it affirms universal salvation; and this is hard to reconcile with a full affirmation of human freedom and responsibility. These are real difficulties, and I do not want to make light of them. It still seems to me, however, that these difficulties are distinctly less than those attaching to the alternative Augustinian doctrines of the prehistoric fall of men or angels, and eternal hell for a proportion of God's creatures.

8 Op. cit., p. 415.

6. God as Necessary Being

'NECESSARY BEING' is one of the terms by means of which christian thought has sought to define the difference between God and man. The notion of necessary being, applied to God and withheld from man, indicates that God and man differ not merely in the characteristics which they possess but, more fundamentally, in their modes of being, or in the fact that they exist in different senses of the word 'exist'.

That such a distinction, however it may be best expressed, is essential to the christian concept of God is agreed virtually on all hands. Paul Tillich has emphasised the distinction to the extent of using different terms to refer to the reality of God and of man respectively. Human beings and other created things exist; God, on the other hand, does not exist, but is Being-itself. This is the most recent way of formulating a discrimination which has been classically expressed in the history of christian thought by the idea of the necessary being of God in contrast to the contingent being of man and of the whole created order.

There are, however, two importantly different concepts which may be, and which have been, expressed by the phrase 'necessary being'. 'Necessity', in a philosophical context, usually means logical necessity, and gives rise in theology to the concept of a being such that it is logically impossible that this being should not exist. But this is not the only kind of necessity referred to in philosophical literature. The non-logical concepts of causal, empirical and material necessity can be grouped together as forms of *factual* necessity. The distinction between logical and factual necessity first appears, so far as I know, in the *Critique of Pure Reason*, where Kant treats of the three modal categories of possibility, existence and necessity. The category of necessity is derived by him from the necessary or analytic proposition in formal logic. But its schema in time is the existence of an object throughout all time;[1] and the corresponding 'postulate of empirical thought' is called by Kant *die materiale Notwendigkeit* and is equivalent to what is often described as causal necessity, i.e. being part of the universal causal system of nature.[2] The schema of necessity as existence throughout all time suggests the notion of a temporally unlimited being, and this is an important part, though not the whole, of the concept of God as a factually necessary being. I shall argue that the notion of factual necessity, when appropriately spelled out, is an essential element in the christian doctrine of God, but that the notion of logical necessity is, in this context, both philosophically and religiously profitless, and indeed even dangerous, to theology.

It is important to distinguish explicitly between logical and factual necessity, not only for the elucidation of the doctrine of within the church, but also in the interests of apologetics. For a number of contemporary philosophers of the analytical school have assumed that christian theology requires the notion of logically necessary being and, having noted that this idea is rendered meaningless by the modern understanding of the nature of logical necessity, have rejected what they suppose to be the christian concept of God. They are, however, I believe, mistaken in their initial assumption. My thesis thus thas a threefold bearing. I wish to suggest, as a matter of theology, that the idea of the divine being as factually necessary is more adequate to the data of christian faith than the idea of God's being as logically necessary; and as a matter of philosophy, that the idea of factually necessary being is immune from the criticisms which have rightly been levelled against the notion of logically necessary being; and as a matter of history, that the notion of God's being as factually necessary has a stronger claim to be regarded as the normative christian use of the term 'necessary being' than has its interpretation in terms of logical necessity.

Let us begin with the idea of logically necessary being. To say that God has logically necessary being, or that his existence is logically necessary, is to say that it is logically impossible that God should not exist; or that the concept of God is such that the proposition 'God exists' is a logical, analytic or *a priori* truth; or

[1] B.184.   [2] B.279-80.

again that the proposition 'God does not exist' is a self-contradiction, a statement of such a kind that it is logically impossible for it to be true. Such a claim, however, contravenes one of the fundamental positions of empiricist philosophy – that an existential proposition (i.e. a proposition asserting existence) cannot be logically necessary. For modern empiricism is largely founded upon the distinction between, in Hume's phrases, 'the relations between ideas' on the one hand, and 'matters of fact and existence' on the other. Given this distinction, logical necessity clearly belongs exclusively to the sphere of the relations between ideas. The ideas of 'larger' and 'smaller', for example, are such that it is a logically necessary truth that if A is larger than B, then B is smaller than A, the necessity arising from the meanings which we have given to the words 'larger' and 'smaller'. On the same principle, such propositions as 'God is omniscient' and 'God is omnipotent' express necessary truths, if 'God' has been defined as 'a being who is omniscient and omnipotent' or, compendiously, as 'unlimited Being'. Given this definition, it is not only a truth but an analytic truth that God is omniscient and omnipotent; for the definition renders it incorrect to call a Being 'God' who is other than omniscient and omnipotent. But, on the other hand, 'God exists' cannot be treated in the same way. God cannot be *defined* as existing. For, in the familiar slogan which has emerged from the critiques of the ontological argument, existence is not a predicate. To say that x exists is not to define, or to expand the definition of, the term 'x', but is to assert that this term refers to some object. And whether a given description has a referent or, to use another terminology, whether a given term has denotation, is a question of fact which cannot be settled *a priori*.

The logical doctrine involved, which had been previously clearly delineated by Hume and Kant, has been formulated definitively in our own time by Bertrand Russell in his theory of descriptions.[3] Russell showed that the question 'Does x exist?' does not imply that in some prior sense the x of which we speak is, or subsists, or has being; and further, that the assertion that x exists is not an attribution to a subsisting x of the further characteristic of existence. It is rather the assertion, with regard to a certain description (or name as standing for a description), that

[3] E.g., *Introduction to Mathematical Philosophy*, 2nd edn. (London: Allen and Unwin, 1920) ch. 16.

this description has a referent. Thus 'horses exist' has the logical structure: 'there are x's such that "x is a horse" is true'. Such an analysis exorcises the puzzle which has tended since the time of Plato to haunt negative existential propositions. 'Unicorns do not exist' does not entail that unicorns must first in some mysterious sense *be* in order that we may then say of them that they do not exist; it means simply that 'there are no x's such that "x is a unicorn" is true'. And 'God exists' means 'there is one (and only one) x such that "x is omniscient, omnipotent, etc." is true'. This Russellian analysis makes plain the logical structure of propositions asserting existence. Their structure is such that they cannot be true by definition, nor therefore by *a priori* necessity. Hence the concept of a being such that the proposition asserting its existence is a logically necessary truth, is a self-contradictory concept. There cannot – logically cannot – be a being whose non-existence is logically impossible. I conclude then that we must on philosophical grounds repudiate all talk of God as having necessary being when the necessity in question is construed as logical necessity.

Granting then that the notion of God's existence as *logically* necessary has to be ruled out as untenable, it is perhaps worth asking, as a matter of history, whether this notion has in fact figured at all prominently in christian thought. The first great thinker of the church who comes to mind in this connection is Anselm. The ontological argument, to the effect that the concept of God, as the concept of the greatest conceivable being, entails the existence of God, appears to be an attempt to show that the proposition 'God exists' is a logically necessary truth. Certainly Descartes's version of the ontological argument has this character. According to Descartes, as the concept of a triangle entails the truth that its internal angles are jointly equal to two right angles, so the concept of God entails the truth that God exists.[4] But in Anselm himself there is another line of thought which stands in conflict with such an interpretation. In the second formulation of the ontological argument, in the third chapter of the *Proslogion*, we read that 'it is possible to conceive of a being which cannot be conceived not to exist (*potest cogitari esse aliquid, quod non possit cogitari non esse*)'. On the face of it this statement would seem to confirm the view that Anselm has in mind what we

4 *Meditations*, v.

would today call the notion of logically necessary being. For the most natural interpretation of his words, at any rate by a twentieth-century reader, is that a being which cannot be conceived not to exist means a being whose non-existence is logically inconceivable, that is to say, logically impossible. However, when we turn to Anselm's reply to Gaunilo we find that he states explicitly what he means by the notion of beings which can and which cannot be conceived not to exist.

All those objects, and those alone [he says], can be conceived not to exist, which have a beginning or end or composition of parts: also . . . whatever at any place or at any time does not exist as a whole. That being alone, on the other hand, cannot be conceived not to exist, in which any conception discovers neither beginning nor end nor composition of parts (*nec initium nec finem nec partium conjunctionem*), and which any conception finds always and everywhere as a whole.[5]

Here we have something quite different from the claim that 'God exists' is a logically necessary truth. We have instead the essence of the contrasting notion of factual necessity – the notion, that is, of God as sheer, ultimate, unconditioned reality, without origin or end. Another aspect of the concept of factual necessity, namely *aseity*, is contributed by Anselm in the *Monologion*, where he draws the distinction between existence *a se* and existence *ab alio*. He says of God: 'The supreme Substance, then, does not exist through any efficient agent, and does not derive existence from any matter, and was not aided in being brought into existence by any external causes. Nevertheless, it by no means exists through nothing, or derives existence from nothing; since, through itself and from itself, it is whatever it is (*per seipsam et ex seipsa est quidquid est*).'[6] The relation between this aspect of Anselm's thought and his ontological argument is another and difficult question into which I do not propose to enter; I only wish, for the present purpose, to point to the presence, often I think unnoticed, of the notion of factually necessary being in his discussions.

Let us now turn the centuries to Thomas Aquinas, who explicitly uses the term 'necessary being'.[7] The conclusion of his

[5] *Responsio editoris*, ch. iv. Cf. *Proslogion*, ch. xxii.   [6] Ch. vi.
[7] *Summa Theologica*, I, q. 2, art. 3.

Third Way argument is that 'there must exist something the existence of which is necessary' (*oportet aliquid esse necessarium in rebus*). But he also, I believe, like Anselm, uses the idea of necessary existence in the sense of factually, and not logically, necessary existence. For in the Third Way passage the mark of contingency is transiency, or temporal finitude – having a beginning and an end in time. And by contrast the mark of non-contingency, or of the necessary being of God, must be not having a beginning or an end in time – in other words, *eternal* being.

Can we then perhaps equate contingent with transient existence, and necessary with eternal existence? The answer that must be given, which is also the answer implicit in Thomas, is No. Eternity is one of the ingredients of the necessary being of the Godhead, but is not by itself sufficient. For it is possible to conceive of something existing eternally, not because it is such that there is and could be no power capable of abolishing it, but only because, although there are powers capable of abolishing it, they always refrain from doing so. Such a being would be eternal by courtesy of the fact that it is never destroyed but not by the positive virtue or power of being indestructible. And it is surely integral to the christian concept of God that God, as the ultimate Lord of all, is not capable of being destroyed.

We must add at this point that, as the ultimate Lord of all, God is also incorruptible, in the sense of being incapable of ceasing either to exist or to possess his divine characteristics by reason of an inner decay or discerption. God can neither by destroyed from without nor suffer dissolution from within.

Indestructibility and incorruptibility, however, even taken together, cannot replace but must supplement the notion of eternal being. For it is possible to conceive of something being both indestructible and incorruptible and yet not eternal in the sense of being without beginning or end. Such a reality would exist only if created, but once created would be indissoluble and indestructible.

In Thomist theology angels and human souls are held to have precisely this character, on the ground that they are simple substances. They have a beginning by divine creation, but once created they exist for ever, unless of course decreated by omnipotent divine action. As incorruptible, such entities are described as necessary beings, and it is presumably these, and perhaps especially angels, that Thomas has in mind when he distinguishes in the Third Way passage between necessary beings which have their necessary existence caused by another, and ultimately necessary being which does not have its necessary existence caused by another but which is uncreated and is God. Some Thomist theologians describe these two kinds of necessary being as, in the one case, intrinsically but not extrinsically necessary, and in the other case, both intrinsically and extrinsically necessary. These definitional refinements do not concern us here except as emphasising that in Thomist thought the notion of necessary being is not an all-or-nothing logical concept but is a factual notion, capable of degrees and qualifications; so that the distinction between necessary and contingent being is not to be correlated with the distinction between logically necessary and contingent truths. Necessity is for Thomas a factual or ontic and not a logical characteristic.

I conclude then, concerning Thomas, that whilst he does not explicitly make the distinction between logical and factual necessity, in practice he cleaved so consistently to one side of the distinction that he was not led into any important ambiguity or confusion by the lack of an explicit separation of the two notions. However, some Thomist writers of our own day do fall into the ambiguity which their master avoided. M. Maritain, for example,[8] uses an instance of logical necessity to illustrate the idea of existence *a se*, thereby revealing that he is not conscious of the difference between these two notions. He first defines necessary existence in these terms: 'a thing is necessary when it *cannot* be prevented, contingent when it *can* be prevented. A thing is *absolutely necessary* when nothing can prevent it from being.' This is a clear enough account of the notion of existence *a se*. But in the next sentence Maritain offers an example from mathematics. 'Thus the properties of the sphere', he says, 'are absolutely necessary'.[9] Now the properties of a sphere – for example, the fact that every point on its surface is equidistant from the centre – are indeed absolutely necessary; that is to say, there could not possibly be a sphere which lacked these properties. But the reason for this is not that there is nothing that can *prevent* a

---

[8] 'Necessity and Contingency' in *Essays in Thomism*, edited by Robert E. Brennan (New York, 1942).

[9] Ibid., p. 27.

sphere from having these properties but simply that these properties belong to the definition of 'sphere'. There is nothing to prevent there being objects which approximate in varying degrees to this particular set of properties, but such objects would not be called spheres for the simple reason that we have chosen to confine the name 'sphere' to objects which fit certain specifications, which thus constitute the defining and necessary properties of a sphere.

II

If a skilled theologian can suppose that the christian concept of God requires the notion of logically necessary existence, we can hardly blame secular philosophers if they make the same assumption and proceed to draw damaging conclusion from it. I should like in this connection to refer to the much discussed article by J. N. Findlay entitled 'Can God's existence be disproved?'[10] in which he derived from the self-contradictory nature of the idea of logically necessary being what he regarded as a strict disproof of divine existence. To see what is amiss with Findlay's argument is by contrast to see a little more clearly the outlines of a religiously and philosophically acceptable account of the unique mode of being of the Godhead.

Findlay is, so far as I know, the first philosopher to have proposed an *a priori* proof of the non-existence of God. He puts the ontological argument into reverse by contending that the concept of deity, so far from guaranteeing the existence of an object corresponding to it, is such as to guarantee that no object corresponds to it.

Findlay defines the concept of God as that of the adequate object of religious attitudes, a religious attitude being described as one in which we tend 'to abase ourselves before some object, to defer to it wholly, to devote ourselves to it with unquestioning enthusiasm, to bend the knee before it, whether literally or metaphorically',[11] such an attitude is rationally adopted only by one who believes that the object to which he relates himself as

---

[10] *Mind*, 1948. Reprinted in *New Essays in Philosophical Theology*, edited by Flew and Macintyre (London: S.C.M. Press, and New York: The Macmillan Company, 1955).

[11] *New Essays*, p. 49.

worshipper has certain very remarkable characteristics. Findlay
lists the most important of these characteristics. First, an adequate
object of religious attitudes must be conceived as being infinitely
superior to ourselves in value or worth. (Accordingly Findlay
refers to this object as 'he' rather than as 'it'). Second, he must
be conceived as being unique: God must not merely be one of a
class of beings of the same kind, but must stand in an asymmetrical relationship to all other objects as the source of whatever
value they may have. Third, says Findlay, the adequate objects
of religious attitudes must be conceived as not merely happening
to exist, but as existing necessarily; if he merely happened to
exist he would not be worthy of the full and unqualified attitude
of worship. And fourth, this being must be conceived as not
merely happening to possess his various characteristics, but as
possessing them in some necessary manner. For our present
purpose we may conflate these two necessities, necessary existence
and the necessary possession of properties, and treat them as one.
It should be borne in mind throughout that in Findlay's argument
'necessary' means 'logically necessary'.

It is the last two in his list of requirements that provide the
ground for Findlay's ontological disproof of theism. 'For if God
is to satisfy religious claims and needs, he must be a being in
every way inescapable, One whose existence and whose possession
of certain excellencies we cannot possibly conceive away. And
modern views make it self-evidently absurd (if they don't make it
ungrammatical) to speak of such a Being and attribute existence
to him.'[12] For, as we have already noted, post-Humean empiricism
can assign no meaning to the idea of necessary existence, since
nothing can be conceived to exist that cannot also be conceived
not to exist. No propositions of the form 'x exists' can be analyti-
cally true. Hence, Findlay argues, the concept of an adequate
object of religious attitudes, involving as it does the notion of a
necessarily existent being who possesses his characteristic in some
necessary manner, is a self-contradictory concept. We can know
a priori, from inspection of the idea itself, that there is and can
be no such being.

We may distinguish in Findlay's argument a philosophical
premiss to the effect that no existential propositions can be necessary truths, and a theological premiss to the effect that an

[12] Ibid., p. 55.

adequate object of religious worship must be such that it is logically necessary that he exists. Of these two premisses I wish to accept the former and reject the latter. I deny, that is to say, the theological doctrine that God must be conceived, if at all, in such a way that 'God exists' is a logically necessary truth. I deny this for precisely the same reason as Findlay, namely that the demand that 'God exists' should be a necessary truth is, like the demand that a circle should be square, not a proper demand at all, but a misuse of language. Only, whereas Findlay concludes that the notion of an adequate object of religious attitude is an absurdity, I conclude that that of which the idea is an absurdity cannot be an adequate object of religious attitudes; it would on the contrary be an unqualifiedly *in*adequate object of worship.

Let us then ask the question, which seems highly appropriate at this point, as to how religious persons actually think of the Being whom they regard as the adequate object of their worship. What aspect of the christian experience of God lies behind the idea of necessary being?

The concept of God held by the biblical writers was based upon their experience of God as awesome power and holy will confronting them and drawing them into the sphere of his on-going purpose. God was known as a dynamic will interacting with their own wills; a sheer given reality, as inescapably to be reckoned with as destructive storm and life-giving sunshine, or the fixed contours of the land, or the hatred of their enemies and the friendship of their neighbours; indeed even more ineluctably so, as the Book of Jonah emphasises. God was not for them an inferred entity; he was an experienced reality. The biblical writers were (sometimes, though doubtless not at all times) as vividly conscious of being in God's presence as they were of living in a material environment. Their pages resound and vibrate with the sense of God's presence, as a building might resound and vibrate from the tread of some great being walking through it. They thought of this holy presence as unique – as the maker and ruler of the universe, the sole rightful sovereign of men and angels, as eternal and infinite, and as the ultimate reality and determining power, in relation to whom his creatures have no standing except as the objects of his grace. But nowhere in the biblical thought about God is use made of the idea of logical necessity. The notion is quite foreign to the characteristically hebraic and concrete utterances found in the Bible and forms no part of the biblical concept or concepts of God.

But, it might be said, was it not to the biblical writers inconceivable that God should *not* exist, or that he should cease to exist, or should lose his divine powers and virtues? Would it not be inconceivable to them that God might one day go out of existence, or cease to be good and become evil? And does not this attitude involve an implicit belief that God exists necessarily, and possesses his divine characteristics in some necessary manner? The answer, I think, is that it was to the biblical writers psycho logically inconceivable — as we say colloquially, unthinkable — that God might not exist, or that his nature might undergo change. They were so vividly conscious of God that they were unable to doubt his reality, and they were so firmly reliant upon his integrity and faithfulness that they could not contemplate his becoming other than they knew him to be. They would have allowed as a verbal concession only that there might possibly be no God; for they were convinced that they were at many times directly aware of his presence and of his dealings with them. But the question whether the non-existence of God is *logically* inconceivable, or *logically* impossible, is a purely philosophical puzzle which could not be answered by the prophets and apostles out of their own first-hand religious experience. This does not of course represent any special limitation of the biblical figures. The logical concept of necessary being cannot be given in religious experience. It is an object of philosophical thought and not of religious experience. It is a product — as Findlay argues, a malformed product — of reflection. A religious person's reply to the question, Is God's existence logically necessary? will be determined by his view of the nature of logical necessity; and this is not part of his religion but of his system of logic. The biblical writers in point of fact display no view of the nature of logical necessity, and would doubtless have regarded the topic as of no religious significance. It cannot reasonably be claimed then, that logically necessary existence was part of the conception of the adequate object of human worship.

What, we must therefore ask, has led Findlay to hold so confidently that logically necessary existence is an essential element in the religious man's concept of God? His process of thought is revealed in these words: 'We can't help feeling that the worthy object of our worship can never be a thing that merely *happens* to exist, nor one on which all other objects merely *happen* to depend.'[13] The reasoning here is that if a being does not exist by logical necessity, he merely happens to exist; and in this case he ought not to be worshipped as God. But in presenting the dilemma, either God exists necessarily, or he merely happens to exist, Findlay makes the very mistake for which he has criticised the theologians. Findlay should be the last person to use this dichotomy, since he has himself rendered it inoperative by pointing out that one half of the dichotomy is meaningless. And to remove half a dichotomy is to remove the dichotomy. If for example it is said that all human beings are either witches or non-witches, and it is then discovered that there is no such thing as a witch, it becomes pointless, and indeed misleading, to describe everyone as a non-witch. Likewise, having concluded that the notion of necessary existence has no meaning, to continue to speak of things merely *happening* to exist, as though this stood in contrast to some other mode of existing, no longer has any validity. From an empiricist standpoint, there are not two different ways of existing, existing by logical necessity and merely happening to exist. A thing either exists or does not exist; or to be more exact a description either has or does not have a referent. But Findlay, after ruling out the notion of necessary existence, in relation to which alone the contrasting idea of 'merely happening to exist' has any meaning, continues to use the latter category, and what is more, to use it as a term of reproach! This is a very advanced form of the method of having it both ways.

Our conclusion must be that Findlay has only disproved the existence of God if we mean by God a being whose existence is a matter of logical necessity. Since, however, we do not mean this, we may take Findlay's argument instead as emphasising that we must either abandon the traditional phrase 'necessary being', or else be very clear that the necessary being of God is not to be construed as *logically* necessary being.

III

We have arrived thus far at an identification of the necessary being of the Godhead with incorruptible and indestructible being

[13] Ibid., p. 52.

without beginning or end. These characteristics, however, can properly be regarded as different aspects of the more fundamental characteristic which the Scholastics termed aseity, or being *a se*. The usual English translation, 'self-existence', is strictly a meaningless phrase, but for the lack of a better we must continue to use it. The core of the notion of aseity is independent being. That God exists *a se* means that he is not dependent upon anything for his existence. In contrast to this the created universe and everything in it exist *ab alio*. For it is true of each distinguishable item composing the universe that its existence depends upon some factor or factors beyond itself. Only God exists in total non-dependence; he alone exists absolutely as sheer unconditioned, self-existent being.

From God's aseity, or ontic independence, his eternity, indestructibility and incorruptibility can be seen to follow. A self-existent being must be eternal, i.e. without temporal limitation. For if he had begun to exist, or should cease to exist, he must have been caused to exist, or to cease to exist, by some power other than himself; and this would be inconsistent with his aseity. By the same token he must be indestructible, for to say that he exists in total ontic independence is to say that there is and could be no reality with the capacity to constitute or to destroy him; and likewise he must be incorruptible, for otherwise his aseity would be qualified as regards its duration. The question might however be asked at this point: Although it is incompatible with the idea of a self-existent being that he should ever be destroyed from without, yet is there any contradiction in the thought of such a being destroying himself? Is it not possible in principle that God might 'commit suicide'? The question perhaps deserves more than the brief discussion that is possible within the limits of this chapter. I am inclined, however, to think that the query itself is as logically improper as it is obviously religiously improper; and this for three reasons. First, the expression 'commit suicide' is highly misleading in this context. The 'suicide' of the absolute self-existent being would not be like a human suicide though on a much grander scale. For the concept of divine death is not analogous to that of human death. The death of a human being means the destruction or the cessation of function of his physical body; but God has no physical body to be destroyed, whether by himself or by another. We have to try to think instead of a purely 'mental suicide'; but so far as I can see this is a completely empty phrase, to which we are able to attach no positive meaning. Second, an absolute end is as inconceivable as is an absolute beginning. Third, there is an additional contradiction in the notion of sheer, unqualified *being* ceasing to exist. Specific modifications of being may alter or cease, but to speak of being itself ceasing to exist is apparently to speak without meaning. I cannot then accept the question as to whether God might commit suicide as a genuine question posing intelligible alternatives.

Finally, to refer back to Findlay's discussion, it is meaningless to say of the self-existent being that he might not have existed or that he merely happens to exist. For what could it mean to say of the eternal, uncreated creator of everything other than himself that he 'merely happens to exist'? When we assert of a dependent and temporally finite being, such as myself, that I only happen to exist, we mean that if such-and-such an event had occurred in the past, or if such-and-such another event had failed to occur, I should not now exist. But no such meaning can be given to the statement, 'A self-existent being only happens to exist', or 'might not have existed'. There is no conceivable event such that if it had occurred, or failed to occur, a self-existent being would not have existed; for the concept of aseity is precisely the exclusion of such dependence. There is and could be nothing that would have prevented a self-existent being from coming to exist, for it is meaningless even to speak of a self-existent being as *coming* to exist.

What may properly be meant, then, by the statement that God is, or has, necessary as distinguished from contingent being is that God *is*, without beginning or end, and without origin, cause or ground of any kind whatsoever. He *is*, as the ultimate, unconditioned, absolute, unlimited being.

On the one hand, the fact that God is, is not a logically necessary truth; for no matter of fact can be logically necessary. The reality of God is a sheer datum. But on the other hand this is an utterly unique datum. That God is, is not one fact amongst others, but is related asymmetrically to all other facts as that which determines them. This is the ultimate given circumstance behind which it is not possible to go with either question or explanation. For to explain something means either to assign a cause to it or to show its place within some wider context in relation to which it is no longer puzzling to us. But the idea of the self-existent creator of everything other than himself is the idea of a reality which is beyond the scope of these explanatory procedures. As self-existent, such a being is uncaused, and is therefore not susceptible to the causal type of explanation; and as the creator of all things other than himself he stands in no wider context – on the contrary, his creative action constitutes the context in which all else stands. He is the ultimate reality, about which it is no longer meaningful to ask the questions which can be asked concerning other realities. For this reason God cannot but be mysterious to us. He is mysterious, not merely because there are questions about him to which we do not know the answers, but because we frame questions about him to which there are no answers since the questions themselves can have meaning only in relation to that which is not ultimate. As the final unconditioned, all-conditioning reality God cannot be included within any system of explanation. This is not to say that we cannot know any truths about him, but that such truths are not logically deduced conclusions but sheer incorrigible facts disclosed within human experience. We may express this by saying that God has no characterising name; he is not of any kind, or for any reason, or from any cause. He just *is*, and is what he is. When he reveals his nature to man he says to Moses 'I shall be what I shall be.'[14]

IV

A further step remains to be taken. For there are two respects in which the concept of aseity is less than adequate to the christian understanding of God, or at least there are two dangers to be guarded against in speaking of God's aseity. One is the danger of understanding aseity in a purely static sense; and the other is the readiness of aseity to be construed in merely negative terms, simply as independence. The next major original treatment of the subject since Aquinas, that of Karl Barth in the present century, would appear to have been undertaken with these two dangers in mind; and it is accordingly to Barth that we now turn.

In his great dogmatic work Barth has a section on the *aseitas*

[14] Exodus 3: 14.

Dei under the heading, 'The Being of God in Freedom'.[15] As against any tendency to think of God as static, self-existent substance, the term 'freedom' reminds us that God is the living God, the Life which is the source of all life, and that he is Life not only as an Agent in human time, but also in his own hidden being, apart from and prior to that which is other than himself. This is an important aspect of the christian concept of God. The scholastic '*actus purus*', and the more biblical term 'life', both point to it; and Paul Tillich, in his own theological system, sought to introduce the same dynamic note when he referred to God as 'the power of Being'. All these terms – pure act, divine life, freedom, and power – are of course symbolic in Tillich's sense of being expressions whose ordinary meaning is partially negated by that to which they point. That is to say (speaking more prosaically) even as we use them we are conscious of certain respects in which they would be misleading if taken literally. However, granting the symbolic character of all these words, the term 'freedom', as Barth uses it, does appear to have special appositeness as supplementing the notion of aseity.

Barth draws a distinction between what he calls the primary, or ontic, and the secondary, or noetic, absoluteness or freedom of God. The former refers to God's absoluteness in himself, the latter to his absoluteness or lordship in relation to his creation. This secondary absoluteness is characterised by Barth as total independence; God does not depend for his existence upon any factor external to himself. From this point of view, he is 'the One who is free from all origination, conditioning or determination from without, by that which is not Himself'.[16] But, Barth insists, we must not think of God's unique mode of being only or even primarily in negative terms, as the absence of dependence upon his creation. God's absoluteness in relation to the world is secondary and derivative. Behind it there lies the primary absoluteness or freedom which is prior to and outside of all relations. God is free, says Barth, 'quite apart from His relation to another from whom He is free'.[17] God, in his own inner being, entirely apart from his creative action, is intrinsically free, and 'the freedom to exist which He exercises in His revelation is the same which He

---

[15] *Church Dogmatics* (Edinburgh: T. and T. Clark, and New York: Charles Scribner's Sons, 1957) vol. II, pt. I, ch. vi, § 28, 3.
[16] Op. cit., p. 307.   [17] Ibid., p. 307.

has in the depths of His eternal being, and which is proper to Him quite apart from His exercise of it ad extra'.[18] This insight of Barth's provides an important balancing note to the traditional discussion of aseity. Instead of being thought of primarily in his relation to the world, even though that relation be one of unqualified independence, God is to be conceived in the first instance as positive self-existence in infinite richness and plenitude. The ultimate Being should not be defined negatively as the One who does not depend upon other beings; on the contrary, his independence of the world is a corollary of his own sheer unique Godness, his infinite and absolute uncreated self-sustaining life.

Finally, a brief summary of conclusions. If we continue (as I think we properly may) to use the expression 'necessary being', we must explicitly interpret it in terms of the concept of factual, as distinguished from logical, necessity. So interpreted, the necessary being of the Godhead is his aseity, understood primarily, however, not as non-dependence upon his creation, but positively, as absolute and unlimited being in infinite plenitude and freedom.

[18] Ibid., p. 305.

7. The Reconstruction of Christian Belief

I

THE CHRISTIAN theologian starts within a continuing society called the church and within an inherited set of ideas called christian theology.

The church as we know it is widely different from anything that can plausibly be said to have been intended by Jesus of Nazareth. The church's history has been that of a human community, developing in acordance with the same principles of social dynamics as other human communities, and revealing under sociological x-ray very much the same kind of power structure. However, our subject is primarily belief rather than the institutional church, and I therefore leave the latter largely out of account in what follows.

The weight and extent of the strain under which christian belief has come can be indicated by listing aspects of traditional theology which are, in the opinion of many theologians today (including myself), either quite untenable or open to serious doubt:

1. There are divinely revealed truths (such as the doctrine of the Trinity, or of the two natures of Christ).

2. God created the physical universe out of nothing n years ago.

3. Man was originally brought into existence as a finitely perfect being, but rebelled against God, and the human condition has ever since been that of creatures who have fallen from grace.

4. Christ came to rescue man from his fallen plight, buying man's (or some men's) restoration to grace by his death on the cross.

5. Jesus was born of a virgin mother, without human paternity.

6. He performed miracles in which the regularities of the natural order were suspended by divine power.

7. His dead body rose from the grave and returned to earthly life.

8. All men must respond to God through Jesus Christ in order to be saved.

9. At death a person's relationship to God is irrevocably fixed.

10. There are two human destinies, traditionally referred to under the symbols of heaven and hell.

I shall not take time at this point to say why each of these propositions has come to be discarded by very many of us, though the reasons are not far to seek.

If we stand back in thought from our immediate situation as twentieth-century Christians, and take note of the character of christian theology as an historical phenomenon, we shall not be greatly disturbed by the current repudiation of so many aspects of the system of ideas in which most of us were brought up.

For theology is a creation of the human mind. Jesus of Nazareth lived, taught and healed, died and then in some way encountered his followers after his death. In his presence people found themselves also in the presence of God and under the claim to love God and their neighbours. But the development of metaphysical systems to conceptualise the significance of Jesus of Nazareth is part of the history of man's civilisation in the west. Most theologians accordingly now understand theological thinking as a human activity which seeks to state the meaning of revelatory events, and above all of the Christ-event. Theology begins with religious experience – the experience of encountering God in Christ and in one's own life – and then tries systematically and consistently to interpret this and to relate it to our other knowledge. But since both the intellectual categories with which we do this and the contextual knowledge within which we do it are parts of the ongoing stream of human culture, theology necessarily changes through time. Accordingly the christian theological tradition has always been a tradition of change. For a complex variety of historical reasons this change has been quicker or slower at different times. The first four centuries A.D., for example, were a time of rapid movement, when the theological scene was one of immense variety and experiment. The medieval period on the other hand was one of relative stability and only gradual change. Our own time is again one of very rapid change. For the most part the metaphysical frameworks supplied by Greek philosophy (principally by Plato and Aristotle), within which christian theologies have been built until now, have been left behind; and our present knowledge of human nature and its environment is so different from that of even fifty years ago that the relating of the meaning of religious experience to our wider knowledge has largely to be done afresh and kept in a continuous state of revision. Thus not only do we stand in a tradition of change but as it faces the future this tradition is open-ended. We cannot say in advance that Christianity, as man's faith-response to Jesus of Nazareth, may not continue to change as the human situation changes, nor can we set any limits to the extent of the change it can undergo without ceasing to be Christianity. So long as the person of Jesus of Nazareth is remembered, and gives rise to a continuing faith-response, the men and women in whom that faith-response occurs will be the church, and the ways in which they conceptualise their faith will be christian theologies.

In this context of the understanding of theology as an ongoing activity in which the church continually adjusts or (in times of rapid change) reconstructs its Christ-affected picture of the universe, let us look at the two main factors which are today in process of transforming christian thought. I take these to be, first, contemporary scientific knowledge and technological power, and second, the newly encountered fact of the other world religions.

It is in principle possible, on the basis of the physical and human sciences, to form a picture of the universe, including man, which is complete and yet involves no reference to God. In other words there can in principle be a complete and consistent non-religious understanding of the universe. In this picture the physical universe is unbounded in both space and time. It has had no initial state, and therefore it does not require to be explained by reference to a prior creative divine reality. The universe just *is*, as the ultimate fact and (to the meditative human mind) the ultimate mystery. It is unlimitedly complex in its potentialities – our own minds being the most complex development now known to us. Given the existence of matter and the basic 'laws' exhibited in its behaviour, the formation of solar systems is intelligible, and on our planet the origin of life through the self-ordering of molecules to form polymers of amino acids constituting the primitive proteins. Given life, its development in response to environmental changes, by means of the mechanism of genetic self-copying with occasional errors (or mutations), is likewise intelligible. It is thus possible to understand the emergence of man within the evolution of the forms of life, and then to understand man's moral and religious experience and beliefs as functional responses to the pressures of his situation as a gregarious animal whose intelligence is able to generate concepts not directly tied to his sense experience. Morality has developed as the method of self-regulation which makes social existence possible; and religion has developed as an outlet for our more fundamental anxieties and wishes, fulfilling a function parallel to but more basic than that of our nightly dreams: in his religions man is day-dreaming. Thus in broad principle the entire phenomenon of human life and experience, and of the physical universe within which it has emerged, are intelligible in exclusively non-religious terms.

What should be the theologian's response to this situation? Should he seek for gaps in the fabric? – emphasising, for example, difficulties in tracing the origin of life or the development of consciousness and intelligence or the growth of moral and religious concepts? Certainly the causal web is at present evident only in principle, and there is a great deal more work to be done before fully convincing descriptive theories will be available. But I think we must assume that the gaps will in fact sooner or later be filled and that our theological picture must be one that can still 'stand up' after this has been done.

The following is a sketch for such a picture, drawing upon the work of a large number of recent and contemporary theologians. Given (i) our belief in the reality of God (the grounds of which belief are not at present under discussion) and (ii) the human situation as we observe it, we form the theological hypothesis that the meaning of human existence, what is going on, is that God is creating finite personal beings, with a real freedom over against himself, who may thus enter into personal relationship with him. Suppose that such beings had been brought into existence in the immediate 'presence' of God, i.e. so that they could not help being aware of the infinite divine reality and of standing in the direct presence of infinite knowledge, infinite power, and infinite goodness and love. They would not in that case have had any real autonomy and freedom in relation to God. In order, then to possess such freedom they had to be created at a distance from their maker – not, needless to say, a spatial distance (for such an idea has no meaning in this case) but an epistemic distance, a distance in the dimension of knowledge. They had to be brought into being in a situation in which they are not automatically conscious of God, but in which they have the possibility of freely becoming conscious of him and freely relating themselves to him. Now our actual human situation, so far as it is known to us, fits these specifications. Man finds himself in a universe which is an autonomously functioning system, of which he is himself part, and in which he can understand both himself and his environment without reference to God. His attention is initially directed upon his natural environment, for he has to struggle to survive within it. He is however also a worshipping animal, with an innate capacity to experience his life religiously. Hence the religions of the world – about which more presently. This religious bias operates, in civilised man at any rate, only as an 'inclining' cause. In primitive man however it seems to have operated as a 'determining' cause. For individual personality and thought seem only gradually to have become separated out from the group mind of the tribe. In primitive societies the individual was so fully merged in the group, and his religious ideas were so entirely moulded by the collective mind, that speculation and doubt were very rare. Critical thinking about the common religious reaction of the tribe, embodied in the primitive cult, was a late development, accompanying economic and social changes making for larger social units and the consequent release of the individual from the close-knit psychic unity of the tribe. It is only in this comparatively recent stage of human development that our cognitive freedom in relation to God has become effective. And occurring, significantly, hand in hand with this development there has been a development within the religious consciousness itself towards deeper and more penetrating conceptions of the demands which the divine makes upon us. There has been a progression from non-rational taboos to an ethically rational demand for righteousness, and from concern for ritual acts and observances to a larger interest embracing the inner thoughts and intents of the heart. There have thus proceeded *pari passu* the gradual liberation of the individual mind from absorption in the group mentality and the gradual realisation by that mind of deeper and more far-reaching demands of the divine reality upon man's life. Thus cognitive freedom in relation to God has increased as the need for it has increased if man was to exist as finite person over against God.

The autonomous character of the physical universe, inviting a comprehensive non-religious account of it, is – theologically – its character as an environment in which man can be cognitively free in relation to his maker. That we can explain our world and our existence within it without God is the obverse of the circumstance that we exist at an epistemic distance from him and so have the possibility of freely relating ourselves to him.

Here we must distinguish between scientific descriptions (or a theoretically possible unified scientific description) of the universe, and a naturalistic theory of it. Whereas the former says, for example, that man is an animal, a primate of the species *homo sapiens*, the latter adds that he is nothing but this – and therefore not a being created for fellowship with a transcendent God. It seems to me clear – though it is not clear to some of the more radical 'death of God' writers – that the naturalistic theory is incompatible with christian belief. But it is far from clear that any actual or foreseeable scientific descriptions are incompatible with the belief-systems of twentieth-century Christians whose faith-response to Jesus of Nazareth, and to God as mediated through him, is articulated in a way which takes account of contemporary knowledge. Our basic picture, then, of the relation between science and religion is this: we exist by God's creative action as parts of a universe which constitutes an autonomous order; and the sciences are the activities in which we systematically explore and to some extent control this order from within it. There is no conflict between science and religion, for any development of scientific knowledge, describing the natural order more and more fully without reference to God, is compatible with the hypothesis that he has deliberately created a universe in which he is not compulsorily evident but is known only by a free personal response of faith.

There can thus be a theological picture which is compatible with the world-view of modern science. This theological picture does not blot anything out of the scientist's picture, but transcends it and thus sets it in a larger context. It does not deny that the processes whereby man has come to be what he is are those traceable by the various sciences. It does not deny that man's moral nature is a function of his social character, or that man's religious nature is a function of his anxiously precarious existence within the universe. There is in fact no point at which the theological claim clashes with scientific descriptions. The theological picture is both supplementary and complementary to the scientific account of the universe. It is supplementary in that it points to a larger context within which the physical universe itself is seen and understood in a new way; and it is complementary in the sense (not precisely that of complementarity theory in quantum physics) that the scientific and religious ways of seeing and speaking of the universe are so related that the truth of the one does not entail the falsity of the other.

More briefly: what about recent technological developments, and their theological implications? For example the possibility of controlling human heredity; of taking apart the DNA code and mixing human beings to selected specification; of cloning – producing multiple copies of the same genetic individual; of repeated organ replacements which prolong human life indefinitely; of the thermo-nuclear self-destruction, or genetic mutilation, of the race. . . . In all these, and other spheres, man is beginning to take charge of his own future evolution. He is acquiring some of the functions of God in relation to subsequent human generations. What theological comment is possible on all this from the kind of standpoint outlined above?

(a) Whatever powers man wrests from his environment must have been written into the structure of the world by God. The potentialities now being realised must be proper to the universe as God has creatively willed it. In this sense they are good rather than evil.

(b) The reality of human freedom, and the immense responsibilities that go with it, are emphasised a hundredfold by these technological developments. We possess terrifying powers; and at the moment we only appear to be muddling our way towards suicide either by over-population or by thermo-nuclear war.

(c) How do we relate together points (a) and (b) above? This is one of theology's major unsolved problems.

(*d*) Because man has the power to mar nature (by cumulative pollution of his environment; or by a level of nuclear fall-out adversely affecting the genes; or by miscalculated genetic engineering; or by human conditioning which undermines moral freedom and responsibility), decisions about the use of technology are not only technical but also moral decisions; and participation in a well-informed and intellectually competent way in the making of these decisions is today a very important form of christian service. Some of the resources now put into the training of the clergy and missionaries should be put into training christian decision-makers for the technological age.

(*e*) The fact that a credible theology has to go all the way with the scientist's picture of the world and then go further on its own, is emphasised by some of these technological advances. For example, genetic engineering makes nonsense of the idea that God at some stage implants a human soul into the foetus, giving it its personal characteristics. We have to say instead that God's creation of the soul – or better, of the person – is through the reproductive processes and also, increasingly today, through human choices.

(*f*) All sorts of new, or restructured, moral problems arise as side-effects of rapid technological development. For example, efficient contraception separates in principle sexual intercourse from the begetting of children and thus removes a major reason for regarding pre- and extra-marital intercourse as morally bad. Again, as another example, the harnessing of thermo-nuclear energy and its application to weaponry removes the basis of the traditional doctrine of the 'just war'.

II

The pressures upon christian theology that we have been looking at so far stem from the secular world, and especially from its scientific and technological advances. But there is another set of pressures which are no less important, coming from the wider religious world. This creates a new context in which theological work will increasingly have to be done in the future. This new context is a world in which the different forms of man's religious life are in increasing contact with one another, and in which therefore the intellectual and religious isolationism of the past

only restricts responsible thinking. Two hundred years ago
Fielding's Parson Thwackum could say, 'When I mention
religion, I mean the Christian religion; and not only the Christian
religion, but the Protestant religion; and not only the Protestant
religion, but the Church of England'. But we today cannot help
being conscious of the wider realms of man's relationship to the
divine, within which Christianity represents one major historical
strand among others. Even without travelling beyond the borders
of this country we find today in some of our big cities – such as
my own city of Birmingham – thousands of Muslims, Sikhs and
Hindus, including deeply devout adherents of those faiths, whose
very presence challenges a christian theology that was developed,
not indeed in ignorance, but nevertheless in essential unawareness,
of the other religions of the world. I do not think it is an exaggeration to say that traditional christian theology simply ignored the
greater part of the human race! For it has had only afterthoughts
to offer concerning God's purpose for all those hundreds of
millions of men and women who have lived and died since man
began either before the birth of Christ or beyond the borders of
Christendom. To this extent our theological tradition is not so
much monotheistic as henotheistic, and is ripe for important
further development and enlargement.

The problem usually thought to be posed by the fact of the
other world religions can be expressed very simply in this way: if
I had been born in India I would probably be a Hindu; if in
Egypt, probably a Muslim; if in Ceylon, probably a Buddhist;
but I was born in England and am, predictably, a Christian.
However, these different religions each profess to be true. Are we
then to say that one is true and the others false – whether equally
false or false in varying degrees? Or are we to say that each is
true subjectively, for its own adherents – with the implication
that none is true objectively?

However, when formulated in these terms the problem is insoluble; for neither alternative will do. The latter amounts, in
thinly disguised form, to the view that religion is illusion. The
former means, in christian terms, that ours is the true faith and
the others valid only in so far as they approximate to it. But whilst
this solution has a certain traditional authority it is ultimately
ruled out by the christian understanding of God. For does not the
divine love for all mankind, and the divine lordship over all life,

exclude the idea that salvation occurs only in one strand of human history, which is limited in time to the last nineteen centuries and in space virtually to the western hemisphere? If God's love is universal in scope, he cannot thus have restricted his saving encounter with humanity. If God is the God of the whole world, we must presume that the whole religious life of mankind is part of a continuous and universal human relationship to him.

With this, then, as our starting point, how may we understand the human religious situation, and how will the understanding of it affect the work of the christian theologian?

I suggest that we shall be moving in the right direction if we follow out the implications of the realisation, increasingly established within western thought in the modern period, that what we call a religion, as an empirical entity that can be traced historically and mapped geographically, is a human phenomenon. Christianity, Judaism, Buddhism, Islam and so on are human creations whose history is part of the wider history of human culture. In his important and illuminating book, *The Meaning and End of Religion*,[1] the Canadian scholar Wilfred Cantwell Smith, now Director of the Center for the Study of World Religions at Harvard, traces the development of the concept of a religion as a distinct and bounded historical phenomenon, and shows that the notion, so far from being universal and self-evident, is a distinctively western invention which we have magisterially exported to the rest of the world. It began in the Roman empire, and reached its present form, in which we virtually equate a religion with a theological system, at the time of the European Enlightenment. This notion of religions as mutually exclusive entities with their own characteristics and histories, although it now tends to operate as a habitual category of our thinking, may well be but another example of the illicit reification, the turning of good adjectives into bad substantives, to which the western mind is prone and against which contemporary philosophy has armed us. In this case a powerful but false conceptuality has helped to create phenomena answering to it, namely the religions of the world seeing themselves and each other as rival ideological communities.

However instead of thinking of religion as existing in mutually exclusive systems perhaps we should see the religious life of

[1] New York: Mentor Books, 1964.

mankind as a dynamic continuum within which certain major
disturbances have from time to time set up new fields of force, of
greater or lesser extent, displaying complex relationships of
attraction and repulsion, absorption, resistance and reinforce-
ment. These major disturbances are the great creative religious
moments in human history from which the distinguishable
religious traditions have stemmed. Theologically, such moments
are intersections of divine grace, divine initiative, divine truth,
with human faith, human response, human enlightenment. They
have made their impact upon the stream of human life so as to
affect the development of cultures; and Christianity, Islam,
Judaism, Buddhism, Hinduism are among the resulting historical-
cultural phenomena.

We know, for example, in our own case, that Christianity has
developed through a complex interaction between religious and
non-religious factors. Christian ideas have been formed within
the intellectual framework provided by Greek philosophy; the
christian church was moulded as an institution by the Roman
empire and its system of law; the catholic mind reflects the Latin
mediterranean temperament, and the protestant mind the
northern Germanic temperament. And so on: it is not hard today
to appreciate the connections between historical Christianity and
the continuing life of man in the western world.

And of course just the same is true in their own ways of the
other world religions. There is no time now to try to spell this
out; but I think that if one has seen it in the case of Christianity
one has no difficulty in seeing it in that of the other religions also.

Now this means that it is not appropriate to speak of a religion
as being true or false, any more than it is to speak of a civilisation
as being true or false. For the religions, in the sense of distinguishable religio-cultural streams within man's history, are expressions
of the diversities of human types and temperaments and thought-
forms. The same differences between, for example, the eastern
and western minds, expressed in different conceptual and
linguistic, social, political and artistic forms, also presumably
underlie the contrasts between eastern and western forms of
religion.

Cantwell Smith examines the development from the original
religious event or idea, whether it be the life of Christ, or the
teaching of Mohammed, or the insight of the Buddha, to a

religion in the sense of a vast living organism with its credal back-bone and institutional skin. And he shows in each case that this development stands in a questionable relation to that original event or idea. Religions as institutions, with the theological doctrines and the codes of behaviour which form their boundaries, did not come about so much because the religious reality required this as because human nature tends to surround truths and values with institutional walls which divide 'us' from 'them'. This development was understandable in terms of human psychology, and its results constitute the situation that we inherit. But now that the world has become a communicational unity we are moving into a new situation in which it is proper for theological thinking to transcend these cultural-historical boundaries. We, as Christians, owe our existence to that intersection of divine grace and human response in the life of Jesus of Nazareth in which we have seen the divine love made flesh. But it is far from self-evident that the activity of God's love in the life of Christ is incompatible with divine activity in other forms, in other times, in other places. On the contrary, if the religious life of mankind is a continuous field of relationship to the divine Reality, the theologian must try to include all forms of religious experience among his data, and all forms of religious ideas among the hypotheses to be considered. His theology should take account of all genuine human experience of the divine transcendent. For the varied but continuous field of the religious life of mankind demands unified theories of commensurate scope. These will not be christian theologies, or islamic theologies, or buddhist theologies, but human theologies, which are not sectional but global in their use of the religious data.

What is such a programme likely to involve? Clearly it must be the work of a multitude of minds and of several generations. There would seem to be two main tasks to be performed: first, the critical sifting of the several accumulated religious traditions to reveal more clearly the forms of religious experience living within them; and secondly the construction of theologies (in the plural) based upon the full range of man's religious awareness. Ideally, no doubt, the first of these tasks would be completed before the second is begun. But in fact they must both go on as best they can, some people working at one, some at the other.

We may perhaps reasonably expect it to be largely among

christian theologians that the second, more synoptic, work will proceed in the more immediate future, since the preliminary sifting process is furthest advanced in the case of Christianity. It has been taking place during the last hundred and fifty years or so in the encounter of christian thought with the rapidly developing sciences. As a result we have learned to distinguish between the central message of the gospel and its expression in the now obsolete thought forms of earlier ages. Of course this sifting process can never be definitively completed and its results agreed. But christian theology has long recognised the presence and function of myth in the scriptures and in the body of traditional doctrine, and has long been concerned to couch the christian message in ways that are intelligible to the demythologised modern mind. What has happened is that the growth of human knowledge in so many fields has forced the christian theologian back behind the interpretations of his ancient and medieval predecessors to the records of the original Christ-event, seeking to restate its meaning for twentieth-century men. Further, Christianity has after long struggles arrived at a conception of the nature of theological thinking which makes possible constructions going beyond the data provided by a single religious tradition. The older view of theology was that it was a body of divinely revealed truths. It is now understood as a continuing process of human reflection and theorising aiming to clarify the meaning of man's religious experience. And given this new understanding of the nature of theology the restriction to the religious data of a single culture becomes artificial.

Similar processes of reinterpretation in the light of modern science are for the most part only just beginning in the other world faiths – although there is of course a large and impressive modern Hindu literature concerned with the constructive understanding of the relation between the truth claims of the various religions. But in many cases (Islam, for example) the task of self-criticism and reformulation has a long way to go, and can of course only be undertaken by the different traditions moving at their own pace. But still the christian observer, with the western experience in mind, can to some extent see how these sifting processes are likely to go. Let us take for a moment one concrete example: the very ancient and widespread eastern idea of reincarnation. The question will inevitably arise whether this can survive philosophical analysis and scientific testing. Will the problem of the nature of the identity between two persons living at different times, one of whom is said to be the reincarnation of the other, be capable of solution; and will the doctrine, when clearly formulated, be compatible with the knowledge provided by modern genetics? Or will it perhaps cease to be an empirical hypothesis and turn into a purely metaphysical idea? Will the idea of reincarnation prove to be a religious myth comparable with, say, the christian myth of the fall of man from primitive perfection at some time in the far-distant past; or will it on the contrary become established as something to be included within any viable theology? This is the sort of question that now demands as careful consideration as such traditional christian topics as trinitarian or sacramental doctrine or theories of the atonement.

Perhaps an aspect of eastern religion that is most likely to withstand rational theological criticism is the experience of the divine as impersonal. From our western personalistic point of view Theravada Buddhism, for example, can be described as atheistic – that is to say, it does not acknowledge a personal deity. But it is deeply aware of a spiritual world-order, a teleological structure of existence, in right relationship to which man's ultimate good consists. And if the whole religious life of mankind is a varying continuum of relationship to ultimate Reality, this eastern experience of divine impersonality must be taken into account, along with the western experience of divine personality, in the construction of a global or human theology. It may be that ecological factors – which ought in that case to be capable of being traced – have in some cultures sharpened human awareness of one aspect of the divine and in other cultures of another aspect. Perhaps the corresponding modes of worship will always differ as between east and west. But this does not necessarily make impossible the construction of a theology which accepts both types of religious experience as valid and seeks to relate them together within a complex understanding of deity based upon both. Why should it not be the case that God is greater and more many-sided than either our individual or our separate community experiences of him? – so that whilst we can never form a fully adequate conception of God's nature, nevertheless we may form a less inadequate one on the basis of the full range of man's religious experience than on the basis of a single segment of it.

It is, of course, no implication of what I have been saying that the labours of theological scholarship in the past have generally been misdirected or wasted. Until recently the different religious traditions have run their separate courses, each more or less ignoring the others in the construction of its own beliefs. This was appropriate in the centuries before human history had begun to coalesce into a single global history. But now we are in a new situation created by the virtual unification of the world as a communicational system. And whereas it was hitherto reasonable to develop our theology in disregard of God's dealings with the non-christian world, it has now ceased to be reasonable to do that. We must be prepared to respond to the new situation by beginning the long-term task of forming a global or human theology.

It should be noted that a global theology would be compatible with the continued existence of a plurality of religions as concrete forms of religious life. For religions, as empirical entities, are human cultural forms reflecting different human mentalities and strands of history, within which God (to use our western word for the ultimate) is worshipped in different ways and under different patterns of religious concepts. There will (presumably) always be people selecting different styles of worship along the spectrum which stretches from the most highly formal and 'liturgical' to the most free and unstructured; and from the most purely intellectual to the most richly emotional. There will (presumably) always be, in William James's classification, once-born and twice-born types of religious believer. Again, there will (presumably) always be people who emphasise the remoteness and unapproachable majesty of God as the Wholly Other, and others who emphasise the nearness and friendship of God as Father; God as love and object of *bhakti*, or God as justice and *karma*; God as divine Thou, or God as infinite ground and depth of being. And if the foregoing thoughts have moved at all in the right direction, we should not assume that these different apprehensions of God are mutually exclusive. God may in his infinite reality be both love and justice, both Thou and *karma*, both king and friend.

It is not, I would suggest, necessary to 'water down' the essential christian understanding of Christ in order to relate it realistically to the wider religious life of mankind. But the divine presence in the life of Christ does not preclude an equally valid awareness of God in other religions. Millions of men and women have in Buddhism come to God as release out of suffering into Nirvana; or in Islam to God as holy and sovereign will addressing the Arab peoples through Mohammed; or in Hinduism to God as many-sided source and meaning of life. And further, it may be that Christ is also present in these other religions, and their several awarenesses of God likewise present in Christianity; so that, whilst a single world religion may well be impossible, nevertheless there may, in our communicationally unified world, be an increasing interpenetration of religious traditions and a growing of them closer together.

8. The Essence of Christianity

WHAT IS the essence of Christianity? As I have just asked it the question is ambiguous and in need of clarification. For there are two different things that we might be looking for. We might be looking for *that which is most important in Christianity*. Or we might be looking for *that which is uniquely christian* and not paralleled in any other faith. In other words we might be asking for the essence of Christianity in the sense of that which is most significant in it, or in the sense of that which is uniquely peculiar to it; and these are two different questions. For that which is peculiar to Christianity may or may not turn out to be the same as that which is most important in it. And so it is well to be clear at the outset what it is we are seeking.

I suggest that we should be looking for that which is most important in Christianity, the religious heart of the christian faith. It is this that we want to be able to compare with the essence of other faiths, rather than any historical peculiarities of the christian tradition which lie away from its religious centre. We are looking, then, for the essence of Christianity in the sense of that which is most religiously significant in it.

Christianity as an organised movement came into existence because it had something to offer that was of vital concern to ordinary men and women; and it will be helpful to start by remembering how the early Christians themselves described this. Quite early on both they and their enemies used the familiar hebraic concept of the Way. In the Acts of the Apostles, for example, we read of Saul the persecutor applying for letters to the synagogues at Damascus authorising him to arrest anyone found following 'the new way'.[1] Christianity appeared in the Roman world as a new and striking way based upon allegiance

[1] Acts 9: 2.

to Jesus as Lord. It was a distinctive way of life arising out of a distinctive loyalty. But it was at the same time a way in a deeper sense, a way of salvation, a way to the ultimate good for which man has been created and which Christianity has variously described as eternal life, heaven, the Kingdom of God, man's humanisation, the full realisation of his potential as a child of God, the fulfilment of the divine intention for his life. When Paul and his party were in Philippi someone followed them shouting, 'These men are servants of the Supreme God, and are declaring to you a way of salvation'.[2] This is a good description of what was and still is most important about Christianity: it is a way of life which is also a way to salvation, to man's wholeness and his eternal life.

Jesus himself had spoken of the narrow road which leads to life, in contrast to the wide road that leads to perdition.[3] And the figure of two ways recurs in the early christian writings as the ways to life and to death,[4] as the way of light and the way of darkness,[5] and as the way to heaven and the way to hell.[6] Christianity as the way, then, leads to salvation, light, life, heaven, the divine Kingdom; it is a way to the ultimate good offered by God to man. In all these variations the concept of the Way implies a goal to be attained; and the basic image in biblical and western thought has been that of movement along a road or (as in *The Pilgrim's Progress*) of an adventurous journey through life to the heavenly kingdom.

To a great extent the christian way is presented in the teaching of Jesus and in the patristic literature as an ethical Way. To follow this way is to live in a certain spirit or according to a certain pattern. It is a practical way, a way of living. To this extent the image of the way agrees with a widespread modern understanding of the essence of Christianity. The heart of the christian religion, many people say today, is not theological doctrine but the Sermon on the Mount. The christian essence is not to be found in beliefs about God, and whether he is three in one and one in three, but in an attitude to man as our neighbour; not in thinking correctly about Christ's two natures, as divine

---

[2] Acts 16: 17. [3] Matt. 7: 13–14.
[4] *Didache*, ch. 1; *Constitution of the Holy Apostles*, bk. VII, sec. 1.
[5] *Epistle of Barnabas*, chs. 19–20.
[6] Lactantius, *The Divine Institutes*, bk. VI, ch. 3.

and human, but in living as disciples who in his name feed the hungry, heal the sick and create justice in the world. In short, the essence of Christianity is not in believing rightly but in acting rightly in relation to our fellows.

There is something very importantly true here. The christian way is a practical way, a way to be lived. But nevertheless it is not simply an ethic. When we look at Jesus' moral teaching we find that it cannot be separated from his religious teaching. His command was to imitate God's attitude to mankind. As God is universally loving, letting his rain and sunshine fall equally on the just and the unjust, so we are to achieve a universal and impartial love for each human individual. As God is merciful so we are to be merciful. Because God is sovereign we need not be anxious or self-seeking. In short, it is because God *is*, and is what he is, that we are to behave in the manner that Jesus describes. Such a way of life is rendered both reasonable and attractive by certain convictions about the nature and ordering of the world; for Jesus presents the world as being such that this is the appropriate spirit in which to inhabit it. Thus the way of life, and the context of belief which makes it a rational way, form an integral whole. Accordingly the christian ethic by itself is not the christian Way. The other element that is also essential is belief or faith, together with the activity of worship in which this most directly expresses itself.

At this point we have to avoid the error of assuming that christian belief and worship constitute a fixed and unchanging substance or structure. For during the nineteen centuries or so of christian history continuous change, development and diversification has been taking place. The change has sometimes been rapid and obvious, and at other times so slow as to be barely perceptible; but it has been taking place all the time. You only have to compare the life of the church in New Testament times with its life in the high Middle Ages, and again with the life of the churches today, to see immense and manifest transformations. Or again, compare the state of christian belief in Britain or the United States, say two hundred years ago, with the state of christian belief in these countries today. Or compare worship in St Peter's, Rome, in an Anglican parish church, in a Baptist chapel, in a Pentecostal Assembly Hall, and in a meeting of the Society of Friends. These spot checks are enough to remind us that in a multitude of ways Christianity has become diversified and pluriform as it has lived through the centuries. There is indeed a fixed basis or, better, a fixed starting point, for christian belief and worship; but proceeding from that starting point there is a still unfinished history of change as the christian way has been followed through the centuries, meeting new human circumstances and new intellectual climates. I shall return later to these diverse and changing aspects of Christianity; but let us turn now to the unchanging aspect.

The permanent and unchanging within Christianity is, I suggest, the set of happenings from whose impact these varying forms of belief, worship and organisation have all flowed. In other words, the unchanging element is to be found in the originating events from which the moving stream of christian history has flowed. The phrase 'the Christ-event' has been coined in modern times to refer to the complex of happenings constituting the life, death and resurrection of Jesus and the birth of the persisting community which was created by its response to him. It is in this complex event that christian faith sees God acting self-revealingly for the salvation of the world. And it is this that forms Christianity's unchanging basis; for it consists of events that have occurred and can never unoccur or be expunged from the process of the universe. The life, death and resurrection of Jesus of Nazareth, his influence upon those who responded to him in faith, their memories of him and of his words, and their experience of a new quality of life in a new relationship with God and with one another — all this is something that has happened and cannot unhappen. And it is this that forms the permanent basis of Christianity.

Let us now ask what sort of an event the Christ-event was. It was not an ordinary item of secular history, but a revelatory event. Revelation necessarily has two sides to it − a divine activity of communication and a human reception of that communication. God signals to man, and when man reads the signals aright divine-human communication has taken place. There has to be both divine action in the world and man's appreciation of the occurrence *as* divine action; both God's self-revealing activity and the answering human response which we call faith. And the Christ-event, as revelation, has these two sides to it. God was acting in human history but acting, as always, in such a way that man remained free to see or fail to see what was happening *as* God's doing. For religious faith, in its most basic sense, is the cognitive choice whereby we experience events and situations as mediating divine activity.[7] In his presence Jesus' disciples experienced the presence of the transcendent God and his claim upon human life. This faith response was focused, in the minds of the first-century Jews who were his disciples, by the traditional Jewish idea of the anointed one – in Hebrew, Messiah; in Greek, *christos*; and in English, Christ. Others, who closed their hearts to Jesus as mediating God's grace and claim, saw him instead as an unauthorised rabbi, or a false prophet, or a dangerous revolutionary. But Christianity has grown out of the small group who saw Jesus as the Messiah, or who were ready to see him retrospectively as Messiah in the light of the resurrection experience which created the early christian community.

Thus to speak of the Christ-event is to speak the language of faith. The Christ-event was not an event in public history, but an event experienced in faith. Jesus of Nazareth was of course a figure in public history, but Jesus the Christ, Jesus as mediating the presence and claim of the transcendent God, is not known and therefore does not exist outside the religious field of vision. The source event from which Christianity in all its still unfolding diversity has flowed is a faith event, and the New Testament documents by which that event is reflected to us across the centuries are documents of faith. For they were written by the community which had experienced Jesus raised beyond death into a life continuous with God's saving activity towards mankind.

To be a Christian today is to share the faith of the New Testament writers, seeing something of what they saw and feeling something of what they felt. But although we can share their faith we cannot, except for occasional glimpses, penetrate behind it to the Jesus of secular history. We cannot, for example, reconstruct his physical appearance, except to say that he was a young Jewish working-class man who died a violent death at about the age of thirty-three. More importantly, we cannot with any certainty reconstruct the actual words that he uttered; for the New Testament reports of his teaching and conversation

[7] See Chapter 3 above.

began to be written down after the lapse of at least a full generation during which the oral tradition interacted with the life of the
church, influencing and being influenced by it. Consequently,
whilst the gospels give us a coherent impression of the *kinds* of
things that Jesus said and did, we cannot press the reports of his
words as actual verbatim records.

Because of these difficulties of historical reconstruction different
christian circles have understood Jesus very differently – as stern
apocalyptic visionary expecting an early end to the world, as
divine therapist probing and healing individual souls, as hebraic
prophet demanding justice for the poor, as preacher of universal
love. . . . Perhaps he was all of these things; perhaps he was
something other than them all. We cannot know. But we can
know, by looking at those who were directly influenced by him,
through those whom they in turn influenced, that he brought
men and women to God with a directness that made all other
ways of salvation needless to them. In following Jesus the
Messiah they encountered God in a manner that entirely filled
their lives.

So the community lived and grew, more and more men and
women experiencing the excitement and peace of the new way,
until before two generations had passed they came to think of
Jesus himself as virtually God. Accordingly we read in Pliny's
report to the Emperor Trajan about the year 112 that the
Christians were accustomed to meet before daybreak and to
recite hymns to Christ as a god.[8]

This deification of Jesus was the first and most important step
in the formation of what we know today as orthodox christian
theology. Before this step was taken there was a great religious
event, within which men and women knew themselves to be
confronted by God, but an event that was not yet intellectually
interpreted in terms of a fixed system of beliefs. Travelling about
Palestine with Jesus as he preached and healed, the disciples had
a sense of being on the inside of a dynamic divine action in the
world, an invasion of human life by God's redeeming power
focused in Jesus. He was God's agent among them, like the
prophets of old. But once the step of deification had been taken
it set in motion a development of christian thought along the path

[8] Henry Bettenson, ed., *Documents of the Christian Church* (London
and New York: Oxford University Press, 1943) p. 6.

which it has followed during the last nineteen centuries. In time the belief that Jesus of Nazareth was God incarnate became entrenched within a comprehensive body of doctrine which both depends upon it and reciprocally supports it. Indeed so central is the belief in the deity of Christ to the established system of christian theology that many people today would identify it as *the* essential christian belief.

It is therefore of the utmost importance, in pursuing again the question of the essence of Christianity,[9] to see that this crucial first step was part of the process whereby the church sought to interpret to itself the meaning of the Christ-event, and not part of that event itself. For it is extremely unlikely that Jesus thought of himself, or that his first disciples thought of him, as God incarnate. He used the mysterious title Son of Man, the meaning of which remains to this day uncertain. He may hesitantly have allowed his disciples to think of him as Messiah, a title which referred in the minds of his contemporaries to a political and military leader, an anointed son of David who would come to institute God's rule over and through his chosen people. This was the category which Jewish thought offered for a man with a special divine calling and authority. Perhaps Jesus permitted himself, at least among his chosen disciples, to be thought of by this title, though at the same time evidently trying to bring about a shift in their understanding of messiahship from a political to a religious meaning.

But if Jesus himself did not think in the categories of later christian theology, how *did* he think of himself, and what understanding of him was involved in the original faith response that was part of the Christ-event? There are certain limited things that we can say with reasonable probability about Jesus' self-understanding, and beyond that we have to acknowledge our ignorance of his inner life and thoughts. But it seems clear that he was, and was conscious of being, genuinely and unambiguously human. He did not descend fully grown from the heavens but was born as a human baby and grew to adulthood through the normal stages of development. When he was baptised at about the age of thirty in the river Jordan he had an experience of

[9] Already significantly reopened for us today by Stephen Sykes in *Christian Theology Today* (London: Mowbrays, 1971) and in 'The Essence of Christianity', *Religious Studies*, Dec 1971.

being called by God to a special vocation. After this, or after the succeeding period of solitary meditation in the desert, he was a soul liberated from selfhood and fully open to the divine Spirit. In eastern terms he was *jivanmukti*, or he was a Buddha, one who had attained to true knowledge of and relation to reality. As a by-product of this he had powers of healing – though he did not wield omnipotent power; and he had deep human insight – though he was not omniscient. He was intensely and vividly conscious of the presence of God as his heavenly Father. And it must have been evident to him that he was experiencing a more powerful sense of God's presence and a closer communion with God, and consequently spoke to men and women about God and his will for them with greater authority, than anyone else whom he encountered, including the religious leaders of Jewry. He must have been aware that within the sphere of his own observation, which covered directly or indirectly the Palestine of his own day, God was impinging upon human life much more powerfully through himself than in any other way. Through his healing and teaching, through his parables conveying the limit-less divine grace and goodness, through his words of challenge and rebuke, through his declarations of the divine forgiveness, opening the possibility of new life to the spiritually and morally impoverished, the divine reality was encountering men and women and seeking their response. As Jesus expressed it, the Kingdom of God had come upon them: St Matthew's Gospel reports him as saying concerning his own healing work, 'But if it is by the Spirit of God that I drive out the devils, then be sure the kingdom of God has already come upon you'.[10]

The language of divine sonship was available to the growing christian community, for it had long been used of the Messiah in the Old Testament. In one of the psalms Jahweh says to the king of Israel, prototype of the Messiah, 'You are my son, today I have begotten you',[11] and in Isaiah Jahweh refers to the suffering Servant as 'my chosen, in whom my soul delights'.[12] This Old Testament language is echoed in the description of Jesus' experi-ence at the time of his baptism. But 'Son of God' in these contexts is Old Testament messianic language and does not imply the trinitarian notion of God the Son as this was to develop in the

[10] Matt. 12: 28.   [11] Psalm 2: 7.   [12] Isaiah 42 : 1.

theology of the church. The beginnings of this trinitarian thought in the New Testament – in such sayings as 'My Father and I are one',[13] 'Anyone who has seen me has seen the Father',[14] 'no one comes to the Father except by me'[15] – belong to the Fourth Gospel and express the understanding of the significance of Jesus that was developing in christian circles at about the end of the first century. What seems to have happened during the hundred years or so following Jesus' death was that the language of divine sonship floated loose from the original ground of Jewish thought and developed a new meaning as it took root again in Graeco-Roman culture.

This language was pitched to the level of the reality which was to be expressed. For whenever men and women encounter God something of absolute importance has happened, something which can only be expressed in the language of absolutes. They have encountered *God*; and no event could be more momentous or final than this. And so when they come to speak of this crucial event they have to find a way of expressing its definitive character and its startling uniqueness within their own experience. The way that was taken by the christian movement as it expanded westwards into the Graeco-Roman world, and had to explain the christian way to that world, was, as we have seen, a redeployment of Old Testament language concerning God's human agent, Messiah, developed in accordance with models offered by the Greek philosophy that constituted the intellectual currency of the age. In particular the notion of substance exerted its influence as a static, all-or-nothing model; for something either is or is not composed of a given substance. Thus the meaning of the Christ-event was first expressed by saying that Jesus was the Messiah, to whom in the Old Testament God had said, 'Thou art my beloved Son'; and then this divine sonship was later understood as his being of one substance with God the Father. This led in turn to the conclusion that Jesus was God incarnate, the second Person of the Holy Trinity – in the words of the fourth-century Nicene Creed, 'the only-begotten Son of God, begotten of the Father before all the ages, Light of Light, true God of true God, begotten not made, of one substance with the Father, through whom all things were made'. Accordingly the christian bodies

[13] John 10: 30.   [14] John 14: 9.   [15] John 14: 6.

forming the World Council of Churches 'are one in acknowledging Him [Christ] as our God and Saviour'.[16]

If, however, Christianity had happened to expand eastwards, so that its basic thinking had been done within an Asian instead of a European culture, its intellectual interpretations would inevitably have taken very different forms. If, for example, it had moved very early into India, in which Buddhism was then becoming a powerful influence and the Mahayana doctrines were being developed, it is likely that instead of Jesus being identified as the divine Logos or the divine Son he would have been identified as a Bodhisattva who, like Gotama some four centuries earlier, had attained to Buddhahood or perfect relationship to reality, but had in compassion for suffering mankind voluntarily lived out his human life in order to show others the way to salvation.

If this had happened, and christian theology had developed within an eastern instead of a western context, would this have been a wrong development or simply a different development? Once we understand that theology is the human attempt to state the meaning of revelatory events experienced in faith, we realise that many different christian theologies are possible – like the many different projections by which the three-dimensional earth can be represented on two-dimensional maps. For theology is part of the human, culturally conditioned response to the Christ-event. The theology that has actually developed, and has acquired a classic or orthodox status, is an aspect of the interaction between the Christ-event and the history of man in the western world during the last two thousand years. And if the main thrust of the christian movement had been into India instead of into Europe the rather different christian orthodoxy that would have resulted would have been an aspect of the interaction between the Christ-event and the civilisation of India. In fact, however, christian thought has been formed in the west. In its first phase the christian way was an increasingly important element within Graeco-Roman civilisation; then it formed the intellectual and imaginative heart of medieval Europe; then it stimulated the Renaissance and the birth of the modern era; and now it exists in the west in uneasy tension with the world of science and

[16] Message of the first Assembly of the World Council of Churches, Amsterdam, 1948.

technology which it has created. But even within this western development, extending now over more than nineteen centuries, the christian understanding of the Christ-event, and the christian picture of the universe of which that understanding is a part, have changed massively and cumulatively. I doubt, for example, whether a medieval christian theologian would be able to recognise as christian at all the theology of a contemporary liberal christian thinker whose mind is post-Darwin, post-Marx, post-Freud, and post a century of biblical criticism, and who is engaged in sympathetic dialogue with non-christian faiths. I doubt whether a fifteenth-century Byzantine bishop would be able to recognise a nineteenth-century British Quaker as a fellow disciple of Christ; and I doubt whether a Scottish Calvinist divine of the seventeenth century would be able to recognise Paul Tillich or Rudolf Bultmann as fellow christian theologians. The changes of outlook and opinion during the centuries of the church's life have immensely broadened the range of intellectual options that can claim the name of christian. Christian theologians have believed that Jesus' death was a ransom paid to the devil; that it was an offering made to satisfy the divine honour; that it was the death of a substitute being punished in place of sinful mankind; that it was a moral example. They have believed that the Trinity consists of three centres of divine consciousness; that it consists of one God acting in three ways; and that the trinitarian doctrine is secondary and speculative. Christians have believed seriously in the existence of the devil and of demons, and have dismissed these beliefs as superstitions. They have believed that the Roman Pope is the Vicar of Christ on earth, and that he is Antichrist. They have believed in the six-day creation of the world, and in the existence of Adam and Eve and the Garden of Eden, the forbidden fruit and the tempting serpent, and they have regarded all this as mythology. They have believed in heaven and hell, and in heaven only, and in neither.

Further, there has been an immense diversification of the modes of christian thought. These have included not only the more closed systems of Augustine or Aquinas or Calvin, but also the more open systems of Origen and of the christian Platonists; and the recent theology of Paul Tillich, which has much in common with Indian religious thought; and again the experimental theologies of Teilhard de Chardin, of John Robinson, of the 'Death of God' theologians, and now political theology, revolutionary theology, black theology, and so on. What all these have in common, making it proper to call them christian, is a common origin in the Christ-event. If Christianity, as a phenomenon spanning the centuries, is the history of man's faith response to Jesus of Nazareth, then all these diverse ways of thinking are part of that phenomenon. Christianity is an ongoing movement of life and thought, defined by its origin in the Christ-event and by its consciousness of that origin. It cannot be defined in terms of adherence to any doctrinal standard, for its doctrines are historically and culturally conditioned and have changed as the church has entered new historical and cultural situations. Accordingly it is impossible to predict or to limit the developments that will take place in the future history of this movement. Christians of a thousand years ago could not have foreseen what it is to be a Christian in our contemporary technological society, and would perhaps have been horrified if they had been given a prevision of it; and no more can we today foresee what it will mean to be a Christian in the world of a thousand years hence.

I am suggesting, then, that in its essence Christianity is the way of life and salvation which has its origin in the Christ-event. It will continue as a way of salvation so long as men and women continue to find salvation – that is, spiritual life and health – through it. And so long as there is a community of people, however closely or loosely organised, who find salvation in the christian way, and who continue to take the name of christian, their religious beliefs will be part of the history of christian theology. Christian belief consists in the beliefs of Christians, and the Christians of one age cannot legislate for the Christians of another age, either past or future. Christianity, then, is an open-ended history which has taken varying forms in varying circumstances, and which has as its essence the way of salvation that was initiated by the Christ-event.

This conclusion will provide the starting point for our inquiry into the relation between Christianity and the other religions of the world.

9. The Copernican Revolution in Theology

CHRISTIANITY has seen itself from the beginning as a way of life and salvation. Our next question is this: Do we regard the christian way as the only way, so that salvation is not to be found outside it; or do we regard the other great religions of mankind as other ways of life and salvation?

Let us begin by going back into history. For fifteen centuries at least the christian position was that all men, of whatever race or culture, must become Christians if they are to be saved. Declarations asserting this are legion; for example, the famous papal pronouncement of Boniface VIII in 1302, 'We are required by faith to believe and hold that there is one holy, catholic and apostolic Church; we firmly believe it and unreservedly profess it; outside it there is neither salvation nor remission of sins. . . . Further, we declare, say, define and proclaim that to submit to the Roman Pontiff is, for every human creature, an utter necessity of salvation';[1] or again the Decree of the Council of Florence in 1438–45 affirming that 'no one remaining outside the Catholic Church, not just pagans, but also Jews or heretics or schismatics, can become partakers of eternal life; but they will go to the "everlasting fire which was prepared for the devil and his angels", unless before the end of life they are joined to the Church'.[2] This side of traditional Roman Catholic teaching is summed up in the dogma, *extra ecclesiam nulla salus*, outside the church there is no salvation.

The Protestant equivalent of this has been the firm assumption,

[1] Denzinger, 468–9. *The Church Teaches: Documents of the Church in English Translation* (St Louis and London: B. Herder Book Co., 1955) pp. 153–4.
[2] Denzinger, 714. *The Church Teaches*, p. 165.

not however explicitly stated as an article of faith in any of the great Reformed, Lutheran or Anglican confessional declarations, that outside Christianity there is no salvation. This note is to be heard not only in older missionary statements but also in declarations made within very recent years from the fundamentalist evangelical groups. For example, the Frankfurt Declaration of 1970 spoke to the non-christian world, saying 'We therefore challenge all non-christians, who belong to God on the basis of creation, to believe in him [Jesus Christ] and to be baptized in his name, for in him alone is eternal salvation promised to them'.[3] Again, 'The adherents of the non-christian religions and world views . . . must let themselves be freed from their former ties and false hopes in order to be admitted by belief and baptism into the body of Christ'.[4] In the same spirit the Wheaton Declaration of 1966 pledged its supporters to work for 'the evangelization of the world in this generation'.[5] And in one of the Messages delivered at the Congress on World Mission at Chicago in 1960 it was said that 'In the years since the war, more than one billion souls have passed into eternity and more than half of these went to the torment of hell fire without even hearing of Jesus Christ, who He was, or why He died on the cross of Calvary'.[6] The controlling assumption behind all these utterances, whether medieval Catholic or modern Protestant evangelical, is that outside the church, or outside Christianity, there is no salvation.

Now I think that most of us who are Christians in this country today have inherited essentially this conception of the christian mission, though we may not have held it so explicitly and emphatically as in the statements I have been quoting. Certainly this view, or rather this assumption, was present in my own mind for at least twenty-five years. I assumed it to be a central christian position that salvation is through Christ alone, and therefore that those who do not respond to God through Christ are not saved but, presumably, damned or lost. However, although I believed

---

[3] Para. 3. *Christianity Today*, 19 June 1970.   [4] Para. 6.

[5] Harold Lindsell, ed., *The Church's Worldwide Mission*, Proceedings of the Congress on the Church's Worldwide Mission, 9–16 April 1966, at Wheaton College, Wheaton, Illinois (Waco, Texas: Word Books, 1966) p. 237.

[6] *Facing the Unfinished Task:* Messages Delivered at the Congress on World Mission, Chicago, Ill., 1960, edited by J. O. Percy (Grand Rapids, Mich.: Eerdman, 1961) p. 9.

this I did not stress its negative implications. My attention was
focused within the area of salvation and not upon those left outside, and accordingly I did not dwell upon the question of what
happens to those outside the faith, and had no clear beliefs about
their religious status or their ultimate fate. Indeed I suppose it
would be correct to say that I simply ignored them, and accordingly ignored the theological problems which their existence
creates. I believed that God has made himself known to mankind
with unique fullness and saving power in Christ, and has ordained
that all men must come to him through Christ. And although it
follows from this that those who do not become Christ's disciples
have missed the way to salvation yet I did not explicitly apply
this conclusion to the hundreds of millions of inhabitants of the
globe. I believed by implication that the majority of human
beings are eternally lost; but I did not believe this explicitly and
whole-heartedly, so as to have to come to terms with its consequences for my other beliefs. This was of course a thoroughly
illogical state of mind to be in. And yet I don't think that such a
state of mind, in which one has certain convictions but refrains
from facing their implications, is so very uncommon; and it may
in this case have expressed a benevolent unwillingness to accept
so humanly repugnant a conclusion. At any rate, this was the
position in which I was for a number of years concerning the
relation of Christianity to other religions. And I suppose it was a
product of two factors: first, an unreadiness to face this range of
problems, and second, the fact that these problems did not particularly force themselves upon my attention.

But as soon as one does meet and come to know people of
other faiths a paradox of gigantic proportions becomes disturb-
ingly obvious. We say as Christians that God is the God of
universal love, that he is the creator and Father of all mankind,
that he wills the ultimate good and salvation of all men. But we
also say, traditionally, that the only way to salvation is the
christian way. And yet we know, when we stop to think about it,
that the large majority of the human race who have lived and
died up to the present moment have lived either before Christ or
outside the borders of Christendom. Can we then accept the
conclusion that the God of love who seeks to save all mankind
has nevertheless ordained that men must be saved in such a way
that only a small minority can in fact receive this salvation? It is

the weight of this moral contradiction that has driven christian thinkers in modern times to explore other ways of understanding the human religious situation.

Let us then look at the ways in which the churches have tried to meet this problem, beginning with the traditional and deeply entrenched dogma: outside the church there is no salvation. This was formed as early as the third century, and was promulgated by Pope Boniface VIII in 1302 in the Bull from which I have quoted. However, it has become increasingly evident in the light of expanding acquaintance with the wider religious life of mankind that such a dogma, as it was understood in the medieval church, is untenable; and accordingly there have been vigorous attempts, particularly in Roman Catholic circles, to rethink the traditional position. As long ago as 1854 Pope Pius IX began the process; and he did it in the characteristically Catholic way of continuing to pay allegiance to the original dogma but at the same time adding an epicycle of subsidiary theory to change its practical effect. In an Allocution Pius IX said, 'It must, of course, be held as a matter of faith that outside the apostolic Roman Church no one can be saved, that the Church is the only ark of salvation, and that whoever does not enter it will perish in the flood. On the other hand, it must likewise be held as certain that those who are affected by ignorance of the true religion, if it is invincible ignorance, are not subject to any guilt in this matter before the eyes of the Lord.'[7] Thus if a non-catholic – whether a non-catholic Christian or an adherent of another faith altogether – is invincibly ignorant of the truth of the Catholic faith, he may be saved even though he dies outside the church; and only God himself knows to whom this doctrine applies.

Another related theory, by which the original intent of the 'no salvation outside the church' doctrine is avoided without the doctrine itself being withdrawn, consists in the two related ideas of implicit faith and of baptism by desire. According to this epicycle there may be people who are consciously outside the church who are nevertheless unconsciously within it. They have an implicit faith in the form of a sincere desire to do God's will. They are not outwardly baptised into the church, but nevertheless they are in the church by a baptism of desire, namely their sincere desire for the truth even though they do not as yet know

[7] Denzinger, 1647. *The Church Teaches*, p. 174.

what the truth is. The effect of these epicycles was summarised in an important letter from the Holy Office in Rome to the Archbishop of Boston in 1949 in the following words, 'To gain eternal salvation it is not always required that a person be incorporated *in fact* as a member of the Church, but it is required that he belong to it at least in *desire* and *longing*. It is not always necessary that this desire be explicit. . . . When a man is invincibly ignorant, God also accepts an *implicit desire*, so called because it is contained in the good disposition of soul by which a man wants his will to be conformed to God's will.'[8] By means of these epicycles the 'no salvation outside the church' dogma is retained, but sincere men of other faiths can nevertheless be held to be in a sense inside the church if their ignorance of christian truth is not culpable and if they have a sincere desire to do God's will.

As a way of acknowledging, in terms of the dogma 'no salvation outside the church', that there is in fact salvation outside the church, these epicycles have served a useful purpose. But nevertheless they can only operate as an interim measure. For they are fundamentally weak arguments accepted for the sake of an intuitively accepted conclusion until better arguments are found! As thus far formulated they either do not go far enough or else go too far. Since presumably only theists can have a sincere desire to do God's will, the doctrine of implicit desire does not extend to adherents of the non-theistic faiths, such as Buddhism and an important part of Hinduism; and thus does not go far enough. But, on the other hand, if the epicycles are developed to the point at which salvation is understood in terms of right relationship to the divine reality as variously known in the different religious traditions, instead of in terms of incorporation into the church of Christ, then it would be time frankly to abandon the original dogma.

I have called these supplementary theories, developed to modify the original dogma whilst leaving it verbally intact, 'epicycles' because they are so powerfully reminiscent of the epicycles that were added to the old Ptolemaic picture of the universe, with the earth at the centre, to accommodate increasingly accurate knowledge of the planets. The stars, including the sun and the planets, were all supposed to move in concentric circles round the earth. This was at that time a feasible theory as

8 *The Church Teaches*, pp. 274–5.

regards the stars; but the planets moved in paths which did not fit such a scheme. But instead of abandoning the scheme the ancient astronomers added a series of smaller supplementary circles, called epicycles, revolving with their centres on the original circles. If a planet was thought of as moving on one of these smaller circles whilst it was in turn moving round the great circle, the resulting path was more complex and nearer to what was actually observed; and this complication of the system made it possible to maintain the basic dogma that the earth is the hub of the universe. Looking back we can see that it was theoretically possible to stick indefinitely to the conviction that the earth is the centre, adding epicycle upon epicycle as required to reconcile the dogma with the facts. However, the whole thing became increasingly artificial and burdensome; and the time came when people's minds were ready for the new Copernican conception that it is the sun and not the earth that is at the centre. Then the old Ptolemaic system was thrown aside and appeared in retrospect utterly antiquated and implausible. And much the same, I cannot help thinking, applies to what I shall call the Ptolemaic theology whose fixed point is the principle that outside the church, or outside Christianity, there is no salvation. When we find men of other faiths we add an epicycle of theory to the effect that although they are consciously adherents of a different faith, nevertheless they may unconsciously or implicitly be Christians. In theory, one can carry on such manoeuvres indefinitely. But anyone who is not firmly committed to the original dogma is likely to find the resulting picture artificial, implausible and unconvincing, and to be ready for a Copernican revolution in his theology of religions.

This then was the state of the Ptolemaic theology up to the time of the Second Vatican Council of 1963–65. As Vatican II addressed itself to the problem of the world religions the great question was whether it would be able to make the Copernican revolution that was called for. But alas it did not. It added yet further epicycles to the old theory. In its Dogmatic Constitution on the Church, promulgated in 1964, the Council said:

Those also can attain to everlasting salvation who through no fault of their own do not know the gospel of Christ or His Church, yet sincerely seek God and, moved by grace, strive by their deeds to do His will as it is known to them through the dictates of conscience. Nor does divine Providence deny the help necessary for salvation to those who, without blame on their part, have not yet arrived at an explicit knowledge of God, but who strive to live a good life, thanks to His grace. Whatever goodness or truth is found among them is looked upon by the Church as a preparation for the Gospel.[9]

And in a Declaration on the Relationship of the Church to Non-Christian Religions made at the end of the Council in 1965 it is said, 'The Catholic Church rejects nothing which is true and holy in these religions. She looks with sincere respect upon those ways of conduct and of life, those rules and teachings which, though differing in many particulars from what she holds and sets forth, nevertheless often reflect a ray of that Truth which enlightens all men.'[10]

In comparison with the much earlier dogmatic statements which I quoted at the beginning the Vatican II pronouncements are magnificently open and charitable. The emotional climate has changed, and has changed radically and for the better; and there can be no question that these new pronouncements represent a major step forward. But still Vatican II has not made the Copernican revolution that is needed in the christian attitude to other faiths. It still assumes without question that salvation is only in Christ and through incorporation into his mystical body, the church. Vatican II sees this incorporation as being possible on the basis of a sincere effort to follow the light available within other religious traditions. But the goodness and truth that men of other faiths have is, the Dogmatic Constitution says, 'looked upon by the Church as a preparation for the gospel'. This suggests that faithful men in other religions are still required by God sooner or later to arrive at an explicit christian faith; and this is made clear in the next paragraph, which says concerning its missionary task that 'the Church is compelled by the Holy Spirit to do her part towards the full realization of the will of God, who has established Christ as the source of salvation for the whole world'.[11] This Ptolemaic framework of thought is equally explicit at the beginning of the Dogmatic Constitution, where it is asserted that at the end of time 'all just men from the time of Adam . . . will be

[9] Ch. ii, para. 16.   [10] Para. 2.   [11] Ch. ii, para. 17.

gathered together with the Father in the universal Church'.[12] This presupposition of Vatican II that human salvation is only in Christ and his church, and involves an explicitly christian faith, was further made unmistakably clear by Cardinal Bea in the words with which he presented the Dogmatic Constitution to the Council in 1964. He spoke of its conception of inter-faith dialogue 'through recognizing the spiritual and moral values to be found in the various religions and through sincere esteem for their followers. For those who live according to the command of their right conscience are united to Christ and his mystical body through implicit faith . . . pending the time when they recognize fully the riches of Christ and share in them. There can be no doubt that the Church in her dialogue with them effectively endeavours to lead them to an explicit and full participation in these riches.'[13] Here is the old Ptolemaic theology, with almost all possible epicycles working!

Almost, but not quite all. For in recent years a number of leading Roman Catholic theologians who had worked for the Vatican II declaration have since used it as a door through which to pass to further elaboration of the church's new respect for non-christian faiths and further explorations of the implications of that attitude. This new thinking begins before the Vatican II pronouncement and goes beyond it, and starts with Karl Rahner's 1961 essay, prior to the Council, on 'Christianity and the Non-Christian Religions'. His new contribution is the idea of anonymous Christianity. 'Christianity', he says, 'does not simply confront the member of an extra-Christian religion as a mere non-Christian but as someone who can and must be regarded in this or that respect as an anonymous Christian.'[14] Thus the non-christian may be a Christian without knowing it, in that he is within the sphere of divine grace although he does not yet know the source of that grace as the God and Father of our Lord Jesus Christ. Clearly Rahner is struggling valiantly to do justice to the reality of religious faith outside Christianity; but equally clearly he has not been able to face the Copernican revolution

[12] Ch. i, para. 2.
[13] Quoted in J. Neuner, ed., *Christian Revelation and World Religions* (London: Burns & Oates, 1967) p. 7.
[14] *Theological Investigations*, vol. 5 (Baltimore: Helicon Press, and London: Darton, Longman & Todd, 1966) p. 131.

that is required and has instead only contributed yet another ingenious epicycle to the old Ptolemaic theology.

We must look at one more attempt, and this the boldest so far, to achieve honesty and realism concerning the wider religious life of mankind without entirely abandoning the 'no salvation outside Christianity' dogma. This is in the notable paper by Hans Küng read to a conference on 'Christian Revelation and Non-Christian Religions' held at Bombay in 1964, just after the Vatican Council had promulgated its Dogmatic Constitution on the Church with its important section on non-christian religions. Küng's central and most striking suggestion is that the world religions, by which he means all religions other than Catholic Christianity, should be regarded as the ordinary way of human salvation and the Catholic Church as the extraordinary way. 'A man is to be saved', he says, 'within the religion that is made available to him in his historical situation. Hence it is his right and his duty to seek God within that religion in which the hidden God has already found him.'[15] Thus the world religions are, he says, 'the *way of salvation* in universal salvation history; the general way of salvation, we can even say, for the people of the world religions: the more common, the "*ordinary*" way of salvation, as against which the way of salvation in the Church appears as something very special and extraordinary'.[16]

If 'ordinary' here simply meant 'majority', and if 'extra-ordinary' simply meant 'minority', Küng's doctrine would be an acknowledgement that most men are saved by God through religions other than Christianity. This would be a decisive move into the post-Ptolemaic theological world. But in fact Küng goes on to make it clear that whilst his terminology is novel, his meaning remains firmly Ptolemaic. For him the ordinary way of salvation through the world religions is only an interim state until the adherents of those religions arrive at an explicit Christian faith. The non-christian's right and duty to seek God within his own religion is, says Küng, 'until such time as he is

---

[15] Neuner, p. 52.
[16] Neuner, p. 53. The same idea is developed by H. R. Schlette in his monograph, *Towards a Theology of Missions* (E.T.: London: Burns & Oates, 1966). Paul Tillich's distinction between the 'latent' and the 'manifest' church offers a related concept. See his *Systematic Theology*, III (Chicago: Chicago University Press, and Welwyn, Herts: James Nisbet & Co., 1963) pp. 152f.

confronted in an existential way with the revelation of Jesus Christ'.[17] People of other faiths, he says, 'are pre-Christian, directed towards Christ. . . . The men of the world religions are not professing Christians but, by the grace of God, they are called and marked out to be Christians.'[18] Again, he says that 'the individual people in the world religions are called upon by the Church of Christ to make the decision of faith in Christ only at that point in time when not only the report, the information about the Gospel of Jesus Christ, but that Gospel *itself* is preached to them'.[19] In other words, they must sooner or later become Christians, but in the meantime they are not condemned, for the gospel has not yet reached them in such a way as to overcome their hitherto invincible ignorance of its truth.

This is plainly the old Ptolemaic system, to which Küng in turn adds his own epicycle in the notion of the ordinary and extraordinary ways of salvation. The finally Ptolemaic character of his thought consists in his separating Christianity from the other religions of the world and according it an unique status as the religion to which all men must eventually come. Thus for Küng Christianity, and indeed the Roman Catholic Church, remains in the end at the centre of the universe of faiths.

There is also a Protestant epicycle which is sometimes heard in discussions although I have not seen it in the published literature of missiology or of the theology of world religions. This is the idea that all who are to be saved must come to God through Jesus Christ, but that those who have not encountered him and his gospel in this life will do so in the world to come and will there have their opportunity to accept him as their saviour. Thus the uniqueness of Christ as the sole redeemer is preserved; but the fact that only a minority know him on earth is rendered compatible with this uniqueness by extending the sphere of Christ's saving activity beyond this world. It is not entirely clear whether Wolfhart Pannenberg is sponsoring this or the rather different anonymous Christianity idea when he says:

The symbolic language of Jesus' descent into hell expresses the extent to which those men who lived before Jesus' activity and those who did not know him have a share in the salvation that has appeared in him. That is an extremely important question

[17] Neuner, p. 52.   [18] Neuner, pp. 55–6.   [19] Neuner, p. 56.

for all Christian missions and for the self-understanding of Christianity in the midst of humanity: Does only the person who believes in Jesus with a conscious decision have a share in the nearness of God that he has opened? Or must account be made for an unconscious participation in salvation by men who never or only superficially came into contact with the message of Christ? The concept of Jesus' descent into hell, of his preaching in the realm of the dead, affirms the latter. It asserts that men outside the visible church are not automatically excluded from salvation.[20]

At any rate the idea of a post-mortem encounter with the person of Christ is available to the liberal Protestant who finds acceptable the idea of a 'second chance' after death; although it is not available to the traditionally orthodox Protestant or to the Roman Catholic, both of whom regard death as ending our period of freedom to respond to God in faith.

This idea does at least, I think, look in the right direction for a final solution to the problem of the relation between religions; for the only unity possible to them must be eschatological. But as an attempt to preserve the traditional claim of Ptolemaic Christianity it does not easily square with the evidences of salvation within other faiths in this present life – the evidence of saints, prophets, martyrs and mystics who have been intensely aware of the divine presence and whose lives have demonstrated the reality of their devotion. One can of course say that this is accepted by God as a basis for the salvation of devout men of non-christian faiths on an interim basis, until they seal it by their conscious response to Christ in the world to come. This would be a similar epicycle to those developed within Catholic theology, except for the addition of the 'second chance'; and it may appeal to some whose primary concern is to hold onto the Ptolemaic dogma. There will certainly be others, however, who feel that the dogma has now been stretched beyond recognition and is due to be replaced.

Now the Copernican revolution in astronomy consisted in a transformation in the way in which men understood the universe and their own location within it. It involved a shift from the

[20] *Jesus – God and Man*, trans. Lewis L. Wilkins and Duane A. Priebe (Philadelphia: Westminster Press, 1967 and London: S.C.M. Press, 1968) p. 272.

dogma that the earth is the centre of the revolving universe to the realisation that it is the sun that is at the centre, with all the planets, including our own earth, moving around it. And the needed Copernican revolution in theology involves an equally radical transformation in our conception of the universe of faiths and the place of our own religion within it. It involves a shift from the dogma that Christianity is at the centre to the realisation that it is *God* who is at the centre, and that all the religions of mankind, including our own, serve and revolve around him. Such a revolution in our understanding was in fact boldly advocated in the Conclusions of the Bombay conference to which Hans Küng's paper was given. The conference asked for a shift from an ecclesio centric to a theo-centric understanding of the religions. But unfortunately the conference did not carry this programme out either in its other conclusions or in the published papers. The task still remains to be done; but before offering a contribution to this work let me put in another and less theological way the case for so radical a displacement of thought.

We have to realise that in principle a Ptolemaic type of theology can be operated not only from within Christianity but equally from within any other faith — just as men on Mars or Jupiter, if there were any, could formulate their own Ptolemaic astronomy with their own planet as the centre of the system. The most striking example of this today in the religious realm is provided by contemporary philosophical Hinduism. This holds that the ultimate reality, Brahman, is beyond all qualities, including personality, and that personal deities, such as the God of the Bible or the Krishna of the Bhagavad Gītā, are partial images of the Absolute created for the benefit of that majority of mankind who cannot rise above anthropomorphic thinking to the pure Absolute. Thus the various religions of the world, with their different proportions of anthropomorphism and mysticism, can be seen as so many approaches to the truth that is fully revealed in the Upanishads. Here then we have a Ptolemaic system with a vedantic instead of a christian centre. And from this point of view the Christian, and the Jew, and the Muslim, and so on, can be said to be a Vedantist without yet knowing it. He is an 'anonymous' Vedantist; he stands within the lower or 'ordinary' realms of the religious life, but will rise eventually into the 'extraordinary' realm of the truly enlightened; if he does not see the truth in his present life then he will come to see it in a future life; he is a Vedantist 'implicitly', and by virtue of his sincere desire for the truth even though he does not yet know what the truth really is. Thus all the epicycles of Ptolemaic Christianity can also be used within a Ptolemaic Hinduism – or a Ptolemaic Buddhism, or Islam, or Jainism, or Judaism, and so on. In other words the adherent of each system of belief can assume that his own system is alone fully true and that all the others are more or less true according as they approximate to or diverge from it. And this is of course a very natural assumption to make. And yet one only has to stand back in thought from the arena of competing systems, surveying the scene as a whole, to see something that is hidden from the Ptolemaic believer. This is the fact that the particular standpoint of a Ptolemaic theology normally depends upon where the believer happens to have been born. And having seen this one can hardly help wondering whether it provides a sufficient basis for a conviction which involves an assessment of all other men's convictions. I myself used to hold a Ptolemaic christian theology; but if I had been born into a devout Hindu family in India and had studied philosophy at, let us say, the University of Madras, I should probably have held a Ptolemaic Hindu theology instead. And if I had been born to Muslim parents, say in Egypt or Pakistan, I should probably have held a Ptolemaic Muslim theology. And so on. This is an evident fact; and an intellectual position which ignores it or fails to make sense of it can hardly be adequate. And having noted that Ptolemaic theologies tend to posit their centres on the basis of the accidents of cultural geography, one can scarcely avoid seeing one's own Ptolemaic conviction in a new light. Can we now be content that our own religion should be a kind of spiritual horoscope read off from the time and place of our birth? And can we be so entirely confident that to have been born in our particular part of the world carries with it the privilege of knowing the full religious truth, whereas to be born elsewhere involves the likelihood of having only partial and inferior truth? Is there, one asks oneself, some vestige here of the imperialism of the christian west in relation to 'lesser breeds without the law'? It remains possible to retain the Ptolemaic point of view; but when we are conscious of its historical relativity we may well feel the need for a more sophisticated, comprehensive and globally valid theory.

10. The New Map of the Universe of Faiths

LET ME BEGIN this chapter by proposing a working definition of religion as an understanding of the universe, together with an appropriate way of living within it, which involves reference beyond the natural world to God or gods or to the Absolute or to a transcendent order or process. Such a definition includes such theistic faiths as Judaism, Christianity, Islam, Sikhism; the theistic Hinduism of the Bhagavad Gītā; the semi-theistic faith of Mahayana Buddhism and the non-theistic faiths of Theravada Buddhism and non-theistic Hinduism. It does not however include purely naturalistic systems of belief, such as communism and humanism, immensely important though these are today as alternatives to religious faith.

When we look back into the past we find that religion has been a virtually universal dimension of human life – so much so that man has been defined as the religious animal. For he has displayed an innate tendency to experience his environment as being religiously as well as naturally significant, and to feel required to live in it as such. To quote the anthropologist, Raymond Firth, 'religion is universal in human societies'.[1] 'In every human community on earth today', says Wilfred Cantwell Smith, 'there exists something that we, as sophisticated observers, may term religion, or a religion. And we are able to see it in each case as the latest development in a continuous tradition that goes back, we can now affirm, for at least one hundred thousand years.'[2] In the life of primitive man this religious tendency is expressed in

[1] *Elements of Social Organisation*, 3rd ed. (London: Tavistock Publications, 1969) p. 216.
[2] *The Meaning and End of Religion* (New York: Mentor Books, 1963) p. 22.

a belief in sacred objects, endowed with *mana*, and in a multitude of nature and ancestral spirits needing to be carefully propitiated. The divine was here crudely apprehended as a plurality of quasi-animal forces which could to some extent be controlled by ritualistic and magical procedures. This represents the simplest beginning of man's awareness of the transcendent in the infancy of the human race – an infancy which is also to some extent still available for study in the life of primitive tribes today.

The development of religion and religions begins to emerge into the light of recorded history as the third millennium B.C. moves towards the period around 2000 B.C. There are two main regions of the earth in which civilisation seems first to have arisen and in which religions first took a shape that is at least dimly discernible to us as we peer back through the mists of time – these being Mesopotamia in the Near East and the Indus valley of northern India. In Mesopotamia men lived in nomadic shepherd tribes, each worshipping its own god. Then the tribes gradually coalesced into nation states, the former tribal gods becoming ranked in hierarchies (some however being lost by amalgamation in the process) dominated by great national deities such as Marduk of Babylon, the Sumerian Ishtar, Amon of Thebes, Jahweh of Israel, the Greek Zeus, and so on. Further east in the Indus valley there was likewise a wealth of gods and goddesses, though apparently not so much tribal or national in character as expressive of the basic forces of nature, above all fertility. The many deities of the Near East and of India expressed man's awareness of the divine at the dawn of documentary history, some four thousand years ago. It is perhaps worth stressing that the picture was by no means a wholly pleasant one. The tribal and national gods were often martial and cruel, sometimes requiring human sacrifices. And although rather little is known about the very early, pre-Aryan Indian deities, it is certain that later Indian deities have vividly symbolised the cruel and destructive as well as the beneficent aspects of nature.

These early developments in the two cradles of civilisation, Mesopotamia and the Indus valley, can be described as the growth of natural religion, prior to any special intrusions of divine revelation or illumination. Primitive spirit-worship expressed man's fears of unknown forces; his reverence for nature deities expressed his sense of dependence upon realities greater than himself; and his tribal gods expressed the unity and continuity of his group over against other groups. One can in fact discern all sorts of causal connections between the forms which early religion took and the material circumstances of man's life, indicating the large part played by the human element within the history of religion. For example, Trevor Ling points out that life in ancient India (apart from the Punjab immediately prior to the Aryan invasions) was agricultural and was organised in small village units; and suggests that 'among agricultural peoples, aware of the fertile earth which brings forth from itself and nourishes its progeny upon its broad bosom, it is the mother-principle which seems important'.[3] Accordingly God the Mother, and a variety of more specialised female deities, have always held a prominent place in Indian religious thought and mythology. This contrasts with the characteristically male expression of deity in the Semitic religions, which had their origins among nomadic, pastoral, herd-keeping peoples in the Near East. The divine was known to the desert-dwelling herdsmen who founded the Israelite tradition as God the King and Father; and this conception has continued both in later Judaism and in Christianity, and was renewed out of the desert experience of Mohammed in the islamic religion. Such regional variations in our human ways of conceiving the divine have persisted through time into the developed world faiths that we know today. The typical western conception of God is still predominantly in terms of the male principle of power and authority; and in the typical Indian conceptions of deity the female principle still plays a distinctly larger part than in the west.

Here then was the natural condition of man's religious life: religion without revelation. But sometime around 800 B.C. there began what has been called the golden age of religious creativity. This consisted in a remarkable series of revelatory experiences occurring during the next five hundred or so years in different parts of the world, experiences which deepened and purified men's conceptions of the ultimate, and which religious faith can only attribute to the pressure of the divine Spirit upon the human spirit. First came the early Jewish prophets, Amos, Hosea and first Isaiah, declaring that they had heard the Word of the Lord

---

[3] *A History of Religion East and West* (London: Macmillan and New York: St Martin's Press, 1968) p. 27.

claiming their obedience and demanding a new level of righteousness and justice in the life of Israel. Then in Persia the great
prophet Zoroaster appeared; China produced Lao-tzu and then
Confucius; in India the Upanishads were written, and Gotama
the Buddha lived, and Mahavira, the founder of the Jain religion
and, probably about the end of this period, the writing of the
Bhagavad Gītā;[4] and Greece produced Pythagoras and then,
ending this golden age, Socrates and Plato. Then after the gap of
some three hundred years came Jesus of Nazareth and the
emergence of Christianity; and after another gap the prophet
Mohammed and the rise of Islam.

The suggestion that we must consider is that these were all
moments of divine revelation. But let us ask, in order to test this
thought, whether we should not expect God to make his revelation in a single mighty act, rather than to produce a number of
different, and therefore presumably partial, revelations at different times and places? I think that in seeing the answer to this
question we receive an important clue to the place of the religions
of the world in the divine purpose. For when we remember the
facts of history and geography we realise that in the period we
are speaking of, between two and three thousand years ago, it
was not possible for God to reveal himself through any human
mediation to all mankind. A world-wide revelation might be
possible today, thanks to the inventions of printing, and even
more of radio, TV and communication satellites. But in the
technology of the ancient world this was not possible. Although
on a time scale of centuries and millennia there has been a slow
diffusion and interaction of cultures, particularly within the vast
Euro-Asian land mass, yet the more striking fact for our present
purpose is the fragmented character of the ancient world. Com-
munications between the different groups of humanity was then
so limited and slow that for all practical purposes men inhabited
different worlds. For the most part people in Europe, in India, in
Arabia, in Africa, in China were unaware of the others' existence.
And as the world was fragmented, so was its religious life. If

---

[4] The dating of the Bhagavad Gītā has been a matter of much debate;
but R. C. Zaehner in his recent monumental critical edition says that 'One
would probably not be going far wrong if one dated it at some time
between the fifth and second centuries B.C.' *The Bhagavad Gītā* (Oxford:
Clarendon Press, 1969) p. 7.

there was to be a revelation of the divine reality to mankind it had to be a pluriform revelation, a series of revealing experiences occurring independently within the different streams of human history. And since religion and culture were one, the great creative moments of revelation and illumination have influenced the development of the various cultures, giving them the coherence and impetus to expand into larger units, thus creating the vast, many-sided historical entities which we call the world religions.

Each of these religio-cultural complexes has expanded until it touched the boundaries of another such complex spreading out from another centre. Thus each major occasion of divine revelation has slowly transformed the primitive and national religions within the sphere of its influence into what we now know as the world faiths. The early Dravidian and Aryan polytheisms of India were drawn through the religious experience and thought of the Brahmins into what the west calls Hinduism. The national and mystery cults of the mediterranean world and then of northern Europe were drawn by influences stemming from the life and teaching of Christ into what has become Christianity. The early polytheism of the Arab peoples has been transformed under the influence of Mohammed and his message into Islam. Great areas of South-East Asia, of China, Tibet and Japan were drawn into the spreading Buddhist movement. None of these expansions from different centres of revelation has of course been simple and uncontested, and a number of alternatives which proved less durable have perished or been absorbed in the process – for example, Mithraism has disappeared altogether; and Zoroastrianism, whilst it greatly influenced the development of the judaic-christian tradition, and has to that extent been absorbed, only survives directly today on a small scale in Parsee-ism.

Seen in this historical context these movements of faith – the judaic-christian, the Buddhist, the Hindu, the Muslim – are not essentially rivals. They began at different times and in different places, and each expanded outwards into the surrounding world of primitive natural religion until most of the world was drawn up into one or other of the great revealed faiths. And once this global pattern had become established it has ever since remained fairly stable. It is true that the process of establishment involved

conflict in the case of Islam's entry into India and the virtual
expulsion of Buddhism from India in the medieval period, and in
the case of Islam's advance into Europe and then its retreat at
the end of the medieval period. But since the frontiers of the
different world faiths became more or less fixed there has been
little penetration of one faith into societies moulded by another.
The most successful missionary efforts of the great faiths continue
to this day to be 'downwards' into the remaining world of relatively primitive religions rather than 'sideways' into territories
dominated by another world faith. For example, as between
Christianity and Islam there has been little more than rather rare
individual conversions; but both faiths have successful missions in
Africa. Again, the christian population of the Indian sub-
continent, after more than two centuries of missionary effort, is
only about 2.7 per cent; but on the other hand the christian
missions in the South Pacific are fairly successful. Thus the
general picture, so far as the great world religions is concerned, is
that each has gone through an early period of geographical expansion, converting a region of the world from its more primitive religious state, and has thereafter continued in a comparatively settled
condition within more or less stable boundaries.

Now it is of course possible to see this entire development from
the primitive forms of religion up to and including the great
world faiths as the history of man's most persistent illusion,
growing from crude fantasies into sophisticated metaphysical
speculations. But from the standpoint of religious faith the only
reasonable hypothesis is that this historical picture represents a
movement of divine self-revelation to mankind. This hypothesis
offers a general answer to the question of the relation between
the different world religions and of the truths which they embody.
It suggests to us that the same divine reality has always been
self-revealingly active towards mankind, and that the differences
of human response are related to different human circumstances.
These circumstances – ethnic, geographical, climatic, economic,
sociological, historical – have produced the existing differentia-
tions of human culture, and within each main cultural region
the response to the divine has taken its own characteristic forms.
In each case the post-primitive response has been initiated by
some spiritually outstanding individual or succession of individuals, developing in the course of time into one of the great

religio-cultural phenomena which we call the world religions. Thus Islam embodies the main response of the arabic peoples to the divine reality; Hinduism, the main (though not the only) response of the peoples of India; Buddhism, the main response of the peoples of South-East Asia and parts of northern Asia; Christianity, the main response of the european peoples, both within Europe itself and in their emigrations to the Americas and Australasia.

Thus it is, I think, intelligible historically why the revelation of the divine reality to man, and the disclosure of the divine will for human life, had to occur separately within the different streams of human life. We can see how these revelations took different forms related to the different mentalities of the peoples to whom they came, and developed within these different cultures into the vast and many-sided historical phenomena of the world religions.

But let us now ask whether this is intelligible theologically. What about the conflicting truth-claims of the different faiths? Is the divine nature personal or non-personal; does deity become incarnate in the world; are human beings born again and again on earth; is the Bible, or the Koran, or the Bhagavad Gītā the Word of God? If what Christianity says in answer to these questions is true, must not what Hinduism says be to a large extent false? If what Buddhism says is true, must not what Islam says be largely false?

Let us begin with the recognition, which is made in all the main religious traditions, that the ultimate divine reality is infinite and as such transcends the grasp of the human mind. God, to use our christian term, is infinite. He is not a thing, a part of the universe, existing alongside other things; nor is he a being falling under a certain kind. And therefore he cannot be defined or encompassed by human thought. We cannot draw boundaries round his nature and say that he is this and no more. If we could fully define God, describing his inner being and his outer limits, this would not be God. The God whom our minds can penetrate and whom our thoughts can circumnavigate is merely a finite and partial image of God.

From this it follows that the different encounters with the transcendent within the different religious traditions may all be encounters with the one infinite reality, though with partially different and overlapping aspects of that reality. This is a very familiar thought in Indian religious literature. We read, for example, in the ancient Rig-Vedas, dating back to perhaps as much as a thousand years before Christ:

> They call it Indra, Mitra, Varuna, and Agni
> And also heavenly, beautiful Garutman:
> The real is one, though sages name it variously.[5]

We might translate this thought into the terms of the faiths represented today in Britain:

> They call it Jahweh, Allah, Krishna, Param Atma,
> And also holy, blessed Trinity:
> The real is one, though sages name it variously.[5]

And in the Bhagavad Gītā the Lord Krishna, the personal God of love, says, 'Howsoever men approach me, even so do I accept them; for, on all sides, whatever path they may choose is mine'.[6]

Again, there is the parable of the blind men and the elephant, said to have been told by the Buddha. An elephant was brought to a group of blind men who had never encountered such an animal before. One felt a leg and reported that an elephant is a great living pillar. Another felt the trunk and reported that an elephant is a great snake. Another felt a tusk and reported that an elephant is like a sharp ploughshare. And so on. And then they all quarrelled together, each claiming that his own account was the truth and therefore all the others false. In fact of course they were all true, but each referring only to one aspect of the total reality and all expressed in very imperfect analogies.

Now the possibility, indeed the probability, that we have seriously to consider is that many different accounts of the divine reality may be true, though all expressed in imperfect human analogies, but that none is 'the truth, the whole truth, and nothing but the truth'. May it not be that the different concepts of God, as Jahweh, Allah, Krishna, Param Atma, Holy Trinity, and so on; and likewise the different concepts of the hidden structure of reality, as the eternal emanation of Brahman or as an immense cosmic process culminating in Nirvana, are all images of the divine, each expressing some aspect or range of aspects and yet none by itself fully and exhaustively corresponding to the infinite nature of the ultimate reality?

[5] I 164.   [6] IV 11.

Two immediate qualifications however to this hypothesis. First, the idea that we are considering is not that any and every conception of God or of the transcendent is valid, still less all equally valid; but that every conception of the divine which has come out of a great revelatory religious experience and has been tested through a long tradition of worship, and has sustained human faith over centuries of time and in millions of lives, is likely to represent a genuine encounter with the divine reality. And second, the parable of the blind men and the elephant is of course only a parable, and like most parables it is designed to make one point and must not be pressed as an analogy at other points. The suggestion is not that the different encounters with the divine which lie at the basis of the great religious traditions are responses to different *parts* of the divine. They are rather encounters from different historical and cultural standpoints with the same infinite divine reality and as such they lead to differently focused awarenesses of that reality. The indications of this are most evident in worship and prayer. What is said about God in the theological treatises of the different faiths is indeed often widely different. But it is in prayer that a belief in God comes alive and does its main work. And when we turn from abstract theology to the living stuff of worship we meet again and again the overlap and confluence of faiths.

Here, for example, is a Muslim prayer at the feast of Ramadan:

> Praise be to God, Lord of creation, Source of all livelihood, who orders the morning, Lord of majesty and honour, of grace and beneficence. He who is so far that he may not be seen and so near that he witnesses the secret things. Blessed be he and for ever exalted.[7]

And here is a Sikh creed used at the morning prayer:

> There is but one God. He is all that is.
> He is the Creator of all things and He is all-pervasive.
> He is without fear and without enmity.
> He is timeless, unborn and self-existent.
> He is the Enlightener
> And can be realised by grace of Himself alone.

[7] Kenneth Cragg, *Alive to God: Muslim and Christian Prayer* (London and New York: Oxford University Press, 1970) p. 65.

He was in the beginning; He was in all ages.
The True One is, was, O Nanak, and shall forever be.[8]

And here again is a verse from the Koran:

To God belongs the praise, Lord of the heavens and Lord of the earth, the Lord of all being. His is the dominion in the heavens and in the earth: he is the Almighty, the All-wise.[9]

Turning now to the Hindu idea of the many incarnations of God, here is a verse from the Rāmāyana:

Seers and sages, saints and hermits, fix on Him their reverent gaze,
And in faint and trembling accents, holy scripture hymns His praise.
He the omnipresent spirit, lord of heaven and earth and hell,
To redeem His people, freely has vouchsafed with men to dwell.[10]

And from the rich literature of devotional song here is a Bhakti hymn of the Vaishnavite branch of Hinduism:

Now all my days with joy I'll fill, full to the brim
With all my heart to Vitthal cling, and only Him.

He will sweep utterly away all dole and care;
And all in sunder shall I rend illusion's snare.

O altogether dear is He, and He alone,
For all my burden He will take to be His own.

Lo, all the sorrow of the world will straightway, cease,
And all unending now shall be the reign of peace.[11]

[8] Harbans Singh, *Guru Nanak and Origins of the Sikh Faith* (Bombay, London and New York: Asia Publishing House, 1969) pp. 96–7.
[9] *Alive to God*, p. 61 (Surah of the Kneeling, v. 35).
[10] *Sacred Books of the World* edited by A. C. Bouquet (London: Pelican Books, 1954) p. 226 (The Rāmāyana of Tulsi Das, Canto 1, Chandha 2, translated by F. S. Growse).
[11] Ibid., p. 245 (A Hymn of Namdev, translated by Nicol MacNicol).

And a Muslim mystical verse:

> Love came a guest
> Within my breast,
> My soul was spread,
> Love banqueted.[12]

And finally another Hindu (Vaishnavite) devotional hymn:

> O save me, save me, Mightiest,
> Save me and set me free.
> O let the love that fills my breast
> Cling to thee lovingly.
>
> Grant me to taste how sweet thou art;
> Grant me but this, I pray,
> And never shall my love depart
> Or turn from thee away.
>
> Then I thy name shall magnify
> And tell thy praise abroad,
> For very love and gladness I
> Shall dance before my God.[13]

Such prayers and hymns as these must express, surely, diverse encounters with the same divine reality. These encounters have taken place within different human cultures by people of different ways of thought and feeling, with different histories and different frameworks of philosophical thought, and have developed into different systems of theology embodied in different religious structures and organisations. These resulting large-scale religio-cultural phenomena are what we call the religions of the world. But must there not lie behind them the same infinite divine reality, and may not our divisions into Christian, Hindu, Muslim, Jew, and so on, and all that goes with them, accordingly represent secondary, human, historical developments?

There is a further problem, however, which now arises. I have been speaking so far of the ultimate reality in a variety of terms – the Father, Son and Spirit of Christianity, the Jahweh of

---

[12] *Alive to God*, p. 79 (From Ibn Hazm, 'The Ring of the Dove').
[13] *Sacred Books of the World*, p. 246 (A Hymn of Tukaram).

Judaism, the Allah of Islam, and so on – but always thus far in theistic terms, as a personal God under one name or another. But what of the non-theistic religions? What of the non-theistic Hinduism according to which the ultimate reality, Brahman, is not He but It; and what about Buddhism, which in one form is agnostic concerning the existence of God even though in another form it has come to worship the Buddha himself? Can these non-theistic faiths be seen as encounters with the same divine reality that is encountered in theistic religion?

Speaking very tentatively, I think it *is* possible that the sense of the divine as non-personal may indeed reflect an aspect of the same infinite reality that is encountered as personal in theistic religious experience. The question can be pursued both as a matter of pure theology and in relation to religious experience. Theologically, the Hindu distinction between Nirguna Brahman and Saguna Brahman is important and should be adopted into western religious thought. Detaching the distinction, then, from its Hindu context we may say that Nirguna God is the eternal self-existent divine reality, beyond the scope of all human categories, including personality; and Saguna God is God in relation to his creation and with the attributes which express this relationship, such as personality, omnipotence, goodness, love and omniscience. Thus the one ultimate reality is both Nirguna and non-personal, and Saguna and personal, in a duality which is in principle acceptable to human understanding. When we turn to men's religious awareness of God we are speaking of Saguna God, God in relation to man. And here the larger traditions of both east and west report a dual experience of the divine as personal and as other than personal. It will be a sufficient reminder of the strand of personal relationship with the divine in Hinduism to mention Iswara, the personal God who represents the Absolute as known and worshipped by finite persons. It should also be remembered that the characterisation of Brahman as *satcitananda*, absolute being, consciousness and bliss, is not far from the conception of infinitely transcendent personal life. Thus there is both the thought and the experience of the personal divine within Hinduism. But there is likewise the thought and the experience of God as other than personal within Christianity. Rudolph Otto describes this strand in the mysticism of Meister Eckhart. He says:

The divine, which on the one hand is conceived in symbols taken from the social sphere, as Lord, King, Father, Judge – a person in relation to persons – is on the other hand denoted in dynamic symbols as the power of life, as light and life, as spirit ebbing and flowing, as truth, knowledge, essential justice and holiness, a glowing fire that penetrates and pervades. It is characterized as the principle of a renewed, supernatural Life, mediating and giving itself, breaking forth in the living man as his nova vita, as the content of his life and being. What is here insisted upon is not so much an 'immanent' God, as an 'experienced' God, known as an inward principle of the power of new being and life. Eckhart knows this *deuteros theos* besides the personal God. . . .[14]

Let me now try to draw the threads together and to project them into the future. I have been suggesting that Christianity is a way of salvation which, beginning some two thousand years ago, has become the principal way of salvation in three continents. The other great world faiths are likewise ways of salvation, providing the principal path to the divine reality for other large sections of humanity. I have also suggested that the idea that Jesus proclaimed himself as God incarnate, and as the sole point of saving contact between God and man, is without adequate historical foundation and represents a doctrine developed by the church. We should therefore not infer, from the christian experience of redemption through Christ, that salvation cannot be experienced in any other way. The alternative possibility is that the ultimate divine reality – in our christian terms, God – has always been pressing in upon the human spirit, but always in ways which leave men free to open or close themselves to the divine presence. Human life has developed along characteristically different lines in the main areas of civilisation, and these differences have naturally entered into the ways in which men have apprehended and responded to God. For the great religious figures through whose experience divine revelation has come have each been conditioned by a particular history and culture. One can hardly imagine Gotama the Buddha except in the setting of the India of his time, or Jesus the Christ except against the back-

[14] Rudolph Otto, *Mysticism East and West*, trans. Bertha L. Bracey and Richenda C. Payne (New York: Meridian Books, 1957) p. 131.

ground of Old Testament Judaism, or Mohammed except in the
setting of Arabia. And human history and culture have likewise
shaped the development of the webs of religious creeds, practices
and organisations which we know as the great world faiths.

It is thus possible to consider the hypothesis that they are all,
at their experiential roots, in contact with the same ultimate
reality, but that their differing experiences of that reality, interacting over the centuries with the different thought-forms of
different cultures, have led to increasing differentiation and
contrasting elaboration – so that Hinduism, for example, is a
very different phenomenon from Christianity, and very different
ways of conceiving and experiencing the divine occur within
them.

However, now that the religious traditions are consciously
interacting with each other in the 'one world' of today, in mutual
observation and dialogue, it is possible that their future developments may be on gradually converging courses. For during the
next few centuries they will no doubt continue to change, and it
may be that they will grow closer together, and even that one day
such names as 'Christianity', 'Buddhism', 'Islam', 'Hinduism',
will no longer describe the then current configurations of men's
religious experience and belief. I am not here thinking of the
extinction of human religiousness in a universal wave of secular-
isation. This is of course a possible future; and indeed many think
it the most likely future to come about. But if man is an indelibly
religious animal he will always, even in his secular cultures,
experience a sense of the transcendent by which he will be both
troubled and uplifted. The future I am thinking of is accordingly
one in which what we now call the different religions will constitute the past history of different emphases and variations within
a global religious life. I do not mean that all men everywhere will
be overtly religious, any more than they are today. I mean rather
that the discoveries now taking place by men of different faiths
of central common ground, hitherto largely concealed by the
variety of cultural forms in which it was expressed, may eventually render obsolete the sense of belonging to rival ideological
communities. Not that all religious men will think alike, or worship in the same way or experience the divine identically. On the
contrary, so long as there is a rich variety of human cultures –
and let us hope there will always be this – we should expect there

to be correspondingly different forms of religious cult, ritual and organisation, conceptualised in different theological doctrines. And so long as there is a wide spectrum of human psychological types — and again let us hope that there will always be this — we should expect there to be correspondingly different emphases between, for example, the sense of the divine as just and as merciful, between *karma* and *bhakti*; or between worship as formal and communal and worship as free and personal. Thus we may expect the different world faiths to continue as religio-cultural phenomena, though phenomena which are increasingly influencing one another's development. The relation between them will then perhaps be somewhat like that now obtaining between the different denominations of Christianity in Europe or the United States. That is to say, there will in most countries be a dominant religious tradition, with other traditions present in varying strengths, but with considerable awareness on all hands of what they have in common; with some degree of osmosis of membership through their institutional walls; with a large degree of practical co-operations; and even conceivably with some interchange of ministry.

Beyond this the ultimate unity of faiths will be an eschatological unity in which each is both fulfilled and transcended — fulfilled in so far as it is true, transcended in so far as it is less than the whole truth. And indeed even such fulfilling must be a transcending; for the function of a religion is to bring us to a right relationship with the ultimate divine reality, to awareness of our true nature and our place in the Whole, into the presence of God. In the eternal life there is no longer any place for religions; the pilgrim has no need of a way after he has finally arrived. In St John's vision of the heavenly city at the end of our christian scriptures it is said that there is no temple — no christian church or chapel, no jewish synagogue, no hindu or buddhist temple, no muslim mosque, no sikh gurdwara. . . . For all these exist in time, as ways through time to eternity.

11. Christ and Incarnation

A COPERNICAN revolution from a Christianity-centred to a God-centred picture of the universe of faiths seems to be demanded by the facts of human religious experience. But before adopting the new picture a Christian must be satisfied that his devotion to Jesus as his personal Lord and Saviour is not thereby brought into question or its validity denied. In this and the following chapter I propose to deal directly with this question of the place of Christ, and the christian affirmations about him, within the proposed new understanding of God's dealings with mankind. It will be well to begin by seeing why this must be the most difficult of all issues for a christian theology of religions.

We can distinguish three kinds of difference and conflict between the world religions – differences in their modes of experiencing the divine reality; differences of philosophical and theological theory concerning that reality; and differences in the key, or revelatory, events to which the different streams of religious experience trace their origins and by means of which they focus their worship.

Prominent examples of the first kind of difference are the contrast between the experience of God as personal and the experience of the divine as non-personal; and within theism, the contrast between the experience of God as stern judge and as gracious friend. There is, however, I think, in principle no difficulty in holding that these can be understood as complementary rather than as rival truths. For if, as every profound form of religion has affirmed, the divine reality is infinite and accordingly exceeds the scope of our human categories, the images of the personal Lord and of the non-personal Ground of Being, and of judge and father, may all be applicable. Here Aurobindo's con-

cept of 'the logic of the Infinite',[1] in which different phenomenological characteristics are not mutually exclusive, deserves
to be explored further.

The second type of difference is difference in philosophical and
theological theory or doctrine. Such differences, and indeed
conflicts, do indeed exist and are not merely apparent. But they
are part of the still developing history of human thought, and it
may be that in the future development of doctrines they will be
transcended. For they belong to the historical, culturally conditioned, aspect of religion, within which almost any degree of
change is possible.

But it is the third kind of difference that presents the greatest
difficulty to a 'Copernican' theology of religions. For each
religion has its holy founder or scripture, or both, through which
the divine reality has been revealed – the Vedas, the Buddha, the
Torah, Christ and the Bible, the Koran. And wherever the Holy
is revealed it claims an absolute response of faith and worship
which seems incompatible with a like response to any other
claimed disclosure of the Holy. Within Christianity this absoluteness of response has been strongly developed in the doctrine that
Christ was uniquely divine, being God the Son incarnate.

The doctrine of the Incarnation has traditionally been expressed by means of the category of substance: Jesus Christ has
two natures, being as human *homoousios* (of one substance) with
mankind and as divine *homoousios* with the Godhead. However
this is only one possible way of expressing the mystery of incarnation. We may freely recognise that in the most generally used
philosophical language of the early christian centuries the term
homoousios was the most emphatic and unambiguous way available of asserting the full Lordship and deity of Christ. However
in contrast to that period there is nothing that can properly be
called *the* philosophical language of the twentieth century. There
are many philosophical languages – analytical, existentialist,
personalist, pragmatist, etc. – no one of which has captured the
mind of the general educated public as had Neo-Platonism in the
early centuries of our era. We are thus free, and indeed obliged,
to return to the biblical starting point of christology, to take our
bearings there independently of the Nicene and Chalcedonian

[1] Sri Aurobindo, *The Life Divine* (New York: India Library, 1949)
bk II, ch. 2.

formulations, and then to try as Christians of our own day to express to ourselves and to our contemporaries the central idea which Nicea and Chalcedon were proclaiming to their own very different intellectual world.

Moreover, substance thinking is not only out of fashion: it has a tendency positively to mislead, which is seen at work, for example, in the doctrine of transubstantiation. In the eucharist the visible and tangible accidents remain those of ordinary bread and wine but their metaphysical substance is changed into that of the body and blood of Christ. This theory, made possible by the Aristotelian notion of substance, and which at one time seemed profoundly satisfactory and illuminating, permits no kind of experiential confirmation or disconfirmation and is a sheer intellectual cul-de-sac. The notion of the hypostatic union in the person of Christ is logically similar. The incarnate Christ is two substances, divine and human, under one set of human accidents. Not only is such a doctrine open to the charge of meaninglessness, but any imaginative meaning that it may have is of a static kind which, in the light of the modern rediscovery of the Bible, seems peculiarly inappropriate for the expansion of the biblical revelation. It is as though one were saying that Christ is made out of the same lump of divine substance as the Godhead and thus shares the divine nature, as two loaves of bread might be made from the same lump of dough and thus be composed of the same substance.

Having been impressed by the static character of the time-honoured category we shall naturally be interested to explore others which are, in contrast, dynamic – categories of action rather than of being. We notice at once that the categories of biblical thinking are themselves predominantly of this kind. The broad distinction between the hebraic and hellenic modes of thought in matters of religion is a commonplace today,[2] and in the light of it one cannot help being struck by the thoroughly hellenic character of the classic christological formulations. Not only did the key categories of *ousia* and *hypostasis* come from Greek thought, but they are peculiar to that side of the ancestry of Christianity and mingle only as foreign bodies with the stream

---

[2] It is a commonplace which can easily be overworked, as James Barr has shown (*The Semantics of Biblical Language*, London: Oxford University Press, 1961), but which nevertheless still has a broad validity.

of markedly hebraic thought and experience which flows through
the Bible. And so it is not surprising that a number of theologians
today should be interested in expressing the religious concern of
Nicea and Chalcedon in categories drawn, not from Greek
philosophical speculations, but from the biblical reports of God's
self-revelation in history.[3] The categories which at once suggest
themselves as the hebraic alternatives to 'substance' and 'essence'
are 'purpose' and 'action'. The Bible does not speak of the substance or of the essence of deity, but it does speak of a divine
purpose for man and of God's mighty acts in human history. The
possibility that suggests itself is accordingly that of expressing
Christ's sonship in these and cognate terms.

As a historical side-issue I wonder whether earlier christian
thought was as monolithically committed to a substance philosophy
as is often assumed? Most of the objections to the *homoousios*
which are liable to occur to us today were familiar to the church
fathers, or at any rate to some of them; and at an otherwise
unimportant Council of Antioch in 363 it was denied that the
term *ousia* is 'taken by the fathers in any usual signification of it
among the Greeks; but it has been employed for the subversion
of what Arius impiously dared to assert concerning Christ, viz. –
that he was made of things "not existing"'.[4] And Gregory of
Nyssa in the fourth century provided the motto for all attempts
to base christology upon the category of action or event when he
wrote that 'the word "Godhead" signifies an operation and not a
nature (φύσιν)',[5] and attempted a doctrine of the Trinity from
this point of view.

This dictum of Gregory of Nyssa's offers a promising starting
point for speculation. I interpret it as implying that the christian
usage of the term 'God' has as its paradigm cases statements
about God's self-revealing activity in human history. Our knowledge of God's nature is derived from our knowledge of his deeds;

[3] For example, John Knox, *On the Meaning of Christ*, 1947; W. R.
Matthews, *The Problem of Christ in the Twentieth Century*, 1950; Norman
Pittenger, *The Word Incarnate*, 1959; Hugh Montefiore, 'Towards a
Christology for Today', *Soundings*, ed. A. R. Vidler, 1962; P. N. Hamilton,
'Some Proposals for a Modern Christology', *Christ for Us Today*, ed.
Norman Pittenger, 1968.
[4] Socrates, *Ecclesiastical History*, bk III, ch. 25.
[5] 'On Not Three Gods', in Hardy and Richardson, eds., *Christology of
the Later Fathers* (London: S.C.M. Press, 1954) p. 261.

we know what he is in so far as we know what he has done. Accordingly, when we use the categories of divine purpose and action, we speak, as all christian thought must, *ex post facto*, in the light of historical events received as revelatory. Hence we may refer, not to divine purpose in general, but specifically to the divine purpose of *Agapé* which we see disclosing itself in the life of Jesus. For everything that Christianity knows concerning the divine attitude and activity towards mankind can be summarised in the assertion that God is *Agapé*; and this assertion is a direct transcript of the faith that the *agapé* which we see in Jesus in some sense *is* the eternal *Agapé* of God. If then we say, with Gregory of Nyssa, that the name 'God' refers not to a nature but to an operation, we mean that operation of *Agapé* which is revealed in the life and death of Jesus. Or if we say with Paul that 'God was in Christ reconciling the world to himself',[6] we mean that in Christ the divine *Agapé* was at work dealing with sinful humanity. And if we say, as twentieth-century theologians, that in the life of Jesus christian faith finds, not divine substance injected into a human frame, but divine action taking place in and through a human life, we mean that in that life is uniquely to be seen the divine *Agapé* directly at work within our human sphere.

The traditional term 'Incarnation' does little to suggest that in christian experience God is known as activity or operation rather than as substance, or to facilitate the understanding of the life of Jesus as the point at which the divine *Agapé* has embodied itself in human actions in the midst of earthly history. There therefore seems to me to be value in H. H. Farmer's inelegant but useful word 'inhistorisation',[7] which brings out just that aspect of God's dealings with men in Christ which we are seeking to explore. By speaking of divine inhistorisation, rather than of divine incarnation, we get explicitly away from the picture of the eternal Logos descending into a temporary envelope of flesh and from there wielding a sovereign power and rule. As against this we must affirm, ultimately on the authority of the New Testament witnesses themselves, that God in Christ has not merely acted *upon* or *into* human history, like a meteor falling from above, but has

---

[6] 2 Cor. 5: 19.
[7] 'The Bible: Its Significance and Authority', *Interpreter's Bible*, vol. 1 (Abingdon: Cokesbury, 1952).

acted *within* and *through* man's life by influencing the course of
our history from the inside.

We must think of the divine *Agapé*, then, as operating not only
externally upon the continuum of men's actions but also within
that continuum as a decisive agency in the developing human
story. There is indeed no other way of acting *within* human
history, as distinguished from acting upon it *ab extra*, than by
becoming one of the human makers of history. All manner of
external circumstances impinge upon and condition man's life –
geographical, meteorological, economic, seismic, etc. – and there
could be (and perhaps are) spiritually sub-human, or demonic,
and supra-human or divine impingements also. But all such
impacts and impingements are to be classified as events and
circumstances modifying man's environment. They contribute to
the stage or setting of his life. Human history, however, is not the
account of man's changing environment but the story of his reactions within and to that environment. And these reactions are,
by definition, the reactions of human beings. To think of the
divine *Agapé* entering into the course of our history it is thus
necessary to think of that *Agapé* as being expressed in the actions
and reactions of a human being or beings.

We may now try to spell out from the New Testament records
the christian claim that the divine *Agapé* has been inhistorised in
the person of Jesus. To say that this has happened is to say that
the compassion and concern which were expressed in Jesus'
dealings with the men and women whom he met were identical
with God's *Agapé* towards those particular individuals. For the
idea which has sustained Christianity is that this *agapé* which we
see reflected in the mirror of the gospel records at work in human
time, in particular finite situations, is none other than the eternal
and universal *Agapé* of God – to which not only some who
happened to be contemporaries of Jesus responded but to which
human beings outside first-century Palestine, in every age and in
every land, may also relate themselves. Jesus' attitude to the sick
persons whom he healed, to the people whom he taught, to the
individuals whom he summoned to be his disciples, and no less to
those whom he condemned as hypocrites and blind leaders, was
God's attitude towards those same people, expressed concretely
in terms of the particular situations in which they then were.
Jesus' *agapé* towards the woman with the issue of blood (for

example) was God's *Agapé* towards her. Jesus' *agapé* towards
Jairus and his daughter was God's *Agapé* towards them. Jesus'
agapé – and now a different aspect of it comes into view –
towards Judas and Pilate and the soldiers at Golgotha was God's
Agapé towards them. It was in each case God's *Agapé* directed
towards particular persons in particular historical situations. And
of course, like all significant actions, these were indicative of the
Agent's character beyond the moment in question. From a
person's behaviour on particular occasions we see how he would
behave on other occasions. And from the narratives of God's
attitudes in Christ to a typical and random assortment of men
and women in first-century Palestine we perceive his attitude
to all men in all ages – as indeed we also see, from the same
narratives, the different ways in which men in all ages respond
to God. The gospels depict God's love inhistorised, operating self-revealingly in relation to certain individuals, but
thereby in principle and in prolepsis taking the initiative to
redeem human life in all its depths, dimensions and predica-
ments.

We may emphasise what the Chalcedonian formula was concerned to emphasise in its *homoousios* by saying that Jesus' *agapé*
towards the men and women whom he met in Palestine was not
like God's *Agapé* towards them (this would correspond to the
Arian *homoi-ousios*), nor was it a reflection or imitation of the
divine *Agapé*, but it actually and literally *was* God's *Agapé*
acting towards them.

At this point, however, typically philosophical questions arise.
For if the suggestion just sketched is to be more than superficially
illuminating, we must clarify its essential claim that the *agapé* of
Jesus *is* the *Agapé* of God. The little word 'is' is perhaps for
philosophers the most troublesome in the language. It bears,
notoriously, a number of different senses, the most frequently
used being the *is* of predication (as when we say 'this paper is
white', thereby attaching a predicate to a subject); the *is* of class
membership (as when we say 'cats are vertebrates' or 'Pompidou
is a Frenchman'); the definitional or equivalence-of-symbols *is*
(as when a dictionary asserts that 'a quadrilateral is a four-sided
plane figure'); and the *is* of identification (as when we say that
"Richard Nixon is the President of the U.S.A.'). But where in the
is-spectrum are we to place the 'is' of the hypostatic union which

occurs when we say that Jesus is divine, or that Jesus Christ is God incarnate?

Let us set aside at once the temptation to dodge this question by claiming that the christological 'is' is unique and that therefore nothing can be said about it – it cannot be either compared or contrasted with other senses of 'is'. This ploy is impermissible. To use a word in a new sense which we declare to stand in *no* explicable relation to its hitherto accepted uses would merely be to misuse the word. We cannot sensibly employ a term if we do not know at all what it means, for in that case we should be intending nothing whatever by it. However, the profession, on the part of a theologian, to have a blank mind on the meaning of the christological 'is' should not be taken seriously. For he says, 'Jesus Christ is God', rather than uttering a nonsense expression, such as 'Jesus Christ fungifies God', or using a word with a definite meaning which differs from the meaning of 'is', and saying, e.g. 'Jesus Christ strangles God'; and he says what he says, rather than something else, because he *does* know at least to some extent what he means by 'is' in a christological context. And it is clearly not allowable thus to select a word, to communicate by means of it and draw inferences from propositions in which it occurs (saying, for instance, that since Jesus is divine he is sinless), but to withhold one's usage from analysis on the plea that it is unique and inexplicable. If we are going to use the christological 'is', we are under an inescapable obligation to say at least to some extent how its use is like and unlike other uses of 'is'.

We return then to our question. What do we mean when we say that Jesus Christ *is* both man and God, or *is* both human and divine?

These two ways of phrasing the query – 'God and man' or 'human and divine' – already point to two different senses of 'is', one of which gives rise to an Arian and the other to a Chalcedonian christology.

To speak of Jesus Christ as being both *human and divine* is to use the *is* of predication; it is to predicate of him the two different characteristics of humanity and divinity. To do this carries with it both philosophical and theological implications. Philosophically, it focuses our attention upon the relation between universals and particulars, and suggests that the union of humanity and divinity in Jesus Christ is a case of the coingredience of two universals in one particular—the *koinonia* or mingling of the Forms, of which Plato speaks.[8] Theologically, it treats divinity adjectivally, and suggests that the quality of divinity is something which may be present in varying degrees in different human beings, Jesus Christ being marked off from the rest of mankind in that he possessed this quality in a greater degree than other men.

On the other hand, to speak of Jesus Christ being both *God and man* is to use, as regards his manhood, the *is* of class membership, and as regards his deity, the *is* of identification. To say that Jesus Christ is a man is to say that he is a member of the class of human beings. This, by itself, does not raise any special problems. To say that Jesus Christ is God is to say that he is identical with God. This does raise special problems, and to these problems we now turn.

In what sense, then, can the *agapé* of the historical Jesus towards, for example, someone whom he healed, be said to be *identical* with the *Agapé* of the infinite God towards that same individual?

There are two senses in which the referents of different terms may be said to be identical – a qualitative sense and a numerical sense.

Consider first the notion of qualitative identity. To speak of two instances of love or, better perhaps, of the loving dispositions or attitudes of two persons, as being qualitatively similar, or even qualitatively identical, has, I think, a reasonably clear meaning. If we say that the love of Mrs *A* for her children is identical in quality with the love of Mrs *B* for *her* children, our meaning is, roughly, that they feel in the same way towards their offspring; if their children's welfare is threatened they will make sacrifices for them to a like extent; their care for them is equally wise and far-seeing; and so on. Such dispositions are difficult, indeed impossible, to measure in any objective way; but nevertheless, although we may never be able to ascertain whether Mrs *A*'s love and Mrs *B*'s love for their children *are* identical in quality, yet I think we can find meaning in this possibility. The difficulty is not in the concept of qualitative identity but in the practical measurement of such qualities.

[8] See for example Anselm's *Letter to Pope Urban II on the Incarnation of the Word*, pt. i.

But, on the other hand, when we turn to the notion of numerical identity, it does not seem to make sense to say that the loving dispositions of *A* and *B* towards *C* are numerically identical. Such a statement would surely be a misuse of the terms. And so one's first inclination is to say that there is meaning in the idea of the *agapé* of Jesus towards the men and women whom he met being qualitatively identical with the *Agapé* of God towards those same individuals, but that there is no meaning in the idea that Jesus' *agapé* towards men was numerically identical with God's *Agapé* towards them. However, it will I think become clear below that this conclusion has to be modified when we try to take account of the uniqueness of the divine nature and therefore of the divine *Agapé*.

We need not at this point elaborate further the possibility that the *agapé* of Jesus was *qualitatively* identical with the divine *Agapé*. A sufficient though rough and ready indication has just been given of an analogical route whereby one might give meaning to it. We have also seen that the notion of qualitative identity, taken by itself, leads to a Degree Christology. If divine incarnation consists in the embodiment in a human life of a certain quality of *agapé*, then incarnation is something that is capable of degrees and approximations. The divine quality of *agapé* has been more fully incarnated in some lives than in others, and has doubtless been intermittently incarnated in a great number of lives, being predicable of some of an individual's actions and not of others. But when we speak of degrees of incarnation we are speaking of the incarnation of divinity, adjectivally construed, and not of the incarnation of the numerically unique life of the Godhead. Thus from the point of view of Nicea and Chalcedon a christology couched in terms of the qualitative identity of Jesus' *agapé* with the divine *Agapé* says too little. The little that it does say is part of the traditional christian claim concerning Christ, and is indeed a very important part of it; but it is a part and not the whole. It does not encompass the central claim that Christ is uniquely the incarnation of God the Son; that, in a phrase of Irenaeus', 'the Father is the invisible of the Son, but the Son the visible of the Father'.[9]

Turning now to the concept of numerical identity, it is clear

---

[9] *Against Heresies*, bk. IV, ch. 6, para. 6.

that we cannot, without talking nonsense, speak of the *agapé* of two human beings, *A* and *B*, as being numerically identical any more than we can speak of their visual fields or their memories or their sensations of pain as being numerically identical. Two human beings are not numerically identical – they are *two* human beings and not one – and likewise the various aspects of their respective selves are not and cannot be numerically one. The 'cannot' here is a logical 'cannot'; to speak of two being numerically one is to divest these words of their meaning. But when we examine the central christian claim concerning Jesus as the Christ we seem to meet precisely the paradoxical assertion that God and a man were numerically identical! That God became inhistorised in a human life can only mean that, in some sense, in that life God and man were one – numerically one. And the like must be said concerning the human *agapé* of Jesus and the divine *Agapé*. That God in Christ was acting in *Agapé* towards mankind must mean that the divine *Agapé* was numerically identical with the *agapé* of Jesus.

I should like at this point to counterfeit a word which will remind us that in speaking of *agapé* we are not speaking of some kind of static substance but of volitional attitudes and operations. Let us speak of activities of 'agapéing', both human and divine. We are then concerned with the relation between the infinite Agapéing of God in relation to mankind and the finite agapéing of Jesus within a certain limited segment of man's history.

It would clearly be without meaning to say of one finite agapéing that it is numerically identical with another. For the concrete action which is *A*'s agapéing is a numerically distinct action from *B*'s agapéing. (*A* and *B* may of course co-operate together – for instance, each contributing to the cost of a gift for *C* – but this is a case of the confluence of two actions, not of their numerical identity.) But it is by no means so clearly without meaning to say of a given finite agapéing that it is numerically identical with the infinite Agapéing of God. For the infinite is not excluded by the finite. On the contrary, the infinite must in some sense include the finite – otherwise the existence of the finite would constitute a boundary reducing the 'infinite' to finitude. In the nature of the case, the finite and the infinite can overlap, can interpenetrate, can (in this sense) be two and one at the same time. It is therefore not self-contradictory to say of a finite agapéing that it is numerically identical with the infinite Agapéing, provided we do not mean that the one is wholly coterminous or congruent with the other – i.e. that the finite agapéing is (in an almost unavoidable spatial metaphor) identical with the *whole* of the infinite Agapéing. But this proviso agrees with what the New Testament prompts us to say of Jesus. If we say that Jesus' agapéing was numerically identical with God's Agapéing, we do not mean that Jesus' agapéing was *the whole* of God's Agapéing. The incarnation was, so to speak, a temporal cross-section of God's Agapéing; but as a cross-section is not the entirety of that of which it is a cross-section, so the divine operation seen incarnate on earth was not the entirety of the divine operation. It was, to continue to speak quantitatively, as much of that operation or nature as could be expressed within the limitations of a particular set of spatio-temporal actions. We want to say of Jesus that he was *totus deus*, 'wholly God', in the sense that his *agapé* was genuinely the *Agapé* of God at work on earth, but not that he was *totum dei*, 'the whole of God', in the sense that the divine *Agapé* was expressed without remainder in each or even in the sum of his actions. We want to say that the *agapé* of Jesus is the divine *Agapé* as this has been seen acting towards us as an agent within human history. Jesus' *agapé* is not a representation of God's *Agapé*; it *is* that *Agapé* operating in a finite mode; it is the eternal divine *Agapé* made flesh, inhistorised. But 'made flesh' and 'inhistorised' signify a finite and hence a limited expression of the infinite love, a disclosure of that love at work, not in relation to every aspect of the created universe, nor in every possible situation, but in a set of specific human situations located in a specific stretch of the human story – beginning 'in the fifteenth year of the reign of Tiberius Caesar, Pontius Pilate being governor of Judea, and Herod being tetrarch of Galilee....'[10]

Is such inhistorisation properly describable as constituting the numerical identity of Jesus' *agapé* with the divine *Agapé*? There are, I think, three related though distinct concepts of numerical identity, or uses of the phrase 'numerically identical'. These are (i) self-identity, as when we say (if indeed in ordinary life we ever do say) of something that it 'is identical with itself; (ii) identity

[10] Luke 3: 1.

through time, as when we say that an object called 'O' at time t¹ is identical with the object called 'O' at time t²; and (iii) identity by continuity or inclusion as, to offer a preliminary example, when an amoeba puts forth a temporary extension of itself, and we describe such a pseudopodium as being one, or continuous, with the amoeba as a whole. The arm and the amoeba are not two objects but one. This relation between part and whole, which can also be termed a relation of continuity or inclusion, is a kind of numerical identity. And it must, I suggest, be some variation of this third concept of numerical identity that is being employed when we speak of the *agapé* of Jesus as being numerically identical with the divine *Agapé*.

However, the example just cited, whilst serving to distinguish this third sense of numerical identity from the other two, fails to illuminate the particular instance of continuity with which we are concerned; namely, the continuity between the divine Agapéing and the agapéing of Jesus. For this latter is a continuity of event rather than of entity. It is a continuity of agapéing considered as an activity, rather than of *agapé* considered as some kind of substance or essence. Our question then is this: Can an instance be found of the continuous identity of actions, which might provide a conceptual model by which to interpret the statement that the agapéing of Jesus is continuous, and in that sense identical, with the divine Agapéing?

The first contemporary writer (so far as I know) to interest himself in this kind of possibility was Dean W. R. Matthews, in a small but significant book, which deserves to be better known, *The Problem of Christ in the Twentieth Century*. He considers the notion of 'pattern' and says:

> I contend that there is no contradiction or absurdity in holding that the moving pattern of the will of God could be also the moving pattern of the behaviour-events which constitute the temporal and historical aspects of a human life. The scale on which the pattern is manifested makes no essential difference. A personal life of which it could be said that it is of the same pattern as the temporal will of God would be the supreme revelation of God; it would be God manifest 'in the flesh'. . . . The pattern of the Father's will, on this hypothesis, is the essential reality of the temporal personality of the Son. It is his

life; without it, or departing from it, he would cease to be himself. And the pattern, like the temporal will of God, is a moving pattern – the work is not yet completed.[11]

This is suggestive. For further help let us go back to an analogy used by several of the early theologians, that of the continuity between a source of illumination and the light which radiates from it. Tertullian, for example, says, 'Even when the ray is shot from the sun, it is still part of the parent mass; the sun will still be in the ray, because it is a ray of the sun – there is no division of substance, but merely an extension. Thus Christ is Spirit of Spirit, and God of God, as light is kindled of light'.[12] Other writers use the same simile; for example Athanasius: 'For the radiance also is light, not second to the sun, nor a different light, nor from participation of it, but a whole and proper offspring of it. And such an offspring is necessarily one light; and no one would say that they are two lights, sun and radiance being two. . . .'[13] During the modern period a change has come about in the accepted understanding of the nature of light which is analogous to the change that is here being contemplated in our christological thinking. The pre-scientific conception of a ray of light, as illustrated in the passage from Tertullian, seems to have been that of a narrow stream of thin ethereal matter proceeding from the sun and remaining continuous in substance with its source. The modern view of the nature of light alternates between the corpuscular and wave theories. According to the former, light consists in a flight of fast-moving particles, called photons. Considered as a basis for a concept of continuity this is only a refined version of the pre-scientific conception. But the rival theory of light as wave motion, which apparently stands today in unresolved alternation with the corpuscular theory, offers a quite different picture and provides a new model for our thought. On this theory light is a pattern of undulations in space initiated and reiterated by the sun's discharging energy. It may be described as something which the sun does, a change which it produces throughout its environment. And the continuous identity of a ray of light is

[11] W. R. Matthews, *The Problem of Christ in the Twentieth Century* (London: Oxford University Press, 1950) pp. 70–1.

[12] *Apology*, ch. 21.

[13] *Four Discourses Against the Arians.* Discourse III, para. 4. Cf. Athanasius, *Defence of the Council of Nicea*, ch. 3, para. 12.

accordingly not that of a continuous piece of homogeneous substance, like an arm stretched out elastically from the sun, nor is it that of a stream of discrete particles shot forth from its surface, but it consists in certain relations holding between certain events. The events whose interrelations define the identity of a ray of light are wave motions in space, and the relations which constitute these 'a ray of sunlight' are twofold: (a) an identity of structure or pattern (i.e. of wave-length) throughout the series of undulations emanating from the sun, and (b) a direct causal connection between the sun, as the source of radiation, and this particular procession of light waves. This second condition is required to distinguish between undulations of the same wavelength proceeding from different sources. These two criteria, if jointly satisfied, entitle us to describe the falling of light waves upon the surface of the earth as constituting a single continuous process with the solar activity which initiated the radiation. The set of light pulsations which affect ourselves is identical, numerically identical, with the radiating activity of the sun.

Using parallel criteria, to assert that the agapéing of Jesus was numerically identical with the divine Agapéing is to assert two things. First, there was an identity of structure or pattern, namely of moral pattern, between Jesus' agapéing and God's Agapéing in relation to mankind. Thus far this constitutes a qualitative identity between Jesus' *agapé* and the divine *Agapé*; and this is as far as an Arian type of christology is willing to go. But a Chalcedonian type of christology goes further, affirming, second, a direct causal connection between Jesus' attitudes to his fellow human beings and God's attitudes to them. This converts the qualitative identity of agapéing into a numerical identity. However, the causal connection postulated here is not, any more than is that between the successive events constituting the emission of a ray of light from the sun, an external relation between distinct entities. To suppose otherwise is to create insoluble because false problems both for physics and for christology. In the case of light we can distinguish earlier and later phases of the single complex event; and in the case of incarnation we can distinguish a noumenal divine activity and its phenomenal correlate in the life of Jesus. We can if we wish apply the category of cause and effect to these distinctions. But this must not lead us to a picture of God (in heaven) causing Jesus (on earth) to act in this way or that, like a puppet-master pulling strings or a general directing his troops by field radio. The neo-Chalcedonian claim is that the eternal divine *Agapé* towards mankind 'caused' Jesus' *agapé* towards the men and women whom he met, in a sense analogous to that in which the radiating energy of the sun 'causes' the falling of its rays upon the earth's surface. That is to say, the sun radiating forth its light, and that light illuminating and warming the surface of the globe, form one continuous complex event; and likewise the divine *Agapé* exerting itself in relation to mankind, and operating on earth as the *agapé* of Jesus, form one continuous event in virtue of which we can say that Jesus was God's attitude to mankind incarnate.

From the standpoint of this suggestion we can try to answer some of the questions that have always been put to christological hypotheses. Did Jesus have one nature or two? He had one nature, and this nature was wholly and unqualifiedly human; but the *agapé* which directed it was God's. Was there one will, or two? There was one will, that of the man Jesus of Nazareth; but again, the *agapé* that was the ruling motive of his life was God's *Agapé* for mankind. Was Jesus conscious that his love for mankind was that of God himself? The answer must be determined by the biblical evidence. My own reading of it is that he was conscious of a special vocation from the time of his baptism by John at about the age of thirty until his death some three years later. It was in virtue of this consciousness that he spoke about God's love with authority and acted it out with power. This does not mean, however, that he was conscious of being God, or the Son of God, or the eternal Logos made flesh. He was consciously a human being, distinct from God, and able to pray to God as his (and our) Father. But he was also conscious within himself of a love for men and women in their plight of estrangement from God and from one another; and he was conscious that in this *agapé* he was at one with God himself, so that in his actions God's *Agapé* was enacting itself and God's Kingdom was being created. How, or why, did all this come about? We can only say that it was an act of grace, God's act of making his *Agapé* towards mankind visible and tangible in the midst of human life for the saving of that human life.

In the end, then, christology must proclaim what it cannot explain. For it is concerned with an action initiated from beyond our world, an action which we observe and respond to and rejoice in, but which we could not have predicted and cannot now profess to understand, except in so far as to see it as an act of love is to understand it. What I have been exploring is not a way of explaining Christianity's traditional claim about Jesus but only of indicating what that claim is. The assertion that Jesus' agapéing was continuous with the divine Agapéing is no more self-explanatory than the assertion that Christ was of one substance with the Father. Neither of these phrases, strictly speaking, explains anything. Each is an expression of faith; and each is an expression of the same faith. But nevertheless I wish tentatively to suggest that the continuity-of-agapéing formulation may today be more intelligible than the oneness-of-substance formulation. Let us proclaim the *homoagapé* rather than the *homoousia*! For we know, at least ostensibly (and what better way could there be?), what we mean by *agapé*, but we do not know what we mean by substance – or at least, whatever meanings of 'substance' we isolate we then have to disavow as failing to provide an interpretation of *homoousios* which would render that term acceptable to twentieth-century Christians – let alone twentieth-century non-christians!

12. Incarnation and Mythology

WE NOW HAVE before us the central christian claim concerning Jesus: that he was/is God the Son incarnate. Or perhaps the Love of God incarnate; for I have suggested that in expressing this claim today we might speak of the identity of divine and human activities of loving rather than of an identity of substance. But it is to be noted that this suggestion does not profess to *explain* the assertion that Jesus was God as well as man but only to present it in terms that have currency today. To repeat what was said above, 'what I have been exploring is not a way of explaining [Christianity's] central claim about Jesus but only of indicating what that claim is. The assertion that Jesus' agapéing was continuous with the divine Agapéing is no more self-explanatory than the assertion that Christ was of one substance with the Father. Neither of these phrases, strictly speaking, explains anything. . . .'[1]

This being so let us go on now to consider the nature of the central christian dogma of the deity of Christ, whether it be expressed in terms of identity of substance or of identity of agapé. What sort of language are we speaking when we affirm divine incarnation in Jesus of Nazareth? What is the logical character of such a proclamation?

I wish to suggest that the language is mythological.[2] In saying this I am distinguishing it from the language of theory or hypothesis. A theory, whether theological or scientific, starts with some puzzling phenomenon and offers a hypothetical description of a wider situation – wider spatially or temporally or both –

[1] p. 164 above.
[2] This suggestion has much in common with the independent speculations of Maurice Wiles in his important paper 'Does christology rest on a mistake?' in *Christ, Faith and History*, edited by S. W. Sykes and J. P. Clayton (Cambridge University Press, 1972).

such that, seen within this wider context, the phenomenon is no longer puzzling. For example, Mendel was puzzled by the apparently haphazard distribution of presumably inherited characteristics in plants, and constructed a complex hypothesis concerning the laws of inheritance such that seen in this context the pattern of characteristics found in each new generation is no longer puzzling but on the contrary predictable. Or a theologian is puzzled by the presence of suffering in a world created by an unlimitedly good and unlimitedly powerful God, and develops a theory such that, if this is a true picture of the larger situation of which human life is a part, then it is no longer puzzling that such a world should contain pain and suffering. A theory is thus a spelling out of a possible state of affairs such that if this state of affairs obtains some otherwise puzzling phenomenon ceases to be puzzling.

A theory is true or false (or partly true and partly false); and any theory that can be of interest to human beings must be capable, in principle at least, of confirmation or disconfirmation within human experience. Otherwise it is 'meaningless' or pointless. Thus the Mendelian theory of inheritance is capable of experimental testing on the basis of which it can be accepted, rejected or improved. A theodicy should likewise be open to confirming or disconfirming evidence by entailing distinctive expectations about the future – for example (as in the case of the theodicy outlined in Chapters 5 and 6), the expectation that good will eventually be brought out of evil universally.

Myths are also responses to problematic phenomena, but a different kind of response which can enable us to relate ourselves to the phenomenon or situation in question without being able to explain it. There has of course been a considerable modern discussion of the place of myth in religion, much of it centering upon Rudolf Bultmann's programme for the demythologising of the New Testament. Bultmann has defined mythology as 'the use of imagery to express the other world in terms of this world and the divine in terms of human life, the other side in terms of this side'.[3] I should like however, for the present purpose, to define myth in a slightly different way: a myth is a story which is told but which is not literally true, or an idea or image which is

[3] *Kerygma and Myth*, ed. H. W. Bartsch, Vol. 1 (E.T., London: S.P.C.K., 1953) p. 10, n. 2.

applied to something or someone but which does not literally apply, but which invites a particular attitude in its hearers. Thus the truth of a myth is a kind of practical truth consisting in the appropriateness of the attitude which it evokes – the appropriateness of the attitude to its object, which may be an event, a person, a situation, or a set of ideas. For example, I may say of a certain happening that it is the work of the devil. If this is not literally true, the statement is mythic in character, and it is a true statement in so far as the attitude which it tends to evoke is appropriate to the actual character of the event in question.

Myths can be classified in many different ways, but one important formal distinction is between narrative myths and mythic concepts or images. A narrative myth evokes a particular attitude to a present situation by telling a story, which is not literally true – usually a story about how the situation came about. Or it may set a body of religious and moral teaching within a narrative framework which evokes a response of faith in the teaching. Again, a mythic image or idea is used to identify, and thus to indicate the significance of, a situation or a person and thereby to evoke a distinctive attitude towards it or him.

It may be useful to note some of the characteristics of myth as exhibited in the narrative myth of the fall of man before turning to the mythic Son of God imagery which is applied by way of identification to Jesus of Nazareth. The same material, whether story or idea, can often be used both as myth and as hypothesis, and it may illuminate the distinction between the two uses of language to observe this in the cases of the fall and the Incarnation.

In the case of the fall the problematic phenomenon is presumably the unsatisfactoriness of human existence, consisting more particularly in our innate selfishness (or sinfulness) and the often painful conditions of human life. Or perhaps this together with the awareness of better possibilities. Treated as theory, the story of the fall is an hypothetical account of actual events in the past. Man existed at one time in a state of innocent goodness in which he dwelt in a paradisal environment and was intimately conscious of God. He then deliberately disobeyed God, thereby ceasing to be either innocent or good, and was deprived of his paradisal life; and his descendants have ever since lived as morally fallen beings in a harsh environment. If this picture of man's early history is true it provides a genetic explanation both of man's wickedness and of the pains and sufferings of his existence. And just as it is in principle possible to confirm or disconfirm other theories about man's prehistory, so it is in principle possible to confirm or disconfirm the story of the fall considered as an account of past events.

Now virtually all Christians who belong intellectually to our contemporary western culture would agree that, so understood, the story of the fall is not literally true. There is no evidence to support it and much that conflicts with it. But nevertheless such Christians may, and indeed usually do, retain the story of the fall, not now as a theory or hypothesis but as a myth. How are they then using it?

So used, the story of the fall would seem to be a poetic, picturesque or parabolic way of saying something that can also be stated in non-mythological language but which is, for most people, conveyed much more effectively, and with much greater power to evoke an appropriate response, by the mythical story. The meaning of the myth may be the way it prompts us to see human wickedness as free and blameworthy and yet as occurring within a corrupt and corrupting inherited situation for which the individual is not responsible. Or it may be the way it leads us to see that as well as being actually wicked man has a potentiality for goodness which ought to be actualised. In this way the story of the fall may remind us that there is a sense in which our 'true' nature is good even though our actual state is bad, and may prompt us to seek to realise our 'true' nature. Thus the myth functions in a way close to that of moral exhortation.

Understood in this way, as a style of persuasive discourse, myth-making is obviously enormously valuable; for most people's minds are much more affected by a concrete than by an abstract expression of an idea. For example, in the *Pilgrim's Progress* Bunyan was expressing christian teaching in a concrete story form, and the work was for several generations possibly the most influential book of christian teaching and exhortation in Britain, evoking a christian attitude to life in many of its readers. Thus the telling of stories which are not literally true, but which tend to evoke a desired attitude in the hearer, is undoubtedly often an effective way of influencing people. And in so far as the attitude evoked is *appropriate*, the myth may be said to be a true myth –

true in that it leads us aright in our attitudes instead of misleading us.

We may turn now to the identifying myth of the Incarnation – the application to Jesus of Nazareth of a family of roughly equivalent images, such as Son of God, God the Son, God incarnate, Logos made flesh, God-Man. What is happening when we identify Jesus by means of one of these ideas?

Careful theologians have always insisted that the Incarnation is a 'mystery'. We do not profess or hope to understand it, but only to affirm it. It is said to be a revealed truth, not discoverable by reason but to be believed by faith. However, as we have seen in Chapter 8, almost certainly Jesus himself did not teach that he was God incarnate. The doctrine of the Incarnation was not revealed by Jesus, but emerged in the mind of the early church as a way of expressing his significance within a world in which it was not uncommon to speak of a great human figure as a son of God. The christian use of the idea, of course, quickly developed a larger meaning in a process that was already far advanced in the writings of St Paul and that was eventually to culminate in the doctrine of the incarnation of the Second Person of the Holy Trinity. We must consider further how the idea developed and what functions it served and now serves. But the immediate question is whether its logical character is that of a theological hypothesis or a religious myth.

It is possible to treat the idea of the incarnation of God the Son in Jesus of Nazareth as a theological hypothesis. (This does not of course mean that it must then be affirmed merely hypothetically, or doubtfully; it may be affirmed as an hypothesis which is known, or asserted, to be indubitably true.) For example, the doctrine of the Virgin Birth can be used to give a literal meaning to the statement that Jesus was God the Son: he was the Son of God because the Holy Spirit played the part of the male parent in his conception. But this interpretation would assimilate the Incarnation to a pagan idea that was applied to many outstanding men in the ancient world; and in modern times thoughtful christian theologians have declined to define the Incarnation in this way. Whether they have affirmed or denied the story of the Virgin Birth they have generally agreed that it is ancillary and not equivalent to the doctrine of the Incarnation.

Again, during the intense christological debates of the first five centuries of the christian era a number of theories were propounded that would have spelled out the idea of divine incarnation as an hypothesis or theory. For example, it was suggested that Jesus' mind was the divine Logos whilst his soul and body were human. But all such theories were in the end rejected by the church on the ground that they failed to do justice either to Christ's humanity or to his deity. Every theory professing to spell out what it means for Jesus to be the God-Man, fully God and fully man, has failed in the judgement of the church for the same reason. On close examination it has been seen to have the effect of denying the very mystery which it undertook to explicate.

Thus it has (so far) proved impossible to 'unpack' the concept of incarnation. Every attempt to specify further the idea that Jesus was both God and man has broken down. It seems impossible to take the thought of the God-Man beyond the phrase 'God-Man' and to find any definite meaning or content in it. But this need not surprise us; for the Incarnation is a mystery. The orthodox believer does not claim to understand it. He believes 'that God the Son became the man, Jesus' but he does not profess to know how this is possible, or how the full humanity of Jesus is compatible with his full deity – how an individual can be at once creator and created; eternal and born in time; infinite, omniscient and omnipotent and yet finite and humanly limited. He simply believes by faith that this is so. And it is significant that the great period of christological discussion in the early church ended with the acceptance of the formula of the Council of Chalcedon (A.D. 451) which simply reaffirmed the mystery in terms of the then readily available language of substance, acknowledging 'one and the same Son, our Lord Jesus Christ, at once complete in Godhead and complete in manhood, truly God and truly man, consisting also of a reasonable soul and body; of one substance with the Father as regards his Godhead, and at the same time of one substance with us as regards his manhood. . .'.

The lesson of those early attempts to understand the Incarnation, each of which misrepresented it by trying to spell it out as an intelligible hypothesis, is surely that the Incarnation is not a theological theory but a religious myth. To say this is not of course to say that the idea has generally been categorised as myth in the christian consciousness. On the contrary, the doctrine of the Incarnation has generally been regarded as a literal truth –

though one which, as a 'mystery', is opaque to human understanding. The suggestion that the language of incarnation is
mythological in character is a critical or second-order suggestion.
Again, the various christological theories, both orthodox and
unorthodox, have probably usually been regarded as explanatory
theories rather than as pointers to a mythological truth. But in
fact the orthodox formulae (such as those of Nicea and Chalcedon) simply reaffirmed the mystery in its full paradoxical character, without explicating it, whilst the heretical theories (such as
the Arian, Eutychian, Nestorian and Appollinarian) explicated
it, but only at the cost of denying one or other of the paradoxical
aspects of God-Manhood. They made incarnation intelligible by
failing to take Christ's humanity, or his deity, seriously. When
we take them both seriously we have a mystery instead of an
explanation. Thus in retrospect we can see that the fundamental
heresy, which the church has rejected in all the many forms
which human ingenuity has devised, is that of treating the myth
as an hypothesis. The same lesson can, I believe, be drawn from
the modern attempts to understand the Incarnation – that is, to
interpret it not as a mystery but as an intelligible theory. I have
tried to show this elsewhere of D. M. Baillie's very influential
'paradox of grace' theory.[4] And Wolfhart Pannenberg, as the
outcome of his massive discussion of both ancient and modern
christologies, concludes that 'The impasse reached by every
attempt to construct Christology by beginning with the incarnational concept demonstrates that all such attempts are doomed
to failure. We found repeatedly that either the unity of Jesus
Christ as person or else his real humanity or true divinity were
lost to view.'[5] Hence he speaks of 'the insoluble problems of an
incarnational Christology constructed "from above to below"'[6]
– although he fails to recognise that the same insoluble problems
are present on his own route 'from below to above'.

The church's rejection of the series of christological heresies
expresses, then, its basic awareness that the idea of divine incarnation in Jesus of Nazareth is a mystery lying beyond human

---

[4] 'The Christology of D. M. Baillie', *Scottish Journal of Theology*,
Mar. 1958. See also John Baillie, 'Some Comments on Professor Hick's
Article on "The Christology of D. M. Baillie" ', *S.J.T.*, Sep. 1958.

[5] Wolfhart Pennenberg, *Jesus – God and man*, op. cit., p. 322.

[6] Ibid., p. 313.

comprehension and not a concept that can be given a precise meaning. Extending this sense of the special character of the incarnational theme, I would say that the reason why no statable meaning or content has been discovered in it is simply that it has no such content. It is not an hypothesis still waiting to be adequately defined; rather, it is not an hypothesis at all. It is a mythological idea. As such it cannot *literally* apply to Jesus. But as a poetic image – which is powerfully evocative even though it conveys no literal meaning – it expresses the religious significance of Jesus in a way that has proved effective for nearly two millennia. It thus fulfils its function, which is to evoke an appropriate response of faith in Jesus.

This response is the attitude to Jesus as saviour. For it is through Jesus that we have encountered God as our heavenly Father and have entered into a new life which has its ultimate centre in God. The absoluteness of the experience is the basis for the absoluteness of the language. For any moment of divine revelation or illumination has an 'absolute' character. Since it is God, the ultimate reality, that is being encountered, the experience cannot fail to have the accent of absoluteness and 'once for all' finality. That *God* has been encountered through Jesus is communicated mythologically by saying that he was God the Son incarnate. The myth is thus an appropriate and valid expression of the experience. It is not the only possible way of expressing it; but amidst the conflict of religions in the early Roman empire this particular mythology was apt and effective. This was a world in which Mithras was to be described as a god of heavenly light whose miraculous birth (also witnessed by shepherds) brought new life to mankind. Such a world virtually prescribed the form to be taken by the mythological translation of christian religious experience. Jesus, in following whom we have found our way of salvation, and in whose shared life we experience the life that is eternal, must be called divine, Son of God, God incarnate: this was an appropriate way of indicating his religious significance.

The question that has now to be raised, however, in the context of our new map of the universe of faiths, is whether we properly understand the function of this christian myth of incarnation if we take it to make an exclusive claim for Christianity as the *only* way of salvation.

We have gone back behind the incarnational mythology to the religious experience which it expresses. Let us look further at this experience and particularly at its quality of psychological absoluteness. For salvation experiences share this quality with a range of other experiences, and it may be instructive to bring some of these into view. The experiences of falling in love, of 'seeing' and being grasped by some important truth, and of being utterly loyal to a monarch or country or to some other group or cause, can also exhibit this absolute and unqualified character. There is nothing tentative or provisional about them; each demands to be expressed in the language of ultimates – the perfect unity of two hearts in love; total illumination; absolute loyalty. Such language is, in the analogy of Chapter 9, inherently and unavoidably 'Ptolemaic' – one's own experience is normative and everyone else's is seen in relation to this as the centre. But in these non-religious cases it is quite clear that it is also legitimate to stand outside the experience itself and to describe it, without in any way thereby downgrading it, from a 'Copernican' point of view. For in the case of the experiences of being in love, of 'seeing' a truth, and of patriotic or other loyalty we can readily acknowledge that it is possible for people genuinely to be in love with others than one's own beloved, genuinely to have the experience of intellectual insight in relation to different truths, and genuinely to be loyal to different groups and causes than one's own. Indeed in these cases we are not seriously tempted to translate the absoluteness of the experience into a doctrine of the exclusive validity of our own experience, even though the language which most adequately expresses and evokes the experience does, if taken literally, suggest such an exclusive claim. We do not suppose that because our own love or insight or loyalty has the unqualified character that it has, other people's love, insight and loyalty must be less authentic. We can appreciate that to each lover, to each intuiter of a momentous truth, to each whole-hearted loyalist, his experience has the same absolute character as our own; and we can be sure of the authenticity of our own experience without supposing that we thereby impugn that of others.

Now why should not the same be true of men's experiences of redemptive encounter with God? The experience has a quality of finality which is most naturally and adequately expressed in language which, taken literally, implies its exclusive validity.

But the analogies with being in love, with intellectual illumination, and with total loyalty remind us that this experienced
absoluteness need not entail exclusiveness. The same 'absolute'
quality of experience may in principle be enjoyed simultaneously
by any number of different consciousnesses. Hence, the christian
experience of saving encounter with God does not in itself entail
that there are not, outside Christianity, other encounters with
God exhibiting the same quality of psychological ultimacy and
finding expression in their own religious mythologies. Ernst
Troeltsch gave classic expression to this thought in his 1923
Oxford lecture on the place of Christianity among the world
religions. He pointed out that Christianity has been a manifesta-
tion of the Divine Life to us in the west.

> The evidence we have for this remains essentially the same,
> whatever may be our theory concerning absolute validity – it is
> the evidence of a profound inner experience. This experience
> is undoubtedly the criterion of its validity, but, be it noted,
> only of its validity *for us*. It is God's countenance as revealed
> to us; it is the way in which, being what we are, we receive,
> and react to, the revelation of God. It is binding upon us, and
> it brings us deliverance. It is final and unconditional for us,
> because we have nothing else, and because in what we have
> we can recognise the accents of the divine voice. But this does
> not preclude the possibility that other racial groups, living
> under entirely different cultural conditions, may experience
> their contact with the Divine Life in a quite different way,
> and may themselves also possess a religion which has grown up
> with them, and from which they cannot sever themselves so
> long as they remain what they are.[7]

And indeed such a thought has always formed a strand, though
usually only a slender one, within the total christian tradition.[8]
It was Irenaeus in the second century who said, 'There is but one

[7] Ernst Troeltsch, *Christian Thought: Its History and Application*
(London: University of London Press, and New York: Meridian Books,
1957) p. 26. Reprinted in Owen C. Thomas, ed., *Attitudes toward Other
Religions* (London: S.C.M. Press, 1969).

[8] This strand is briefly traced by Metropolitan George Khodr in
'Christianity in a Pluralist World – the Economy of the Holy Spirit', in
Living Faiths and the Ecumenical Movement, ed. S. J. Samartha (Geneva:
World Council of Churches, 1971).

and the same God who, from the beginning to the end and by various dispensations, comes to the rescue of mankind'.[9]

This is of course precisely what the reports of the great non-christian faiths suggest. The Jew claims that God has revealed himself through hebrew history as interpreted by the faith of the prophets. The Muslim claims that God has, through his prophet Mohammed, revealed his truth in the Koran. The Buddhist claims that in his enlightenment at Bodh-Gaya Gotama attained to unity with ultimate reality and has revealed to others the way to the same fulfilment. The monistic Hindu claims that the divine truth revealed in the Vedas is confirmed in the mystical experience of *jīvanmukti's* in all ages. The Hindu of the theistic bhakti tradition claims that God has revealed himself through the gods and is known in worship. The Sikh claims that God has revealed his will through Nanak and the Granth. And in each case the true believer experiences divine revelation, divine activity, divine claim, divine grace, divine love with the same quality of absoluteness. In each case the human capacity for faith and worship is fully activated and a total response of devotion takes place. Why not, then, presume that the ultimate divine reality is in fact encountered and responded to in different ways in all these different streams of religious experience?

The conception of a religious myth as a story which is not literally true, or an identifying concept or image which does not literally apply, but which may be 'true' in virtue of its power to evoke an appropriate attitude, enables us to see the mythological character not only of the christian concept of the Incarnation but also of the corresponding concepts of other religions. That the Koran was dictated by God to Mohammed and constitutes a direct verbal revelation of God to man, divinely inspired down to the last syllable, is an identifying myth whose function is to evoke an attitude of reverent obedience to the holy book; and in so far as this attitude is appropriate the myth is true. That the Lord Krishna became incarnate as Arjuna's charioteer before a great battle, and spoke at length about the nature of the universe and the divine purpose, is a mythological narrative whose function is to evoke a receptive attitude to the profound teaching of the Bhagavad Gītā; and in so far as such an attitude is appropriate the myth is true. And so on. The religions of the world are rich in

[9] *Against Heresies*, bk. III, ch. 12, para. 13.

myths of every kind. But we are not required to set these different mythologies against one another as though they were mutually exclusive theories. They are more like different art forms, each of which is at home in a different culture, than like rival scientific hypotheses.

I have argued that the christian image of divine incarnation lacks a content or meaning in virtue of which the statement that Jesus is God made man could be literally true or false. It is not a theological theory but a religious myth, and its function is to evoke an attitude to Jesus as 'the way, the truth and the life' – so that in following him we find salvation, in believing as he believed we are believing rightly concerning God and man, and in living in his fellowship we participate in the life eternal. Through our response of faith to him which sets us on this way, with this truth, and in this life, he is our saviour. But can this christian attitude to Christ be appropriate if he is not literally God the Son incarnate? The truth of an identificatory myth, I have suggested, consists in its aptness to evoke an attitude which is *appropriate* to the real character of that which is being identified. If, then, the appropriate attitude to Jesus the Christ is the attitude of saved to saviour, how can this be justified if he is not literally God incarnate?

If, as I have argued, the idea of divine incarnation in Jesus of Nazareth has no literal meaning, the question has to be posed in a different form – whether, in spite of the mythic character of the idea of incarnation, salvation through Christ can be a reality and his God-Manhood an effective expression of that reality? However, we do not, as Christians, need to ask *whether* salvation through Christ can be a reality, for we start from the fact that it *is* a reality! Through their responses to the person of Jesus countless people have been opened to the divine presence; changed in the direction of their lives; reconciled to themselves, to their neighbours and to God; have become conscious of the reality of their loving heavenly Father who has forgiven and accepted them. This experience of salvation began in Jesus' own lifetime. Indeed the saving impact of his person and teaching must have been at its most intense in his personal historical presence. But we have noted that in all probability the historical Jesus, whose effect upon many people was their experience of salvation, neither thought of himself nor was thought of by his disciples as

God incarnate. It was not he but his heavenly Father who saved. But Jesus was so fully God's agent, so completely conscious of living in God's presence and serving God's love, that the divine reality was mediated through him to others.

Let us raise at this point the traditional question of the uniqueness of Christ. Did he mediate the presence and saving power of God in an unique sense, in which no other religious figure has ever mediated it or ever could? Before answering we must clarify the question itself. It has a clear meaning if it is interpreted as a factual question, to be determined by observation. The idea of the unique saviourhood of Christ would then entail that only those who have been saved through him are really saved. It would follow from this that the experience of salvation, of consciousness of God, of liberation from the bondage of sin, of new life in response to the divine call, reported from within other faiths is illusory. Now it is of course always open to the adherents of one religion to claim that the experience of salvation, liberation or re-creation reported by the adherents of all other religions is illusory and that only their own such experience is genuine. But this has to be asserted as a sheer dogma, as impossible to support as to refute – and a dogma of a kind which can equally well be directed against one's own religion as for it. But if we do not want to make such a dangerous claim, the idea of the unique saviourhood of Christ ceases to have a factual content. What we then have is not an assertion of unique saving effectiveness in human life, but a particular redemption-myth attached to one great historical way of salvation.

Finally, the question of the worship of Christ. Whilst the Christian worships God *through* Christ, 'in the name of our Lord Jesus Christ', he also sometimes worships Christ himself as Lord and Saviour. This is, indeed, the attitude which the language of incarnation is designed to evoke and express. But is such an attitude possible, and is it appropriate, in view of the mythological character of the incarnation concept? Can we and should we worship a human being who is not literally God incarnate?

We have to acknowledge here the elasticity of the concept of worship. In a sense only the ultimate – in Anselm's formula, that than which no greater can be conceived – is to be worshipped, and the worship of any lesser reality is idolatry. But in practice we are only able to worship the ultimate under some more proximate, and indeed anthropomorphic, image. Every human concept of God, in terms of which worship is directed, is a finite image, or mental picture, of the infinite divine reality that exceeds all human thought. In the words of Metropolitan Khodr, 'all concepts of God are idols'.[10] When two Christians – *A* and *B* – pray, *A* thinking of God as the inscrutable sovereign power which predestines some of his creatures to eternal life and others to eternal death, whilst *B* thinks of God as the loving heavenly Father who accepts and redeems us all, they are worshipping God as mediated by two different, though overlapping, images. Indeed all our concepts of God are 'images' of the infinite divine reality: Christ is the Christian's image of God.

Characteristically, in the history of religions, the images through which the divine reality is worshipped have been thought of as beings who are immensely – indeed for all practical purposes infinitely – superior to ourselves spiritually, immensely 'nearer' to God, but who are nevertheless servants of God rather than the infinite Deity himself. To worship such a mediator is not to regard him as the Infinite but to regard him as so vastly 'higher' than ourselves in the direction of God as to be for us an image through whom the ultimate divine reality can be worshipped. This is the way in which christian devotion has very often regarded Jesus. There is a comparable development in Mayahana Buddhism in the idea of the Bodhisattva Amida, thought of as a supremely holy and enlightened being of such spiritual power that to follow him is to receive salvation. There are analogies again in the attitude to the gods – Rama or Krishna or Kali or Durga or another – of the religiously educated Hindu who thinks of these as finite 'images' of the ultimate reality, Brahman. And when we conceive of a spiritual being as so far above us, in the direction of God, that he (or she) can bring us and seeks to bring us to the infinite good of salvation, or nirvana, or eternal life, then our attitude may well be called worship; and it may well be evoked and sustained by a mythology such as that of the Incarnation.

Thus I am suggesting that we have to distinguish between the distinctively christian faith-response to Jesus as Lord and Saviour, and the expression of this response in the mythological

[10] S. J. Samartha, ed., *Living Faiths and the Ecumenical Movement*, op. cit., p. 141.

identification of him as God incarnate. Jesus is the concrete image of God through whom our worship is focused, and the idea of the Incarnation is an effective mythic expression of the appropriate attitude to him. In regarding the attitude as appropriate we are regarding the myth as true. But if we make the mistake (which lay at the root of all the christological heresies) of trying to turn the myth into an hypothesis, we not only falsify its character but also generate implications that would make impossible any viable theology of religions.

13. Towards a Theology of Death

IN ORDER that we may start from where we are, and may be reminded of where this is by contrast with somewhere else, let me quote two passages from the world we have lost – the world in which the belief in a life to come was a pervasive factor in most people's minds, affecting their attitudes both to life and to death. The first passage comes from a book of legal precedents published in London in 1592, when the first Elizabeth was on the throne of England and when Will Shakespeare was a rising London playwright. The book offers 'a verie perfect form of a Will', which begins as follows:

> In the name of God, Amen. The twenty-sixth day of April in the year of our Lord God, one thousand five hundred and ninety two, A.B.C. the unprofitable servant of God, weak in body, but strong in mind, do willingly and with a free heart render and give again into the hands of my Lord God and Creator, my spirit, which he of his fatherly goodness gave unto me, when he first fashioned me in my mother's womb, making me a living creature, nothing doubting that for his infinite mercies, set forth in the precious blood of his dearly beloved son Jesus Christ our alone saviour and redeemer, he will receive my soul into his glory, and place it in the company of the heavenly angels and blessed saints. And as concerning my body even with a good will and free heart I give over, commending it to the earth whereof it came, nothing doubting but according to the article of my faith, at the great day of general resurrection when we shall all appear before the judgment seat of Christ, I shall receive the same again by the mighty power of God, wherewith he is able to subdue all things to himself, not

a corruptible, mortal, weak and vile body, as it is now, but an uncorruptible, immortal, strong, and perfect body in all points like unto the glorious body of my Lord and Saviour Jesus Christ . . .[1]

and then the testator proceeds to the disposition of his property.

Now this is of course a consciously correct form of words according to the ideas of the time, offered as a paradigm for the framing of wills; and we may perhaps be tempted to wonder if it is more correct than sincere. But I think that any such suspicion would be uncalled for. These words reflect the real beliefs of real people.

As indirect evidence of this I cite a second passage. This was written nearly 200 years later, and is to be found in Boswell's *Life of Johnson*, where he transcribes a page of Johnson's diary for Sunday, 18 October 1767.

Yesterday, Oct. 17, at about ten in the morning, I took my leave for ever of my dear old friend, Catherine Chambers, who came to live with my mother about 1724, and has been but little parted from us since. She is now fifty-eight years old.

I desired all to withdraw, then told her that we were to part for ever; that as Christians, we should part with prayer; and that I would, if she was willing, say a short prayer beside her. She expressed great desire to hear me; and held up her poor hands, as she lay in bed, with great fervour, while I prayed, kneeling by her, nearly in the following words:

'Almighty and most merciful Father, whose loving kindness is over all thy works, behold, visit, and relieve this thy servant, who is grieved with sickness. Grant that the sense of her weakness may add strength to her faith, and seriousness to her repentance. And grant that by the help of thy Holy Spirit, after the pains and labours of this short life, we may all obtain everlasting happiness, through Jesus Christ our Lord; for whose sake hear our prayers. Amen.'

I then kissed her. She told me, that to part was the greatest pain she had ever felt, and that she hoped we should meet again in a better place. I expressed, with swelled eyes, and great emotion of tenderness, the same hopes. We kissed, and parted. I humbly hope to meet again, and to part no more.

---

[1] William West, *Symbolæography* (London, 1592) sect. 689.

Here there is I think no mistaking the genuine and full sincerity of the beliefs that are expressed.

These documents, with their presuppositions, come as I have said from the world we have lost. The firm assumption that this life is part of a much larger existence which transcends our earthly span is no longer a part of the thought world of today. Post-christian secular man believes only in what he experiences, plus that which the accredited sciences reveal to him. The afterlife falls outside this sphere and is accordingly dismissed as a fantasy of wishful thinking. Of course not everyone you meet in the streets is an example of post-christian secular man come of age, as depicted after Bonhoeffer. On the contrary, many different phases of pre-christian, christian, and post-christian life coexist in our culture and even sometimes within the same individual. There may even in our society as a whole be more pre-christianity than post-christianity, with more people believing in astrology than astronomy, or putting their faith in horoscopes rather than in microscopes as means to knowledge. So far as afterlife beliefs are concerned, a B.B.C. report of 1955 suggested that about 43 per cent of its public (which is virtually the population as a whole) believes in a life after death. If such is the nation-wide state of mind on the subject, there is good evidence that this has influenced opinion within the churches, drawing it down towards this half-hearted (or to be more precise 43 per cent-hearted) level of belief. For example, the Mass Observation document *Puzzled People*, published in 1948, reported that 'Of those who say they believe in a Deity, one in five are definite in their assertion that they do not believe in a life after death'. And in the Gallup Poll's *Television and Religion* survey, published in 1964, it emerged that some 74 per cent of Roman Catholics in England believe in an afterlife, some 56 per cent of Free Churchmen, and some 49 per cent of Anglicans. These figures are for the official or nominal memberships. The figures for regular church attenders are higher and are grouped closer together, namely Roman Catholics 88 per cent, Free Churchmen 86 per cent, and Anglicans 85 per cent. But that there are 12–15 per cent of regular committed worshippers who do not believe in a life after death is surely significant, and indicates a fairly marked movement away from traditional christian teaching on the matter. And this negative attitude, which may for some 15 per cent of church members be simply an assumption absorbed from the surrounding culture, has been turned by some of our more radical theologians into a principle for the reinterpretation of Christianity. Authentic Christianity, they say, has no place for afterlife beliefs. Christians are not and ought not to be interested in the possibility of an existence after death. We ought instead to be wholly interested in this world and in our contemporary neighbours, with their and our pressing human needs and problems.

In commenting upon this point of view may I begin by indicating my personal starting point?

In general I have far more sympathy with the new theologians than with the old theologians. I regard the contemporary breaking of long-established religious thought forms as good, and as having inaugurated a period in which there are exciting possibilities of reconstruction and challenging scope for originality. Thus in face of the contemporary theological ferment I do not, when I try to look into my own mind, feel reactionary, censorious or defensive. I have even, when I was in the United States, been involved in a heresy case, when a very conservative minority sought to exclude me from the ministry of the United Presbyterian Church for declining to affirm one of the more manifestly mythological aspects of the christian tradition. I mention this simply to indicate that if I now proceed to criticise the understanding of death offered by the new theology this criticism does not necessarily come out of a generally reactionary attitude, nor out of a constitutional failure to comprehend or sympathise with the new. But I am nevertheless bothered by a tendency in popular radical theology today to set up false, because over-simple, alternatives, and to be led thereby to unwarranted conclusions.

It appears to me that in this matter of the afterlife we have a case in point. On the one hand, it seems obviously true that we should not so set our thoughts upon a life to come as to undervalue or fail to engage unreservedly with this present earthly existence. Christianity is concerned with the transformation of human life here and now. Salvation is not something to be postponed to another sphere beyond the grave; eternal life (whatever else it may be) is a quality of living to be entered into now. All this is surely both true and enormously important. But it does not follow, or even begin to follow, that there is no life after death. I shall suggest a little later how the two themes of immortality and this-worldliness are fully compatible with one another. But I would simply point out at the moment that the fact that we ought not, in the midst of this life, to distract ourselves by dwelling upon a life to come, does not entail that this earthly existence, upon which we are now meant to be concentrating, is all. The question of a life after death must be decided in some other way.

Unless, then, we choose to regard ourselves as simply the priests of human culture, affirming – only more so – what our culture affirms and denying what it denies, the fact that the public mind of our day is tending away from belief in a life after death does not settle the matter. There remains the possibility that Christianity is committed by its sources and its nature to the claim that the structure of reality is other than that which our contemporary culture as a whole believes it to be. And so we have to raise directly the question whether the belief in an after-life is or is not an essential part of the christian faith. Upon this issue every other aspect of our theology of death necessarily hinges.

There are two broad divergent alternatives for christian thought in relation to each of its main traditional tenets, including eschatology (i.e. its discourse concerning 'the last things', one of which is death). In philosophical terms, one of these alternatives is realist and the other reductionist. To outline the latter first: it claims that the meaning of the various christian doctrines can be wholly stated in terms of present human experience and involves no claim that goes beyond this. The meaning, for example, of the doctrine of creation is that we accept the world as basically good; the doctrine expresses (I quote Paul van Buren) 'an affirmative view of the world of men and things'.[2] And in the same pattern the meaning of the doctrine of eternal life is our affirmation that the life of faith has unlimited value and significance. There is thus in each case a reduction of – to use a variety of terms – the metaphysical to the psychological, or the ontological to the existential, or the transcendent to the immanent. In contrast to this, theological realism affirms both dimensions and refuses to reduce the one to the other. It does not of course deny that it is part of the meaning of creation that the world is good; or that it is part of the meaning of eternal life that the life of faith has unlimited

---

[2] *The Secular Meaning of the Gospel* (New York: The Macmillan Company, 1962, and London: S.C.M. Press, 1963) p. 177.

worth. It is not concerned to say less than this but in each case to say more than this. And so far as eternal life is concerned it claims not only that the life in relation to God has unlimited value but also that this value is embodied in unlimited existence. The ultimately valuable is also the ultimately real. That which God affirms is held in being by his creative love; and accordingly eternal life is also the life everlasting.

There are two main grounds on which this may be affirmed. One is that the teaching of Jesus is so pervaded by the belief in a life after death that it is hardly possible to base one's religious faith upon him, as the revelation of God's love to man, and yet to reject so integral a part of his conception of the divine purpose. I don't think that I need cite a series of New Testament passages to establish that Jesus believed in a future life. I will only mention, by way of reminder, the parables of Dives and Lazarus and of the sheep and the goats; the controversy with the Sadducees about the general resurrection; and the numerous sayings about future judgement. I have in fact never heard of a New Testament scholar who denied that Jesus believed in an afterlife; and the point can probably safely be taken as non-controversial.

If we now go on to ask *why* Jesus believed so firmly in an after-life, the answer points to the second possible ground for this faith, namely, that it is a corollary of belief in the sovereign heavenly Father. For there would be an intolerable contradiction in affirming on the one hand that God knows, values and loves each of his human creatures as unique individuals, and evokes in them the desire to realise the highest potentialities of their nature in response to his claim upon them, and yet on the other hand that he has ordained their extinction when they have only just begun to fulfil the divine purpose which has endowed them with those potentialities and aspirations. The divine love and the divine demand alike bestow upon man a dignity transcending that of the beasts that perish. As Martin Luther said, 'Anyone with whom God speaks, whether in wrath or in mercy, the same is certainly immortal. The Person of God who speaks, and the Word, show that we are creatures with whom God wills to speak, right into eternity, and in an immortal manner.'[3]

Luther is of course here making the large assumption that

[3] Quoted by Emil Brunner, *Dogmatics*, II (Philadelphia: Westminster Press, and London: Lutterworth Press, 1952) p. 69.

eternal life must mean, or at least must include in its meaning, the continued existence of distinct individual human personalities after their bodily death. But – let us now ask – is not this a rather crassly literal idea, the sort of thing that today we almost automatically demythologise? May we not think instead, for example, of some kind of merging of consciousnesses in a larger whole, a losing of individual personality in something more inclusive, a fulfilment of human existence which does not involve the perpetuation of separate strands of consciousness? Here one time-honoured picture is that of the drop returning to the ocean from which it was temporally separated.

Needless to say, we *can* think in such terms as these; but the question is whether they will satisfy the exigencies of christian faith which led us to speak of eternal life in the first place. If we affirm the life to come because of Jesus' teaching, it seems that we shall find ourselves affirming continued individual personal existence. If we affirm it as a corollary of the love of God for his human children, again it would seem that we shall be affirming the continuance of the individual personality. It is indeed hard to see on what specifically christian ground one would affirm human immortality and yet not affirm it as involving continued personal identity.

But if a conception of eternal life in which human personality is explicitly denied a place fails to satisfy the two interlocking motives of christian eschatology, may we not fall back upon complete agnosticism concerning the form of the life to come and simply declare that in some unimaginable way God's good purpose for mankind will be fulfilled? Death does not cancel God's love for us; and we must rest in this faith without attempting to picture its implications in quasi-earthly terms. Whether it involves continued separate individuality we do not know and we ought not to care. Sufficient that, whatever its nature, our destiny will be determined by the goodness of God. Such a modest and undogmatic approach can hardly fail to appeal to all of us. And yet I think we can also see that it stands in real danger of meaninglessness. Is it a responsible use of language to speak of eternal life, immortality, the life to come, heaven and hell, and then to add that this language carries no implications whatever regarding the continuation or otherwise of human personality beyond the grave? Are we not evacuating our words of all meaning – whilst however retaining their comforting emotive overtones – if we speak at the grave side of the 'sure and certain hope of resurrection to eternal life' and yet add as theologians that this hope is completely neutral as between the deceased's present and future existence and his non-existence?

I must confess that this seems to me to come perilously close to double-talk. And yet this kind of language is often heard. Let us consider an actual example, which is to be found in the chapter on 'Life after death' in Bishop John Robinson's popular book *But That I can't Believe!*[4] This is a book to which on the whole I respond sympathetically. It seems to me a bold and largely successful attempt to communicate the christian faith in the language of the *Sunday Mirror*; and this is both a difficult and an important thing to do. But the subject of death and resurrection inevitably stands out as an embarrassment for the 'new theologian'; for it confronts him with an unmistakable form of the issue which his whole theology is designed to de-emphasise, the issue of transcendence. On the one hand he does not want absolutely and definitively to deny transcendence, for he is aware that ultimately only this can give religious substance to his faith. But on the other hand, knowing that contemporary post-christian secular man has no use for the idea of the transcendent, he does not want to rely upon it in communicating the gospel. He finds himself wanting both to affirm it and not to affirm it; hence the air of double-talk that is so liable to pervade his discussion. To turn to our example, we find Robinson saying that in the New Testament eternal life is not a doctrine of survival after bodily death but of 'a quality of life – here and now – which death cannot touch. Death is put in its place, as powerless to make any difference' (p. 45). This, he notes, agrees with the contemporary attitude that 'Death may be the end. So what?' (p. 45). Accordingly, Robinson concludes that 'nothing turns on what happens after death' (p. 46). He is apparently saying in this aspect of his discussion that eternal life is a quality of existence available to mankind now, and that to affirm it as the gift of Christ is compatible with the contemporary secular assumption that death means personal extinction. But then, talking in a different vein, Robinson also says (p. 46):

[4] London: Collins (Fontana), 1967.

As a Christian, I know my life to be grounded in a love which will not let me go. It comes to me as something completely unconditional. If it could really be put an end to by a bus on the way home it would not have the quality I know it to have. From such a love neither cancer nor the H-bomb can separate. Death cannot have the last word. . . . As St Paul says, 'If in this life only we have hoped in Christ, we are of all men the most foolish.'

Here, if words have any stable meaning, he is saying that eternal life is a relationship to God which is not terminated by bodily death. And, if it is not terminated by bodily death, then presumably it goes on after bodily death. Surely, then, the secular reader will rightly want to know whether Robinson is affirming a life after death or not; and in either case he will want to have the matter stated unambiguously and its consequences explicitly acknowledged. (It is worth adding that this criticism does not apply to Robinson's main book on this subject, *In the End, God . . .*).

It is I think to be noted that the logical relationship between the two views which are found side by side in Robinson's chapter is an asymmetrical relationship. The first excludes the second, but the second does not exclude the positive part of the first. We do not have to choose between the alternatives of eternal life as a present quality of existence and eternal life as immortal existence; still less between an infinitely valuable quality with a brief duration and a relatively valueless quality with unlimited duration. These are not the only possibilities. The more authentically christian view of the matter, I would suggest, goes beyond this false alternative to the conception of eternal life as unlimited both in value and in duration, the link between the two being forged by the love of God which unqualifiedly affirms and supports this mode of creaturely existence.

This is perhaps the point at which to identify a red herring which sometimes misleads thought on these matters. It is said – correctly – that the distinctively christian doctrine is not one of immortality but of resurrection. So far from being naturally immortal, as Plato for example taught, the Bible teaches that man is made out of the dust of the earth and is destined to be dissolved again into that dust. But God by his own will and sovereign power recreates us after death in another sphere of being, bestowing upon us a new life which is not a natural immortality but a free gift of the creator. From this starting point, which represents in capsule the biblical view, some have inferred that there is no christian doctrine of immortality and/or of human survival after death. But this does not follow at all. The doctrine of God's resurrecting of the dead is not the opposite of a doctrine of human immortality, but is a form of that doctrine – namely, one in which man's immortality is seen as a divine gift and as dependent upon the will of God. This is quite clearly a doctrine of human survival of bodily death and in that sense of man's immortality.

However, if Christianity is indeed committed to belief in personal survival after death, both by its starting point in the life and teaching of Jesus and by the logic of its faith in the love of God for the finite beings made in his image, there now opens before us a further set of options. For there are two major alternative theological frameworks within which the christian belief in an afterlife has developed; and these tend to produce two rather different attitudes to death.

The tradition which has for the most part dominated the western christian mind until our own time is based upon the great imaginative picture, or myth, of the drama of salvation beginning with the fall of man and ending in the division of humanity into the saved and the damned, segregated in heaven and hell. Man was originally created as a finitely perfect creature, but wickedly misused his freedom to rebel against God; and it was this original sin that, in Milton's words, 'brought death into the world, and all our woe'. Death is thus a punishment for, or a divinely ordained consequence or fruit of, sin – a consequence brought upon the whole race by the sin of our first forefather, Adam. St Paul wrote that 'sin came into the world through one man and death through sin, and so death spread to all men'.[5] But it was St Augustine in the fifth century who, elaborating Paul's thought in his own way, definitively projected the picture that has informed the christian imagination for 1500 years. In the *City of God* he said that 'the first men were so created, that if they had not sinned they would not have experienced any kind of death; but that, having become sinners, they were so punished

[5] Rom. 5: 12.

with death, that whatsoever sprang from their stock should also be punished with the same death'.[6]

On this view our mortality is not an aspect of the divinely intended human situation, but is an evil, a state that ought never to have come about, a disastrous consequence of man's turning away from his maker. Death is a punishment, and the emotions that appropriately reverberate around it are those of guilt and sorrow, remorse and fear.

But the christian mind has never adhered consistently and exclusively to this understanding of mortality and to the attitude which it renders appropriate. In addition to this dark, punitive conception of the meaning of death there has always been the very different picture of human life as a pilgrimage, with bodily death as the end of one stage of that pilgrimage and, by the same token, as a passing on to another stage. This picture has in it a glint of gold, a note of fulfilment, of triumph, even of adventure in face of death, a note which is perfectly caught in John Bunyan's passage about the passing of that great pilgrim, Mr Valiant-for-truth:

> After this it was noised abroad that Mr Valiant-for-truth was taken with a summons by the same post as the other, and had this for a token that the summons was true, that his pitcher was broken at the fountain. When he understood it, he called for his friends, and told them of it. Then said he, I am going to my fathers, and tho' with great difficulty I am got hither, yet now I do not repent me of all the trouble I have been at to arrive where I am. My sword I give to him that shall succeed me in my pilgrimage, and my courage and skill to him that can get it. My marks and scars I carry with me, to be a witness for me that I have fought his battles who now will be my rewarder. When the day that he must go hence was come, many accompanied him to the riverside, into which as he went he said, Death, where is thy sting? And as he went down deeper he said, Grave, where is thy victory? So he passed over, and all the trumpets sounded for him on the other side.

This pilgrim attitude to death is only at home within a different theological framework from the official Augustinian understanding of our mortality as a divinely inflicted punishment for sin.

[6] XIII 3.

This different framework is to be found within the history of christian thinking, though for most of the time only as a minority report overshadowed by the dominant Augustinian tradition. The alternative goes back through strands of eastern Christianity to the early hellenistic Fathers, and has been developed more fully in the modern period since it reappeared in the work of the great nineteenth-century German Protestant thinker, Friedrich Schleiermacher. On this view man was not created in a finitely perfect state from which he then fell, but was initially brought into being as an immature creature who was only at the beginning of a long process of moral growth and development. Man did not fall disastrously from a better state into one of sin and guilt, with death as its punishment, but rather he is still in process of being created. Irenaeus, in the second century, provided a vocabulary for this teleological conception when he distinguished between the image (*imago*) and the likeness (*similitudo*) of God in man. Man as he has emerged from the slow evolution of the forms of life exists as a rational and personal creature in the image of God. But he is still only the raw material for a further stage of the creative process by which this intelligent animal is being brought through his own free responses to his environment to that perfection of his nature which is his finite likeness to God.

From this point of view the wide gap, marked by the doctrine of the fall, between man's actual state and the state intended for him in God's purpose, is indeed a reality. But the ideal state, representing the fulfilment of God's intention for man, is not a lost reality, forfeited long ago in 'the vast backward and abysm of time', but something lying before us as a state to be attained in the distant future. And our present mortal embodied earthly life is not a penal condition, but a time of soul-making in which we may freely respond to God's purpose and become, in St Paul's phrases, 'children of God' and 'heirs of eternal life'. For such a theology the proper function of our earthly existence, with its baffling mixture of good and evil, is to be an environment in which moral choices and spiritual responses are called for, and in which men and women are being formed in relationship to one another within a common world.

This theology prompts an understanding of the meaning of life as a divinely intended opportunity, given to us both individually and as a race, to grow towards the realisation of the potentialities of our own nature and so to become fully human. Life is thus aptly imaged in terms of the ancient picture of an arduous journey towards the life of the Celestial City. This pilgrimage crosses the frontier of death; for its final end is not attained in this life, and therefore if it is to be attained at all there must be a further life, or lives, beyond bodily death in which God's purpose continues to hold us in being in environments related to that purpose.

Accordingly death does not have the absolute significance that it has in the Augustinian theology as the moment when the individual's eternal destiny is irrevocably decided. In that tradition the soul as it is at the moment of bodily death faces a definitive divine judgement and receives either the gracious gift of eternal life or the just wages of eternal death. But this traditional picture has to be criticised in the light of modern biological, psychological and sociological knowledge. The conditions of a person's life as these are determined by his biological inheritance, and by the influence of the family and the wider social matrix upon his early development, are often such as to make it virtually impossible that God's purpose for the individual will be fulfilled in this life. It would thus be intolerably unjust for such a victim of adverse circumstances to be eternally penalised. From the christian premiss of the goodness and love of God we must accordingly infer continued human life beyond death leading eventually to the far-distant fulfilment of the purpose for which we exist.

Within such a theological framework the question has to be encountered, why is there any such thing as death? If we die only to live again beyond death, why should we die at all? What can be the function of death within the divine purpose, as this kind of theology conceives of it?

I think that some of the things that existentialist writers have said about death point in the direction of an answer by stressing the way in which our mortality determines the shape and character of our lives. This is, I think, an important insight, to which I shall return presently. But before coming to that there is another related suggestion to be considered. It is sometimes said that a man's death gives *meaning* to his life. This is in fact said in two senses, each of which is worth looking at.

First, there is a sense in which a man's death, by completing his life, makes it possible for others to see its meaning. For only when a life has been rounded off by death are we able to see it in its totality and so to characterise it as a whole. And to be able to characterise it as a whole as a good life, or bad, as happy or unhappy, heroic or banal, creative or wasted, and so on, might be equated with seeing its nature and quality, or discerning its meaning. This seems to be true enough; but so far it supplies only a relatively trivial sense in which death gives meaning to life. It applies the general truth that you only see a process in its totality once it has been completed; from which tautology it follows that one can only see a man's life as a totality after he has died. But nevertheless a life may *have* a meaning – a value, a direction, a purpose – whilst it is still being lived, even though it is only at death that the accounts can finally be closed and audited. Bertrand Russell, for example, before he died at the age of ninety-eight, had already produced much more than an average life-span of activity and writing to be surveyed, evaluated, praised, criticised. One did not have to wait until he died to be able to see in his life a remarkable living out of the rationalist spirit. We could see his relentless intellectual honesty; the narrowness of some of his thinking as well as the extreme clarity of all of it; the shape of his life as fulfilling Plato's ideal of the philosophic life, which begins by attending to mathematics and logic and ends in engagement with the concrete human problems of ethics and politics. And so massive and consistent was the quality of his life over this long period that nothing he might do or fail to do in his last year or two could undo the meaning of the life he had already lived. We are thus reminded that the tautology that we can see a life as a whole, and see the meaning of that whole, only when the life has terminated is in some cases merely trivial and unilluminating.

But there is a second sense in which a man's death may give meaning to his life, namely that the manner of his dying may throw a flood of retrospective light upon his character throughout life. The analogy has been used of the final resolving chord of a melody: only when this last chord is heard does the melody as a whole emerge. The last act, the act of dying, instead of being just one more event in a man's biography, may constitute a peculiarly crucial and illuminating climax. For example, one who had seemed through lack of severe temptation to be a person of integrity may die ignominiously trying to save himself at the expense of a number of others, and this selfish end then colours our appreciation of his character and of his life as a whole. Or on the other hand an apparently very ordinary man, living an inconspicuously decent and honest life, may in some great crisis sacrifice his life to save others; and then this death reveals to us a quality that was implicit in his life as a whole. He was all that time a man capable of heroic self-sacrifice, though until this last crisis that quality showed itself only in the quiet integrity of his life. Now, however, there is a final burst of illumination in the light of which that integrity takes on a stronger and more dramatic colour.

In parenthesis let me say that by analogy this may suggest a way of understanding the significance, for Christianity, of the death of Jesus. That is to say, Jesus' death has special significance as revealing the significance of his life and work as a whole. His life was a complex event in which the divine love towards mankind was seen at work on earth in the midst of human history; and the depth of that love was finally and definitively revealed by Jesus' willingness to be crucified rather than deny the saving significance of his own life and teaching. In contrast to the traditional satisfaction and penal-substitutionary atonement theories this means that the significance of Christ's death did not reside in the event itself considered in isolation and as effective *ex opere operato*. Christ's saving work was his ministry as a whole. But within this his passion and death have special significance as revealing the dominant motive and meaning of his life.

There is, then, a sense in which a death may give meaning to a life by illuminating the significance already inherent in it. But such illumination is somewhat exceptional. It occurs only in the case of a death, such as a martyrdom, that is in some special way striking and significant. But most deaths are simply the chronological end of a life, and throw little or no additional light upon the meaning of that life. Or they may be the kind of death that is positively destructive of meaning because it breaks into a life prematurely and yet stands in no organic relation to that life and its quality. It is this that makes the atheistic existentialist Jean-Paul Sartre speak of 'the absurd character of death'.[7] He notes that death may at any moment violently strike a man down in mid-career by accident or disease, leaving his work unfinished,

---

[7] *Being and Nothingness*, op. cit., p. 533.

his relationships unfulfilled, his plans disrupted, his potentialities undeveloped. We are all of us, at least until old age, subject to this possibility. And for Sartre the fact that death as arbitrary destruction may befall·anyone vitiates the meaning of life. 'Thus,' he says, 'death is never that which gives life its meaning; it is, on the contrary, that which on principle removes all meaning from life.'[8]

Sartre is surely exaggerating – and indeed does not a good deal of existentialist thought consist in precisely this kind of exaggeration? – when he says that the possibility of premature death renders all life meaningless and absurd. (Did, for example, the possibility that Bertrand Russell might be run over by a bus in his ninety-eighth year render his already long life meaningless?) However, just as others have been right in saying that in some cases a man's death discloses the meaning of his life, so also Sartre is right in saying that in some cases death deprives a life of meaning. Death can have both this meaning-bestowing and this meaning-destroying effect. And what, as it seems to me, Christianity has to say at this point is that neither this meaning nor this meaninglessness are absolute and final. Death is the end of the chapter but not of the book; or better, it is the end of the volume but not of the whole work. This life has its own autonomy and may have its own completeness; and all our present activities have to be related to it and to terminate within it. And yet, according to Christianity, death is nevertheless not extinction. The meaning developed in this life, in so far as it is good, is to be taken forward into a larger pattern of larger value; and the meaningless thread of a life without value is not to be cut but is to be carried forward and eventually woven into the same pattern of larger and indeed unlimited value.

And yet it remains a valid insight that it is the boundaries that give to anything its shape; and there is an important sense in which the boundary of death provides the distinctive shape and character of our human life. Consider as an analogy the contribution which the regularly recurring boundaries of sleep make to the nature of our human experience. Even if we did not need this relapse into unconsciousness after every eighteen hours or so for the sake of physical rest we should still need it in order to divide life up into manageable sections. Continuous consciousness from

[8] Ibid., p. 539.

the cradle to the grave, without regular pauses and partial new beginnings, would be intolerable. The ceaseless bombardment of sense impressions, the unremitting engagement of the self with other people and with the circumstances and problems of our lives, would mount up to an unbearable pressure. But in fact this pressure is relaxed every night by the disengagement of sleep, making it possible to begin afresh in the morning. Of course the new day offers only a relative beginning. The world has continued through the night, and yesterday's problems are still there waiting to be taken up again. But nevertheless the very fact of taking them up again offers the possibility of a varied approach. The new day opens up new possibilities. Time has passed; tension has been relaxed; emotions have calmed; our mind has surveyed its problems again and perhaps come to see them slightly differently. And this continually repeated new beginning plays an important part in forming the structure and quality of our experience.

Now perhaps this effect of sleep in dividing our life into parts which, having their own terminus, have each their own shape and character, suggests an analogous function for death. Perhaps we are not ready for the endless vista of eternal life because our life lacks that quality which would alone make welcome the prospect of a limitless future. But perhaps it is the function of mortality to bracket a space within our immortal existence, making a limited span within which to live. Within this horizon there is the possibility of finite achievements and failures in finite situations, and consequently of the growth and development of character.

This view involves both an attitude to life and an attitude to death. As regards the first, it means that we have a limited vista of life set before us, bounded by an end beyond which we cannot see; and upon this limited scene we have to concentrate all our thoughts and efforts. It is long enough for the greatest human plans and achievements, and yet short enough to give shape and urgency to life. Because time is limited it is precious. Because we do not live in this world for ever we have to get on with whatever we are going to do. Thus the attitude to life that follows from this view is in practice a this-worldly attitude involving a full concentration upon the affairs of the present life. And as regards our view of death, this is now related to the eternal life which consists in being eternally the object of God's love. Against this background, death will still always be faced with a profound awe and apprehension which engulfs our whole consciousness. But christian faith seeks to match death as the totally unknown with a total trust in the love of God. Of course in fact this trust is usually far from total. It shares the wavering and fluctuating character of the believer's consciousness of God in the midst of his long pilgrimage. And accordingly the facing of death is often an ordeal of doubt and fear when for perfect faith it would have the different character of a great transition, coloured by the sadness of parting but not evoking deep dread or terror. We can only say that in so far as the trust is real and operative it must take the final sting out of death, the sting of ultimate meaninglessness and vacuity, and must thereby deprive the grave of its victory over life. There can be meaning and hope even in the moments prior to dissolution. And in the minds of those who are now left with an irreparable void in their lives there can be, mingled with their grief, the solemn thought of the trumpets that are sounding on the other side, and a sense of the loving sovereignty of God both here and beyond the dark mystery of death.

My suggestion, then, is that christian thought is still committed to belief in a life after death; that there is no advantage in concealing this either from ourselves or from others; but that the Augustinian type of theology in which death is held to be the wages of sin should be replaced by an Irenaean type of theology which sees our mortality in relation to a positive divine purpose of love; and that ministry to the dying and to the bereaved, and the ceremonies of death and disposal, should so far as possible be brought to reflect this theological conception of death.

Index

The word 'God' is not indexed because it occurs on almost every page.